A TASTE *for* WAR

The Culinary History of the Blue and the Gray

William C. Davis

STACKPOLE
BOOKS

Published by
STACKPOLE BOOKS
5067 Ritter Road
Mechanicsburg, PA 17055
www.stackpolebooks.com

Printed in the United States of America

10 9 8 7 6 5 4 3 2 1

FIRST EDITION

Library of Congress Cataloging-in-Publication Data

Davis, William C., 1946–
   A taste for war : the culinary history of the Blue and the Gray / by William C. Davis.— 1st ed.
      p. cm.
   Includes bibliographical references and index.
   ISBN 0-8117-0018-6
   1. United States—History—Civil War, 1861–1865—Social aspects. 2. United States—History—Civil War, 1861–1865—Food supply. 3. Cookery, Military—United States—History—19th century. 4. United States—Armed Forces—Messes—History—19th century. 5. Confederate States of America—Armed Forces—Messes. I. Title.
   E468.9.D285 2003
   973.7'83—dc21

                                                        2003003849

*"I am thinking seriously
of writing a cookbook when I get home."*

Dayton E. Flint,
15th New Jersey Infantry
February 1, 1863

CONTENTS

ACKNOWLEDGMENTS

SEVERAL FRIENDS AND FELLOW HISTORIANS HAVE OFFERED ASSISTANCE IN the course of research for this book, and in the compilation of recipes and illustrations. Most notably, Thomas and Beverly Lowry contributed a wealth of information on food-related trials gleaned from their epic survey of the 80,000 Union military courts-martial in the National Archives. Also at the National Archives, Michael Musick, that perennial friend to all researchers, pointed out hidden culinary treasures. At the United States Army Military History Institute, Richard J. Sommers and his staff made available much rich food lore from the largest extant collection of Union soldier letters and diaries. Jack Welsh made available some of the wealth of material he has accumulated on Confederate medical practice. James Kushlan and Sue Miller of *Civil War Times* magazine gave assistance with the loan of illustrative material, and collector John A. Hess was very generous with material from his unparalleled collection of soldier portraits. Old friends Robert Krick, Richard McMurry, T. Michael Parrish, and Melissa Meisner also volunteered aid, as did Kathy Olson. To all of them and more, I offer sincere thanks and a hearty *bon appétit*.

INTRODUCTION

"AN ARMY IS A BIG THING," WROTE A YANKEE OFFICER IN OCTOBER 1863, "and it takes a great many eatables and not a few drinkables to carry it along."[1] So it did. Pvt. Amos Breneman of the 203rd Pennsylvania Infantry noted in 1865 that the primary "vegitable of life" is women, alcohol and tobacco. Most soldiers got along just fine throughout the conflict of 1861–65 without any of these three staples.[2] But the real "vegitables" and everything else that made up a man's diet remained a constant concern and for most, something of an obsession. If an army really "marches on its stomach," as Napoleon put it, then few armies in history did more abdominal traveling than those of the North and South in the American Civil War. From the picnic baskets that Washington tourists brought with them to watch the first battle along Bull Run in July 1861 to the need for rations that fatally slowed Robert E. Lee's army on its retreat from Richmond to Appomattox in April 1865, the soldier and sustenance were inseparable. "No government ever provided more liberally for the wants [of] its soldiers in respect to food," a New York medical professor declared of the Union's catering effort at the war's end.[3] Perhaps so, but nevertheless, at one time or another—and far too much of the time for many—every soldier knew hunger. No one completely escaped the rotten meat, the worm-infested bread, the illness from want of fruits and vegetables, or the utter absence of even the basic principles of nutrition and a balanced diet. As it was a nightmare in so many ways, the Civil War, even with the advent of forward-looking techniques in food preservation, was essentially a bad dream on a plate.

No wonder every soldier's letters and diary commented more on the awfulness of his diet than on anything else except perhaps his poor health and bad officers—and all three could be interconnected. Through the millennia armies have groused about their meals, generally with good cause. North and South started a war for which neither was prepared, and though they rapidly got up to speed—with the Confederacy often running behind—they never completely solved the problems of getting adequate food to the armies on time, or in the right place, or in palatable condition, let along educating millions of strangers to the kitchen in how to cook and eat what they got. No wonder the armies fed as much from hapless local farmers' fields and livestock as from their commissaries. No wonder that food itself became a staple of army humor, to remain so ever after. They named mess halls for their favorite generals, dishes and drinks for their leaders good and bad, and created tall tales of Paul Bunyonesque proportions around the mythical properties of the things they put in their stomachs.

Even Shakespeare and politics did not escape being drawn into the imaginations of those who saw food and the war as integrally linked. C. Chauncey Burr, a one-time emancipationist turned race-baiter—and incidentally a part-time bigamist—published an intemperate monthly journal, titled *The Old Guard*, in which he vented his venom at what he perceived to be the tyrannies of the Lincoln administration, particularly those of Secretary of War Edwin M. Stanton. In his 1864 poem "Cooking the Hell Broth," Burr turned Stanton into one of Macbeth's three witches and adapted the Bard's most famous recipe into a diatribe against the administration, its antislavery supporters like Benjamin Butler and Orestes Brownson, fears of racial integration, and reformist clerics like Theodore Parker:

> Double, double, toil and trouble,
> Fire burn and cauldron bubble,
> Liver of the Parker school, Spleen of preacher,
> tongue of fool,
> Socinian's eye and Athiest's heart,
> Of any, Brownson's better part;
> Or Butler's, for the charm will kill
> With poisons which they may instil;
> With wine from chalice, foeman's blood,
> Sacred bread and preacher's rations,

> Life-blood of the States and nation's,
> Negro's wool and white man's brains,
> To miscegenation our vapid veins,
> And cherry cheek and ebon lip,
> And slime of live that devils sip,
> And make the gruel thick and slab,
> In throw the heart of brothel's drab,
> Add thereto a Sambo's liver,
> Fished from old Charon's sluggish river.[4]

Presumably, no one actually attempted to prepare the dish.

From the other side of the contest came a far more imaginative and comprehensive, if just as bitterly cynical and vindictive, proposition to end several separate ills by culinary device. George W. Bagby of Richmond was a venomously partisan and intemperate journalist who wrote for a number of Confederate newspapers, including the Charleston *Mercury*, the organ of Robert Barnwell Rhett, Sr., and his namesake son. In the days before the war, Bagby led "fire-eating" secessionists who became the most implacable foes of the administration of Jefferson Davis, upon whom they blamed all of the war's ills. Bagby's reputation for biting satire made him popular with the other anti-Davis press, and in Richmond itself in the fall of 1863. After two years of war with no end in sight, and the Confederacy severely wounded by losses at Vicksburg and Gettysburg the previous summer, Bagby was in a mood to unleash a prescription for a hellfire meal of his own.

Mirroring the bigotry that characterized his Rhett employers, the journalist decried the presence in the Confederacy of "the Jews, a class which includes not only the unworthy Israelites but all who indulge the alleged Hebraic propensity for exacting the pound of Christian flesh and amassing riches at the expense of the life blood of their fellow-citizens." In his rather broad definition of Jewry, Bagby included just about everyone who irritated him, chiefly those whose prices in their business concerns seemed to reflect profiteering in the crisis: "Yankee tradesmen of whatever denomination, restaurant-keepers, confectionary and apple-sellers, oyster-cellar men, proprietors of hotels and boarding houses and the like." He figured there must be a half million of them in the Confederacy. The Jews especially were noted for peddling rotten shoestrings, alleged meerschaum pipes made of cheap plaster, and penny lead pencils priced at a dollar. Yet, Bagby believed, they owned the finest houses in Richmond and had their cellars stocked with hoarded flour, bacon, sugar, coffee, and more, all of which were being denied the poor gentile citizens. Of just whiskey alone they had enough to keep Richmond's gambling dens, canal packets, Congress, and even the notoriously inebriate Gov. John Letcher grinning for three months. And they had enough fabric to make two suits of clothes for every one of the shivering Southern soldiers in rags.

Bagby asserted that the Jews must be evicted from their homes and shops, their property confiscated, and their riches appropriated to the care of the poor and refugees from Yankee armies. The Jews and merchants themselves should be put to hard work doing what such miserly miscreants ought to do best—skin flints. Then the remains of the flints could be turned over to any remaining butchers "who will have no trouble in vending them as beef-knuckles or lamb-chops, to which, indeed, they will be generally preferred as being considerably less gritty and decidedly more juicy and nutritious" than what the butchers were then selling.

But the Jews were only the start. There were 600,000 free blacks in the Confederacy whose presence Bagby did not appreciate. The thought they should be confined to caves beneath Church Hill in the capital. Then there were more than 900,000 "men and women of pleasure," by his calculation, who should be banished to Belle Isle in the middle of the James River, where already thousands of captured Union soldiers languished. The Jews were to be confined at labor in old factories and warehouses, and the one million poor and indigent could be housed in empty tobacco barrels, one hogshead neatly accommodating up to a family of six, with peanut shells packed in around them for insulation against the cold. That would leave only the president, Congress, the legislature, government clerks, and functionaries, and they would have the run of the city to live in the pomp and style that they deserved.

But there remained the problem of feeding the three million others thus displaced. "Can this be done?" he asked his readers. In fact, it was easy. First, the Negroes did not need to be fed. They could live on edible dirt. That still left almost a quarter million to feed, but he had the solution, a rather "final solution" at that:

> It has been suggested to me by the learned and original author of "Cannibals All" that the common repugnance to human food is but a foolish prejudice, born of modern

philosophy and political economy, and that the best course
for me to pursue if I am, in accordance with an act of Congress, appointed Commissary-General, as I expect to be, will
be to disregard the weak vagaries of philanthropists and veg-
etarians and proceed at once to feed the people copiously
with the most accessible animal diet, which will, of course,
be human flesh.

So there it was. The gamblers and prostitutes should take turns eating
each other. The Jews should eat the restaurant keepers in an act of poetic justice, and then the Hebrews, thus fattened, ought to be fed to the poor, who
should gladly eat them. Then the blacks could be diverted from their dirt diet
to consume the poor "so that the dangerous classes will be destroyed at a
blow, and nobody be left but Government and negroes, and the Sociology of
the South established on the only firm basis possible—a basis which the slow
cannibalism of modern antagonism between labour and capital would hardly
reach in a century."

But of course, Bagby realized that society might not be ready just yet for
self-consumption. "The problem, then, is to feed two and a half millions of
poor wretches on some article of food, which gentlemen cannot or will not
eat, and which shall be, at the same time, abundant and cheap." The answer
was confederate money. No gentleman would eat it, and no one would take
them in payment for goods or debt. In fact, all that worthless money was really in the way, and they had to get rid of it somehow. "They must, therefore,
be eaten as food." While admitting that the notes in and of themselves were
rather dry and less than tasty, Bagby had a solution for that and a recipe. In
their factory workhouses, the Jews should skin the rinds from pork, which,
with typical suspicion of their fidelity to their dietary laws, Bagby believed
most Jews secretly preferred. Take equal portions of Confederate money and
ground bran, use the grease from bacon rinds as a binder and flavoring, and
the result would be a dish to subsist the poor indefinitely, "the most wholesome, appetizing and uncostive diet that can possibly be devised." Of one
thing he was certain: "If Confederate notes will pass in no other way they certainly will in this."[5]

To soldiers in the field, who were known to boil old boots to flavor a thin
broth from the leather, a bit of paper and ink with the president's picture on it
might not have tasted bad. Short of that extreme, however, Johnny Reb and

Billy Yank went to extraordinary lengths to get food on their plates, and then to get it into their stomachs and keep it there. In the process, they overturned centuries of cultural and gender habit, demonstrated enormous ingenuity in devising things to eat from the raw materials at hand, and endured untold privations that often haunted their health for the rest of their lives. From 1861 to 1865 their menu was a three-course meal of monotony, insufficiency, and improvisation.

CHAPTER ONE

SKIM, SIMMER, AND SCOUR

IN LATE APRIL 1861, THOUSANDS OF ENTHUSIASTIC YOUNG VOLUNTEERS
came by train and steamboat to the capital of the new Confederate States of
America at Montgomery, Alabama, to be forwarded by the new government
to the anticipated fronts in Virginia and elsewhere. In a panoply of uniforms
and civilian dress, the "Southrons" teemed in the city parks and fairgrounds,
some staying in hotels, but most under fresh white canvas tents. As a result,
one journalist found on April 28 that "the aspect of Montgomery at this time
is anything but peaceful." Drumbeats of drilling companies interrupted civilians in their sleep and at their meals, and the complexion of the streets
changed dramatically. "No one thinks of anything but war," the newspaper-
man observed, and indeed he was almost right. But these young men did
think of one other thing at least, and that about three times a day. Outside
the fairgrounds buildings that barracked the volunteers, open pit fires burned
almost constantly, and there "with good fat pork, camp fires and cooking
utensils, wholesome food is easily attained."[1]

If only it were so. The problem was that none of them knew anything
about cooking for themselves. "Every corps stationed in this place is divided
into messes," noted the reporter. "Each mess has its cook and bottle-washer,
and the process of cooking is as much a source of amusement to the troops as
it was to myself." He could hardly stifle a laugh at the sight of six-foot-tall
young men struggling to figure out a coffee grinder that they had likely seen
their mothers operate effortlessly for years, and often breaking into unbecom-
ing profanity when the mill slipped from their grasp and all their precious lit-

1

tle store of grounds fell into the dirt. It proved more hilarious yet to stand beside the fires and watch the neophytes try to figure out what was supposed to happen to all the stuff they had thrown into the cauldrons and pans, and their chagrin at the result. "I saw the cook, his face beaming like the coals, the perspiration streaming down his cheeks, watching a huge fat mass of salt junk [pork] bubble up and down in the great pot." The cook kept looking at his watch to assess how long the congealing blob of pork had been cooking and then looking up at the sky, scratching his head, and muttering under his breath that he wondered "if the d——d thing was done yet."

It was enough to convince the journalist that "the poor fellow was evidently in as big a stew as the object of his solicitude," a conclusion confirmed when the befuddled man asked the cook at another mess's fire how he could tell when the steaming concoction was done.

"Stick a stick into it," came the reply.

"Stick a stick into it!" replied the cook of the first part. "What'll that do?"

"Why if the thing is done the stick will go easy," replied the cook of the second part. "If it ain't done it won't go in."

Immediately, the cook of the first part found a pointed stick of suitable length. "He made several vigorous lunges at the white mass in the pot," noted the reporter, "but all his efforts were unavailing." In frustration he threw the stick and swore. "No use—the infernal thing won't get cooked," he grumbled to the other cook. "It has been boiling for three hours this way. I believe you are hoaxing me." His only recourse was to ask a woman in town to borrow a cookbook from her "to find out how long pork must be boiled before it is done."[2]

That frustrated anonymous cook, whom the journalist did not identify, but who would probably be remembered eternally in the stomachs and curses of his company, spoke for legions of the "blind" feeding the "blind." More than 5,000 units eventually served North and South, from oversize heavy artillery regiments to small independent companies. Those fortunate enough to be stationed for long periods at forts and other substantial installations often enjoyed the services of specifically detailed cooks who acquired experience at least, if not culinary skill. Even in the field armies men experienced at making soft bread performed the work of baking at least. But otherwise, every one of those units detailed multiple enlisted men to act as cooks on an ad hoc basis, sometimes one or two per company and often one for every informal "mess" of a half dozen soldiers. The task of cooking often rotated among the men within a company or mess, and almost every soldier had to cook for himself at sometime on isolated picket duty or off on the occasional foray into the country looking for something to eat. Scarcely one of them was ready for the apron and pot.

No wonder the hapless Montgomery cook sent for a woman with a cookbook. Young men in nineteenth-century America grew up in a world in which men did not stand at the stove or hearth. Except perhaps for some of the better restaurants in the cities, women did all the cooking in poor and middle-class families, and slave or hired servant women did the same in the finer homes. Men were not taught to cook, and few would have been willing to demean themselves by handling pots and pans. On ceremonial occasions like public barbeques and outdoor political meetings, men generally managed the ox roast or made the stew-like "burgoo," and in the deep forest on a long hunt, a man might fry a fish or boil a bit of salt beef or pork, but those were exceptions. Overwhelmingly, the young men who went off to become soldiers in 1861–65 were culinary virgins. They came from cities and towns where they had been clerks and students, or from farms where they might have learned to kill and dress a chicken and butcher a cow or a pig, but they knew more about tanning the hide than preparing what once had been inside. Moreover, even those few who might have risked embarrassing their manhood by asking mother or sister for a few hints when they went off in 1861 expected it to be a short war, so why learn a skill they would never need again? As a result, in Montgomery and throughout the Union and Confederacy alike, many who took up arms did not know how to wield a spoon.

Perhaps worse, there were few aids to help them in the new role suddenly thrust upon them. Officers usually brought their own cooks or managed to have specially detailed cooks provide for their tables, but the men in the ranks almost always were left to their own devices to cook and often to find their own food by foraging. As early as Roman times, authors like Apicius wrote cookery books, but in the absence of printing, copies reached only a few homes of the wealthy and certainly did no good for the poor—usually illiterate—soldier in the field. In the prewar United States, the tiny professional Regular army usually had detailed cooks who, if not previously trained or experienced, at least acquired some competence by rote thanks to the units being almost permanently assigned to fixed posts and fortifications. Still, there was no consistent fixed policy coming out of Washington. In the Army Regulations of 1825, an article ordered that in each squad, every private soldier should take his "tour" at preparing meals and stipulated that "the greatest care will be observed in scouring and washing utensils employed in cooking."

However, nothing provided for the specific length of that tour of duty, a decision left to individual commanders of posts. At Fort Snelling on the upper Mississippi, for instance, the post commander ordered that detailed company cooks serve for one full month, with assistants detailed from the company a day at a time.[3]

At that rate, a career soldier might expect to act as company cook only once in several years, unless he proved so good at it that the clamor of the men could induce officers to detail him more often. Still, after one month at the pots, a man might at least have acquired sufficient rudiments that he could repeat his performance in the future whenever necessary, especially with the limited and monotonous army diet prescribed. The same Army Regulations of 1825 also provided to cooks some rather rudimentary guidelines for food preparation that remained almost unchanged for the next thirty-seven years, many of them betraying the nineteenth-century male's abhorrence of the possibility of eating anything not completely cooked. Bread should not be burned when baked, and it should not be eaten hot from the oven. Rather, it should be eaten only after being toasted, which rendered it "nearly as wholesome and nutritious as stale bread." Times of cooking were rudely approximate, as with "five or six hours" for soup, and the best water came not from springs or wells, but from rivers. Soldiers ought also to have plenty of vinegar. Stale bread, overcooked food, and river water spoke volumes for the military's grasp of nutrition.[4]

During field operations and wartime, as in 1812 and again in the war with Mexico in 1846–48, such month-long assignments broke down and the Regulars predominantly cooked for themselves in camp and on the march, as did the temporarily raised state volunteer regiments that made up the bulk of the military in wartime. This same arrangement was to be the model and expectation for the men in blue and gray—and all the visual cacophony of other colors of uniform early on—as they went to their war. Unfortunately, when they arrived for their training and first figurative and literal taste of army life, there were still no guides for them to use at the cook fire other than those vague regulations.

A few of mother's cookbooks did go to war with the boys, however, and by 1861, the field of guides for cooking and preserving food in the home had become surprisingly broad. Scores of books of recipes and "receipts" were in print. Many, if not most, middle- and upper-class households had at least one, and many housewives regularly gleaned recipes from women's periodicals such as Godey's Lady's Book. Most popular, perhaps, was Mrs. N. K. M. Lee's The

Cook's Own Book, first published in 1832, which had gone through thirteen editions by the time the war started. Like most receipt books of the time, it contained, in addition to 2,500 recipes, guides for preserving foods, proper care of pots and pans, and even a section for making candy. Though primarily offering New England regional dishes, it had penetrated Southern kitchens widely by 1861.

But such guides would be rarities in the camps, except perhaps in the officers' messes or in winter quarters, when campaigning went dormant and soldier and officer wives often came to live near and cook and wash for their husbands. Besides, cookery books presumed an abundant variety of ingredients, fruits, vegetables, seasonings, and spices, which ran counter to army theories of efficiency. Variety was the enemy of simplicity, which made sensible military doctrine, especially when governments would have to provide subsistence for perhaps hundreds of thousands at a time. Large quantities of relatively few staples were easier to procure and distribute as rations, but that meant a certain inevitable reduction in variety on the mess plate. For something to eat beyond the routine, the soldiers would have to provide for themselves by either purchase or foraging. Thus, civilian cookbooks simply offered too many options not practical in camp.

It took the governments awhile to realize that they needed to do something to enable soldiers to cook for themselves, but in the early days of the crisis, when many still thought that either there would be no war or it would be a short summer's affair, the young men found other alternatives. Never again in the war would produce be so abundant or restaurants and hotels so well stocked. Rarely again, especially in the Confederacy, would enlisted men have as much discretionary hard money in their pockets. And so in the North and South, when not in camp, the volunteers descended on the hostelries and chophouses. Even then, the result could be indeterminate.

In late April 1861, a party of soldiers and civilians on a train bound for Pensacola stopped just across the Florida line for the volunteers aboard to dine at a roadside eatery. "We supped upon a mockery of coffee, good corn bread, bad butter, excellent ham, and a dish over which the Georgians and Alabamians disputed at length," noted a fellow diner. One faction believed it to be turtle—which they called "grouper," while the other was just as certain that it was fowl, the truism presumably being already current that any cooked reptilian or amphibian tasted like chicken. "The dish before us tasted more like fowl than anything I had ever known, therefore, I uttered a declaration as to my impressions," recalled one, but as he had never admittedly tasted turtle, the rest refused to yield. The keeper of the eating house, when asked what it was, became suspicious of their motives and refused to answer. "We are yet in the dark," the chicken advocate complained a few days later, "and our party of four yet remains divided, rallying each to the separate war cry 'Grouper!' 'Chicken.'"[5] There would be many other mystery meals on their plates before the war was done.

The idea of actually teaching the soldiers to cook for themselves was not long in coming, though as with so much else in a war in which events outran preparedness, there was little or no system at first. The Confederacy would never be able to address the subject, and first to last its soldiers were left almost entirely to themselves, their officers, and exigency as they learned which end of the spoon went in the pot. In Tennessee, Pvt. Spencer Talley of Company F, 28th Tennessee Infantry, recalled after the war that when his regiment was in its initial training, the men drilled most of the time and then spent the rest of their days "taking lessons in cooking."[6]

It went better for the Yankees. Guns and butter may be the chief concerns of an army in wartime, but at the outset, the guns came first, and state and national governments were too busy raising and training regiments to fight to think about tutorials in the finer points of cuisine. Happily, there were more than enough patriotic civilian relief groups forming to take on such duties. William S. Chapman of Cincinnati, Ohio, called on Gov. William Dennison in the summer of 1861 just after Bull Run regarding the inadequate knowledge of cooking in the camps and the deleterious impact it was having on soldier health. He told the governor that he could "teach soldiers in camp how to cook their rations to the best advantage, and to care for themselves in other particulars in such manner as will best favor the highest degree of comfort and health."

Dennison took him at his word and arranged for him to conduct an experiment in the training camps of the 2nd Ohio Infantry early in October. It worked. After first instructing the colonel of the regiment, who practiced cooking himself as a trial, Chapman instituted what he called a "system of imparting practical instruction to the men in camp on the subject of their cooking." After only a few days, officers reported that "our men entirely approve of and fall into his suggestions, finding therein a decided addition to their table which must result greatly to their benefit," and adding proudly that now "our camp cooks can offer as fine coffee as any hotel." After the 2nd Ohio had gone to the front, its officers testified further that the health and well-being of their regiment had improved, and sent recommendations to Dennison and to the War Department in Washington urging "the importance of teaching the men this art, so essential to their health and efficiency."[7]

Washington did not need to hear from the Ohioans, as it happened, for others had been at work east of the Alleghenies that summer. Within days of the outbreak of war at Fort Sumter on April 12, 1861, civilian relief groups began to form, knowing that the government would be swamped just with raising, clothing, equipping, and training the volunteers, let alone ministering to their physical health and welfare. Following the model of the British Sanitary Commission a decade before in England's war in the Crimea, a number of local and state relief groups appeared, most headed by women and many merging into the Women's Central Association of Relief in New York, which in turn would become the United States Sanitary Commission on June 9. It would spend the rest of the war trying to work in cooperation—sometimes uneasy—with the government in ministering to the physical health and comfort of the men.

Naturally, what the soldiers ate became one of the earliest priorities of the commission or, as the men colloquially called it, "the Sanitary." Even before Bull Run, James M. Sanderson, a New York hotel operator and member of the Sanitary, noticed that already the press seemed full of letters from volunteers in the field complaining of the awful quality of their food and its inadequate preparation. Concerned by what he termed "the injurious and unwholesome mode of cooking now existing in the Volunteer regiments," Sanderson decided to turn his experience to the problem. He got in touch with Gov. Edwin D. Morgan and asked for money and authorization to visit men in the field to experiment with teaching them a simple system of cookery, as did Chapman in Ohio. Morgan gave the Sanitary $200, and the commission sent Sanderson and an experienced cook to Washington to the camps of the 12th New York, the designated guinea pigs for his trial, a regiment chosen "as most deficient in the proper culinary knowledge."

Within three days in early July, Sanderson had two companies of the 12th New York doing markedly better. However, he reported that the rest of the regiment, "owing to the criminal indifference of their officers, the consequent apathy of the men, and the absence of all military authority on the part of the undersigned," was not yet properly organized or ready to receive instruction, and in fact, the regiment itself would be disbanded to be remustered in August. "Checked, but not defeated," as Sanderson said a few weeks later, he secured an invitation from the colonel of the 15th New York Infantry to try his system on them, and in six days, he had the men cooking for themselves and saw a consequent reduction in the cases of diarrhea from twenty a day to just five. The soldiers thanked him, while the regimental surgeon and officers gave him hearty praise in reports to the Sanitary.

Based on that success, and seconded by the recommendations from the 15th New York, Sanderson approached the War Department on July 22, just the day after the defeat at Bull Run, a timing that was surely coincidental, yet still advantageous. In the wake of a humiliating beating at the hands of the Confederates, Washington was rethinking its priorities and expectations and was in a mood to accommodate the comfort of soldiers whom it now expected would be in the field not just for three months, but possibly for years before the rebellion died. Sanderson suggested that "a respectable minority" in each company could acquire "a perfect knowledge of a few of the most essential principles of the art of cookery" if tutored by an expert, and he proposed that the War Department appoint one skilled cook to each regiment as teacher. He should have detailed to him as company cooks two privates from each 100-man company, one position permanent and the other rotating among the men of the company, classified as noncombatants, and he should bear the rank of sergeant major at a salary of $50 a month and the title of "cook major." The cook major ought to be put in charge of all regimental rations "and all matters appertaining to the preparation thereof, giving daily instructions to each and every private detailed as company cook." An officer of suitable rank and experience who has sufficient experience at cookery to know good from bad should be appointed to select and supervise the regimental cooks. This would be a check against the presumed dishonesty of the quartermasters, whom many men in the ranks believed misappropriated their best rations or spent regimental food allowance on inferior goods in order to pocket the savings. At the same time, the volunteers being by nature lazy and improvident when it came to food, such measures would prevent their ruining their food in preparation. Proposing his "thorough, comprehensive, and well-regulated reform, alike conformable to health and military discipline," Sanderson believed that he could all but eradicate grumbling and disease from the camps.[8]

Sanderson's proposal, backed by his experiments, excited the endorsement of the Sanitary Commission and Governor Morgan and was soon referred to the Military Affairs Committee of the United States Senate.[9] The committee did not act on his specific recommendations for instituting formal military ratings and ranks for cooks, but the War Department did give him a commission as a captain in the office of the commissary general of subsistence.

There, during the balance of 1861, he wrote for the army his ponderously titled *Camp Fires and Camp Cooking; or Culinary Hints for the Soldier: Including Receipt for Making Bread in the "Portable Field Oven" Furnished by the Subsistence Department,* published in January 1862.

It was pathbreaking in its way, the first attempt at a cookbook for distribution to the military, though in this case specifically intended just for the Army of the Potomac. "The author has been actuated by a desire to aid the efforts of those of his countrymen who, with the best intentions, lack the knowledge to utilize them," he began, "and having personally assisted in the concoction of the various dishes he treats of, using only camp fires, camp kettles, and soldiers' rations, he knows that a little attention on the part of any sensible man—and none other should ever attempt to cook—will produce the most savory and gratifying results."[10] Perhaps so, but it did not look that way at the outset. Inattention during the editing process resulted in a most unappetizing assertion that the iron mess pan "is to be consumed as taste or ingenuity may dictate." As if the food was not bad enough.

Grammatical oversights aside, Sanderson offered good advice on setting up a campfire and an apparatus over it to suspend cooking pots and went on to recommend as much more efficient—and less inconvenient to a cook—lining a trench with brick with a small chimney at one end and iron bars overhead to hold pot hooks and kettles. Using observations in his native New York of ground boilers used for boiling the salt from seawater, he described one such affair as markedly superior, as indeed it was. But the latter expedients were only practical for men stationary in winter quarters for long periods of time, while the simple trench and wooden sapling for cooking would have to do on the march. Sanderson offered sensible thoughts on what the officers ought to purchase in addition to the meager government issue of utensils, recommending large iron spoons and forks, strong knives, a colander, and without explaining its use, a yard of flannel, perhaps for straining.

Situated as he was in an office in Washington, it is too bad that Sanderson could not have heard the howls of derisive laughter that must have greeted his assertions that "no army in the world is so well provided for, in the shape of food, either as to quantity or quality," and, worse, that "no one man can consume his daily ration, although many waste it." Consequently, he expected that cooks could actually save money from the allotted company fund for extra purchase of food beyond issued rations, money to be used for the occasional delicacy. Just as amusing was his aphorism that "cleanliness is next to Godliness, both in persons and kettles; be ever industrious, then, in scouring your pots." But he did reveal that he well understood that improperly cleaned utensils bred illness. "Better wear out your pans with scouring than your stomachs with purging," he advised; "it is less dangerous to work your elbows than your comrade's bowels." Dirt and grease betrayed the bad cook and ruined the soldier's health, but clean kettles meant good food and good health.

Then there were Sanderson's general tips for cooks. They ought to be sparing with sugar and salt, for it was easy to add more to taste, but impossible to remove too much after added to the pot. "Remember that beans, badly boiled, kill more than bullets," he said, "and fat is more fatal than powder." In cooking, more than in any other worldly endeavor, cooks ought to "make haste slowly." An hour of overcooking was better than five minutes too little. "A big fire burns your face, scorches your soup, and crisps your temper," he said. "Skim, simmer, and scour, are the true secrets of good cooking."[11]

Sanderson followed with eighteen recipes for soups, stews, and boiled and fried meats and vegetables, along with the constant staples of bread and coffee. Considering that the soldiers would be expected to eat three times a day for enlistments of three years or more, this meant about 3,285 meals, which provided for precious little variety. Given that there were really only ten "entrees" and the rest vegetable accompaniments, a soldier could expect in the term of a full hitch of service to face each of those ten dishes an average of 328 times—9 times a month for each—enough to make him heartily sick of every one of them. But the army was not in the business of epicurean variety. It must marshal enormous quantities of basic foodstuffs for distribution through a network that would eventually, in the Union, reach nearly two million mouths, from Maine to California. Thus, the basic ingredients of beef, corned beef, and pork, with mixed fresh or dried vegetables as available, beans, peas, hominy, rice, and potatoes, would have to make do in simple recipes easily prepared on a large scale by men unaccustomed to the finer points of cooking.

With the recipes came some general observations on men's tendencies when they tried to cook, especially their proneness to overcooking everything for fear of eating something raw. They would boil beef soup too hot, toughening the meat and trapping its undefined "impurities" inside. They would not wash peas and beans carefully before making soup, thus producing dirty and gritty dishes that the men would not eat. They would forget to soak the dried beans overnight, resulting in hard and unchewable pellets in their soup. When frying meats, they would not have the pan hot enough, and thus fail to seal in juices and flavor. "Every cook thinks he can cook potatoes," observed Sanderson, "but the number that can cook them well is very small," the tendency being to overboil them. Men would scorch and ruin rice, make dirty coffee, and use bad yeast for their bread.[12] Just as with his simplified ingredients and recipes, Sanderson also offered simple guidelines to avoid such pitfalls.

Just how much *Camp Fires and Camp Cooking* was distributed got through the armies, even the Army of the Potomac, is uncertain, but evidently it was not universal. In any event, there would be similar works to follow, including C. L. Kilburn's 1863 *Note on Preparing Stores for the United States Army*, and E. N. Horsford's *The Army Ration* in 1864. Additionally, several publishers tried to capitalize on an interested market by issuing guides of their own, as well as publishing new editions of some of the prewar standard receipt books. Some would be disseminated by the War Department itself, but more reached soldiers through the efforts of the Sanitary Commission and other relief organizations.

Even then, individual commanders sometimes found that their men either did not receive any such books or else discarded or ignored them. At least one general issued instructions and a set of his own recipes to his men. Maj. Gen. Silas Casey spent years before the war on frontier duty and revising a standard army manual known as *Infantry Tactics*, which was forever associated with his name after the War Department published it in 1862. When war came, Major General Casey saw service in the Army of the Potomac in the abortive spring campaign of 1862 on the Virginia peninsula south of Richmond, but the poor performance of his division and possibly his age—he was fifty-five—saw him removed from important field duty thereafter. In the fall of that year, he commanded a division of three brigades in the Military District of Washington, both training troops and defending the Union capital.

In that capacity, Casey had a chance to see firsthand how lax the attention was given to instructing volunteers in cooking for themselves, and how inattentive their equally green officers could be in overseeing them. As a result, on November 19 he issued a circular directive to all troops in his command. "The attention of those having charge of new troops cannot be too often called to the importance of seeing to the proper preparation of the food provided for the men under their command," he began. Thus he reminded all of Army Regulation 116, which required company officers to visit camp kitchens daily to inspect the kettles and regimental colonels to do the same on frequent occasions. In a variant of the recommendations of Chapman and Sanderson, Casey directed that two men should be permanently detailed as cooks from each 100-man company, one of them as chief cook "to be held responsible for the proper dressing of the food" and the other as his assistant.

Better to have men serve throughout their enlistment and thereby gain experience than to rotate the assignment daily or even monthly. Moreover, he advised detailing officers that "the cook should be a *punctual* man," for it was important for the men to eat their meals at regular hours. "The cooking is every thing," he added.

"Care should be taken to vary the diet as much as possible, for sameness of diet, when long continued weakens digestion," he proposed, perhaps well aware of that awful repetition even in Sanderson's otherwise admirable book. "A judicious use of the ration will furnish a diet of considerable variety, which may be still further extended, by the purchase, from the company fund, of vegetables, butter, milk etc." As Sanderson had suggested, the company fund could also cover buying utensils not issued by the government, and he reminded them that Army Regulation 118 required kitchen pots and equipment to be kept clean at all times. Further with regard to sanitation, Casey went beyond Sanderson by requiring that cooks dig pits at least 150 feet from the kitchen, in which to deposit cooking refuse, covering each day's scraps with six inches of earth until the pit was full.

Casey declared that bread and soup were "the great items of a soldier's diet in every situation," and thus preparation of both must be an essential part of a new cook's instruction. Interestingly enough, he plagiarized most of his instructions thereafter for bread baking from Sanderson's manual, simply shortening the instructions and concluding with the widespread notion that bread should not be eaten fresh from the oven, as it became more healthful as it went stale. He recommended that at least twenty-four hours pass between baking and eating. Going beyond Sanderson's complaint that Americans ate too little soup, Casey boldly asserted that it "cannot be too highly esteemed" and ought to be eaten more than it was. To be best, it ought to be boiled slowly for a long time; "it cannot be boiled too much." As for beef, it should never be used freshly killed, but ought to be cold before cooking, but then, as with the stale bread, he added another admonition either from his own preference or from some folk wisdom that nevertheless had within it some nutritional sense. "All fried meats are unwholesome," he said. "They should be boiled or broiled."

When it came to vegetables, Casey said that they ought to be thoroughly cooked, especially desiccated vegetables—shredded carrots, potatoes, turnips, and the like, dried, shrunken, and pressed into cakes for preservation, which swelled and softened when boiled in water. The soldiers derisively called them desecrated vegetables and bales of hay, and already camp legends told of soldiers who ate them dry, only to have them expand in their stomachs until the men themselves exploded. Over and over, like Sanderson and almost everyone else, Casey stressed that it was crucial to cook everything thoroughly, even to the point, alas, that flavors and textures were liable to disintegrate into a homogenous goo. He also recommended that cooks use money from the company fund to buy dried apples and peaches as soldier treats, revealing that he had at least some understanding of the need for fruit in a healthy diet.[13]

The Confederate government seems to have produced no cookery manuals for its volunteers, but in this, as in almost every other aspect of feeding the men, the South would lag woefully behind its better-funded and better-resourced foe. On both sides of the lines, however, books and guides would be only as good as the degree of attention the men at the pots chose to give to what was, after all, a duty forced on many rather than a craft. Only the actual experiences of the soldiers in the field would show how well—if at all—their cooks served them and, for that matter, how well their governments supplied them with ingredients. Certainly Washington did learn lessons from its culinary war, however. No officer could possibly come out of the conflict without the endless complaints of the men over their meals echoing in his memory, and once peace came again, the War Department was able, in leisurely fashion, to turn its attention to a systematic approach to cooking throughout the postwar army.

In 1877, the government convened a board of officers to study food preparation in America and in the British army and then to experiment with and recommend a body of recipes, subsequently published in the 1879 *Manual for Army Cooks*, a work that in several editions would be the accepted standard for army cooking for more than a generation. Many of Sanderson's basic observations on cookery and baking reappeared in it, somewhat altered, but the postwar *Manual* dramatically expanded on his elemental store of less than two dozen recipes, offering more than twenty for soup alone and including weekly menus for variety, as well as new cooking techniques such as sautéing. There were even such refined delicacies as cheese straws, Welsh rarebit, cake icing, lemonade, and ice cream. Those who came after Johnny Reb and Billy Yank were going to eat a great deal better than they had, thanks in no small part to some of the most bitter, sarcastic, yet witty "reviews" that diners ever offered, as well as to what was learned in the 1860s, an advance paid for in hunger, indigestion, illness, and even death.[14]

CHAPTER TWO

EVERY FELLOW
FOR HIMSELF

MANY A YOUNG VOLUNTEER HAD NO IDEA WHAT TO EXPECT ON HIS MESS plate as he went to war, especially since early in the war meals, friends, family, and relief organizations on both sides often feted the new enlistees before they went off to the armies. In February 1862, when Wilbur Fisk's 2nd Vermont arrived in Washington, he found that "we generally get a generous handful of doughnuts, which, considering the limited resources of our cooking department, I may safely set down as first-rate. This, with the usual 'regimental' bread and 'salt junk,' is amply sufficient to satisfy the inner man."[1] A month later he was still eating far better than he would in months hence. Though thinking he painted a portrait of soldier hardship, Fisk described victuals then available that would seem luxurious to him a year later.

> First then, on the list of edibles, stands wheat bread, sometimes sour, but nevertheless containing the principal element of nutrition. Of course it is wholly unadulterated by milk, lard, cream, or any superfluities of that kind. To eat with this, we sometimes have fresh meat, but most generally boiled salt meat; the boys call it *'salt hoss,'* and I am not inclined to risk my reputation for veracity by disputing its merit to that title. The want of no one thing is felt so much as the lack of butter, or its substitutes, in our rations. . . . Meat and bread, or, for a change, bread and meat, with a cup of coffee forms the principal staple of fodder for all except

the officers. Potatoes are sometimes furnished us. . . . Beans
we have occasionally, say once a week. Peas, semi-occasion-
ally. Boiled rice and hominy are thrown in as incidentals.
The hominy being made of coarse white Southern corn does
not taste bad, from the fact that it requires a pretty hungry
man to perceive that it has any taste at all. A plate of soup,
twice as greasy as any dishwater ought to be, is sometimes
served to each of us, and it relishes first-rate.[2]

When the new volunteers reached their training camps, they were perhaps only hours away from attempting their own cooking, and certainly by
the time they had been shipped to Washington or Richmond or other admin-
istrative centers, they were already encountering a taste of what lay ahead as
the untrained were set to work feeding the ignorant. As a result, the designated company cook system often broke down sooner rather than later, "because of the selection for the trying position of the most uncouth and
disqualified men in the companies, as the men found to their chagrin."[3]

"We get plenty of rations and if we had any way of cooking them we
could live very well, but we are not allowed to cook in mess," complained a
soldier in Missouri early in the war. "So we have to trust to a couple of dirty
cooks which are detailed out of the company and they care but little how they
cook for it is every fellow for himself and the devil for the pile in this case."[4]
A New York soldier looked at the cooks being selected in each of the companies of his regiment and despaired: "Every one smokes or chews tobacco here,
so we find no fault because the cooks do both. Boxes or barrels are used as
kitchen tables, and are used for seats between meals. The meat and bread are
cut on them, and if a scrap is left on the table the flies go right at it and we
have so many the less to crawl over us. They are never washed, but are sometimes scraped off and made to look real clean. I never yet saw the cooks wash
their hands, but presume they do when they go to the brook for water."[5] It
was never wise to presume. Some better-off Confederate volunteers early in
the war tried to improve their lot by employing their own cooks. In the 5th
Kentucky Infantry, a free black named Mose cooked for one mess at the rate
of ten dollars a month, "washing not included." Presumably the men managed
to wash their own dishes.[6]

And when they put food over fire, these neophytes all too often ruined it.
Thanks to the salted or pickled or dried preservative methods in the meat
issue, twenty-four of twenty-five times the only way it could be cooked at all

was by boiling. "For this reason among others the cooks did not always receive the credit which they deserved for their efforts to change the diet or extend the variety on the bill of fare," remarked John D. Billings. On the rare occasion when the commissary furnished proper roasts, cooks roasted them in ovens and served them rare, middling, or well done. Even then the cooks so mangled the meat that the men came to prefer getting their ration raw so they could fry it themselves. Moreover, suspicious as the soldiers were of everyone who came in contact with their rations before they did, it became a common complaint that the cooks kept the largest or choicest portions for themselves. Indeed, some were allowed to profit by selling the livers, hearts, and tongues for what they could get from the men.[7]

Yankees in Tennessee in March 1863 found that it was worth paying the exorbitant prices charged by sutlers to get good food, but the food was ruined by their hired cooks. "When we can get soft bread and other things that are fit to eat, by paying two prices for them, I don't believe in living on such fair as our Quartermaster has been in the habit of furnishing us lately," said William Richardson of Iowa. "The grub we draw would do very well if it was half cooked but it is no use trying to get a g. d. nigger to do anything right unless you stand over him with a club. That would be more trouble than it would be to do it ourselves which we have not time to do and we would not be allowed to do our own cooking if we had time."[8]

Early in the war Lawrence VanAlstyne of the 128th New York observed that "some get mad and cuss the cooks, and the whole war department, but that is usually when our stomachs are full." When they were hungry they would "swallow anything that comes" and were thankful for it. The cookhouse in his regiment, as in so many, was just a part of the field where they camped, and little more than a pole suspended across a couple of cleft sticks over a fire, on which hung kettles. Every company had its own, and all were more or less alike. The mess kettles issued to them were sheet-iron pails that nested one inside another for packing. If they were having meat and potatoes, meat went into one and potatoes into the other. "The one that gets cooked first is emptied into mess pans," said VanAlstyne; "then the coffee is put in the empty kettle and boiled." Cooks cut the soft bread into thick slices and sounded the breakfast call.

> We grab our plates and cups, and wait for no second invitation. We each get a piece of meat and a potato, a chunk of

bread and a cup of coffee with a spoonful of brown sugar in it. Milk and butter we buy, or go without. We settle down, generally in groups, and the meal is soon over. . . . We save a piece of bread for the last, with which we wipe up everything, and then eat the dish rag. Dinner and breakfast are alike, only sometimes the meat and potatoes are cut up and cooked together, which makes a really delicious stew. Supper is the same, minus the meat and potatoes.[9]

Wilbur Fisk recalled mealtime in camp in the 2nd Vermont early in the war.

When the drum beats, or the cooks halloo, "Company —— fall in" for breakfast, dinner, or supper, as the case may be, we all rush pell-mell for the cook's stand, which is a log shanty or a tent, or both, and crowding our way up to the door receive our bread and meat and coup of coffee. Now if we can back out without having our coffee spilled, and our bread knocked out of our hands, why, all right; if not, a volley of oaths and threats are pretty apt to be the consequence. Those that have fire-places in their tents can improve the flavor of their bread by toasting it before the fire. Toasting-sticks are the most important culinary utensils that we use . . . most of us have frying pans, and we hash up our meat and bread together and make it quite palatable. . . . As regards etiquette and politeness we are not one whit behind the most fashionable of swine.[10]

It did not help that the cooking pots were also used in many camps for boiling their dirty clothes. "Not a very nice thing for a soup pot, especially when they were full of vermin," said Private Alfred Bellard.[11] It was just one more reason that gradually the men simply formed themselves into three- and four-man messes and took over their own cooking. It was hardly trying in the event, since most meals on the march were just bacon or salt meat fried in a pan with the hardtack.[12] Later in the war, when away from camp, every man had to do his own cooking, and with no utensils, they used their pint cups or "dippers" for almost everything. "Whether it was coffee, beans, pork or anything depending on the services of a fire to make it palatable, it was accomplished by aid of the dipper only," said one Massachusetts man. There were so few frying pans in camp that only the better off could afford the dollar to buy one. In the 13th Massachusetts, five men went together to buy one, creating what they called the Joint-Stock Frying-Pan Company. "It was understood that each 'stockholder' should take his turn at carrying the frying-pan when on a march, which responsibility entitled him to its first use in halting for the night," said Private Charles Davis. They also rented it to others for an occasional "dividend."[13]

Such things as cutlery rapidly became even more basic. In Missouri in January 1862, "all we have in the shape of cupboard utensils is a butcher knife and tin cup," said William Richardson. "With the knife we cut our pork which is called by the soldiers 'sow belly' and the tin we use to drink our dirty coffee."[14] Later that year in Memphis he found that "our cupboard and table consist of a small box in which we keep our dishes; they are two tin cups, one old knife and a spoon with the handle broke off." But then, that was all they needed, given their rations on the march. "A soldier has no use for more than one tin, for when we have coffee we have no soup and when we have soup we have no coffee. So you see we have no trouble of washing dishes."[15]

While few Yankee soldiers were in want of government-issue camp ovens, usually sheet-metal stoves sufficient to take care of a mess of a half dozen or so, Confederates found them in short supply, along with frying pans and everything else. In North Carolina, a clergyman was talking with some Confederate soldiers on a rail platform as they awaited shipment to the front. Finally, they boarded the train, and as it was pulling out, one of them yelled back to the preacher that they had forgotten to load their small portable oven onto the car and it was sitting there on the platform. "We can't cook without it," one of them called out. "Please throw it up here." He did so, only to learn that it belonged to a Negro waiting elsewhere on the platform.[16]

"I fancy our tidy New England housekeepers, who take honest pride in setting a well furnished table, would smile to see what splendid novices we are in the culinary art," Wilbur Fisk boasted to his family. Referring to a then-popular would-be nutritionist—and inventor of an eponymous "health" cracker destined to far outlast his memory—Fisk said that some of his mess mates at the stove could "out-Graham Sylvester Graham himself in his most radical ideas of simplicity in diet."[17] Some soldiers achieved minor distinction among comrades for their ability to turn monotonous rations into something palatable. In the 2nd Vermont, one man made a very tasty hash from boiled salt beef and hardtack. "He has a very excellent way of making such material eminently palatable," Fisk marveled, even sharing the recipe with his family at home.[18] That was no mean feat considering that, as Bellard testified, "the salt junk as we called our pork was sometimes alive with worms."[19]

When the company cook system died and the men took over their own cooking, it was necessary to revise the method of issuing rations, and almost universally, in both North and South, the same system developed. In the absence of accurate weights and measures, especially in the Confederacy, a kind of blind distribution evolved to weed out favoritism and caprice. Berry Benson recalled of his Confederate service that "when we first went into the army, we had scales for weighing, and measures for liquids, but long before this time the commissary of a company was reduced to dividing out to the men in a much more primitive fashion."

> The meat (usually bacon) was divided carefully into as many "piles" as there were men, a "pile" usually being one little flat piece about the size of a small cake of toilet soap. Having arranged the "piles" on a log, the commissary would get some fair-minded member of the company to review with him their comparative values. Some such colloquy as this would then take place:
> "Don't you think this here piece is a *little* too big?"
> "W-e-e-ll, maybe it is. Where'll I cut it?"
> "About there."
> "Now where'll I put the scrap?"
> "Put her over here with *this* feller; it's end and about the littlest one you got. But, I say, here's a right smart sized chunk; don't you think it's too big?"
> "Well, I don't know; she *looks* pretty big, but if you'll notice she's got a dog-gone sight of bone in her."

And so it went. Then a man was asked to volunteer to call, meaning he turned his back on the company and as the commissary pointed unseen to a particular piece of meat, the soldier called the name from the roll of who should get it, keeping it up until the whole ration was gone. Flour, rice, meal, sugar, and the rest they divided by measure of spoonfuls in their cups, the first pass being a little light to ensure that every man got something, and then a second pass to give out the rest.[20]

On such a basic scale of cookery, certain foods became ever-present staples and achieved legendary status, none more so than the army bean. "No edible, I think, was so thoroughly appreciated," said Billings. Cooks stewed them with pork "and when the pork was good and the stew or soup was well done and not burned—a rare combination of circumstances—they were quite palatable in this way."[21] They made ovens of field stones, and baked the beans in mess pans or kettles, but most often they simply dug a hole in the ground about three inches wider than the diameter of a kettle. Laying a flat stone on the bottom of the hole, they kept a fire going in the pit for several hours and then removed the coals and put in the kettle of pork and beans. That done, they covered the top of the kettle with a board and shoved the coals back in around the sides of the pot. They spread a sack or cloth over top of the hole, supporting it on poles, and spread a few inches of earth over it to retain the heat. On opening the hole the next morning, they found what Billings declared to be "the most enjoyable dish that fell to the lot of the common soldier."[22]

No wonder the bean was commemorated in song and poem.

> There's a spot that the soldiers all love,
> The mess-tent is that place that we mean,
> And the dish that we like to see there
> Is the old-fashioned, white Army bean.
>
> Tis the bean that we mean,
> And we'll eat as we ne'er ate before,
> The Army bean, nice and clean;
> We will stick to our beans evermore.[23]

Boiled potatoes and onions were favored when the soldiers got them. Indeed, the potato stood second only to the bean. Boiled, baked, mashed, sliced and fried, mixed into stews and hashes—there was almost no limit to the ways in which the noble tuber could stretch a soldier's diet. And not surprisingly, it too earned immortalization in verse by an unnamed poet, whose work went before the Northern public in 1863 in the popular press.

THE LAST POTATO[24]
'Tis my last, last potato!
Yet boldly I stand

With the calmness of Cato,
My fork in my hand.
Not one in the basket?
Must you also go?
(With sorrow I ask it)
Shall I peel ye or no?

Let's make an incision
(There's no need to peel ye),
'Twill let in the vision,
To judge if ye're mealy.
How wholesome! How truly
It smells through the mist
Good-by, my sweet Murphy,
Oh, who could resist?

If in that blest Eden
Potatoes had been
Of fruits the forbidden,
We still should have sin;
For who in his senses
Would long be in doubt
'Twixt earth with potatoes,
Or Eden without.

No one wrote songs about split peas, which were sometimes issued and stewed with pork to make "Peas on a Trencher." They never attained much popularity, as the cooks usually burned them. Confederates boiled peanuts—the tuneful 'goober peas' of the popular marching song—sometimes using them to make coffee of a sort as well as a meal. Boiled rice, also usually burned, appeared occasionally, but it was rarely popular. In the Confederate Vicksburg garrison in 1862, soldiers of the 28th Tennessee Infantry received "almost a single diet of sugar and rice," recalled Spencer Talley. "We lived on rice until we became so tired of it, as to despise it, and for thirty years after the war I never saw a day that I could eat it . . . it has found no favor in my menu yet."[25]

If a large soap boiler could be found, a few pumpkins boiled down to a pulp, without salt, and dipped with improvised wooden spoons were not to be sneezed at.[26] But for vegetables, other than what they might purchase or forage from the countryside, the Yankee soldiers at least had to depend on something else far less appetizing—desiccated vegetables. Abner Small of the 16th Maine gave vent to the customary soldier attitude toward this particular viand when he wrote that "too many beans with salt junk demanded an antiscorbutic." The result was that the government advertised for "some kind of vegetable compound in portable form, and it came—tons of it—in sheets like pressed hops." He supposed it might be healthful. Certainly he found in it variety enough in its composition to satisfy any condition of stomach and bowels, though "what in Heaven's name it was composed of, none of us ever discovered." One messmate brought in a chunk of it and asked if it was celery or cabbage, and no one could answer. "I doubt our men have ever forgotten how a cook could break off a piece as large as a boot top, put it in a kettle of water, and stir it," Small continued. "When the stuff was fully dissolved, the water would remind me of a dirty brook with all the dead leaves floating around promiscuously. Still, it was a substitute for food. We ate it, and we liked it, too."[27]

But they did not like it much. Charles Davis of the 13th Massachusetts recalled that "it was at Darnestown that we were first made acquainted with an article of food called 'desiccated' vegetables." For the convenience of handling, it was made into large, round cakes about two inches thick, and when cooked it tasted like herb tea. "From the flow of language which followed, we suspected it contained powerful stimulating properties," he added. "It became universally known in the army as 'desecrated' vegetables, and the aptness of this term would be appreciated by the dullest comprehension after one mouthful of the abominable compound."[28] Billings found that "when put in soak for a time, so perfectly had it been dried and so firmly pressed that it swelled to an amazing extent, attaining to several times its dried proportions." It seemed to reveal layers of cabbage leaves and turnip tops stratified with layers of sliced carrots, turnips, parsnips, and a bare suggestion of onions "with a large residue of insoluble and insolvable material." One inspector even found what appeared to be ground glass.[29]

Jonathan Letterman, medical director of the Army of the Potomac, recommended that desiccated vegetables should be steeped in water two and hours then boiled with a soup broth for three hours. "Half a ration of desiccated vegetables previously soaked in cold water for an hour, with a few small pieces of pork, adding salt and pepper, with water sufficient to cover well the ingredients, and stewed slowly for three hours, will make an excellent dish," he argued. "The secret in using the desiccated vegetables is in having them thoroughly cooked. The want of this has given rise to a prejudice against them which is unfounded; it is the fault of the cooking, and not of the vegetables."[30] Few would have believed him. "I ate a lot of desiccated vegetables yesterday and they made me the sickest of my life," moaned Sgt. Cyrus Boyd of the 15th Iowa. "I shall never want any more such fodder."[31]

At the beginning of the siege of Vicksburg in May 1863, the Confederates in the works around the city had plenty to eat, with ample cattle and sheep, but nowhere to graze them. Eventually, they were allowed to feed on grass just outside the defensive works, but Union sharpshooters brought them down faster than the defenders could kill and butcher them, and much went to waste rotting in the hot sun. By mid-June, the Confederates were down to a quarter ration of bacon per man per day, which they often preferred to eat raw.[32]

The meat ration, thanks to its method of preservation, occasioned the most outrage and almost none of the rather affectionate epithets reserved for hardtack. "The meat generally came to us quivering from the butcher's knife, and was often eaten in less than two hours after slaughtering," complained Billings. Fresh issues of beef were variable, as the quartermaster and his butchers simply went from back to front on the animal. Stringy meat went into the lobscouse with onions or garlic. If more solid, the beef would be eaten as a steak, whether from a traditional steak cut or not, and fried in pork or beef fat or roasted on a ramrod over coals.[33] They would have broiled steaks only very occasionally.[34] Salt pork was a staple, of course, and the cooks usually boiled it. "There was little else they could do with it," said Billings, and when issued to the men raw, it would be fried instead. It went into soups, lobscouse, and baked beans. Bacon came black or "rusty" with mold and not very savory.[35] The salt beef was rarely served on the march, for it was too salty and water was too scarce, but even in camp, men often turned away from it, for according to Billings and innumerable others, "without doubt, it was the vilest ration distributed to the soldiers." Briny, soaked with saltpeter, and stinking, it sometimes had to be soaked in a running brook overnight to make it at all palatable.[36]

Confederates ate mule meat in Vicksburg and at Port Hudson in the summer of 1863, but there only. Some called it "blue beef," and one Kentuckian said it "was much sought after, and when jerked was the thing for a march."[37] At Port Hudson, Confederate defenders found themselves reduced to a few

ears a day of corn so puny it was called "pinewoods nubbins." Their commissary announced mealtime by singing out "Pig-gee, pig-gee, pig-goo-ah!" and
the men got down on all fours and squealed and grunted like hogs to pick up
their ears. They boiled the corn or roasted it, and some toasted it enough that
they could smash it into a rude meal. Late in June, the men asked their officers to kill their horses and mules that they might have some meat. Linn Tanner was seated on a log with a juicy mule steak on his plate when a teamster
came by complaining that his favorite mule had been killed. Tanner, chewing
his first few bites, said that it was either the men or the mules in their extrem-
ity, and that he was even then eating a piece of the teamster's favorite jack.
The teamster then said that he had hoped that if his mule had to be eaten, he
might at least have had time to cure a big sore on the animal's back, at which
Tanner spat out his bite and threw the plate and mule steak at the teamster.[38]

"The flesh of mules is of a darker color than beef, of a finer grain, quite
tender and juicy, and has a flavor something between that of beef and venison.
There was an immediate demand for this kind of food," wrote a veteran of the
Vicksburg mule meals. "Some horses were also slaughtered, and their flesh was
found to be very good eating, but not equal to mule." Another soldier recalled
that "it was a delicacy," though he also remembered that "I saw some delicious
looking rats broiled one evening, but they were not numerous enough to be of
much use."[39]

"During the final months of the war, more than a few horses, mules, dogs,
cats and even rats were eaten by soldiers," said a Confederate doctor.[40] Rats
especially were found to be quite a luxury—"superior, in the opinion of those
who eat them, to spring chicken . . . and there were few among the garrison
whose natural prejudices were so strong as to prevent them from cooking and
eating their share."[41] Nor did rats appear on the starvation menus of only besieged Confederates. In the winter of 1862–63 in Virginia, Benson and others
on picket found many rats, and they teased each other about trying them.
Soon someone killed a few and roasted them. They found that they tasted
rather like squirrel. "If that time were back, I don't think I would not be
squeamish," Benson said later. He also overcame his antipathy to bull frog
"and found him very nice."[42] A South Carolinian in 1864 spoke of eating a
muskrat and then looking covetously at his officer's dog.[43]

Some men actually ate their meat ration without cooking it, as it made little difference in the taste, which was generally abominable. It often came covered in flies and maggots, "rusty" with mold or with a disgusting greenish and

gelatinous appearance from decay. Men were more than once seen giving their meat ration a funeral rather than eating it. Others put it in the sun to dry out, discouraging the flies, before they somehow got it down. The government suppliers sometimes pickled beef and pork in brine, which made it too salty to eat without boiling first or too smelly to swallow. It soon acquired a host of sobriquets—"salt horse," "salt junk," "bully beef," and more. "We have eaten so much salt pork of late that we are inclined to speak in grunts, prick up our ears, and perform other animal demonstrations," one Rhode Island soldier quipped.[44] Some meat issued to Confederates was so impregnated with salt or saltpeter that soaking all night did not help, and it would not have made it more palatable after 1863, when soldiers learned that the South was now making the preservative by collecting and drying human urine collected in cities and towns. As for salt to season their meat once cooked, Confederates sometimes had to dig up the dirt floors of smokehouses and boil the earth; then they strained and evaporated the result to extract a dirty, unappetizing condiment.

Lawrence VanAlstyne recalled that when his regiment came to Morganza on the Mississippi in 1863, they found that cattle for their rations had already been shot and were just lying on the ground. "It was everyone for himself," he said. "Chunks were cut out and were being eaten before the animal was done kicking. A pack of wolves never acted more ravenous and bloodthirsty. I managed to get my hand between the ribs of one and hold of the liver. I couldn't pull my hand out without straightening the fingers and so got only shreds, but I kept it up until I had taken the edge off my appetite."[45] Even at war's end, on May 14, 1865, a Maine soldier saw that when the men were issued their meat ration, they ate it "in a jiffy and finding it did not throw us into convulsions," they went to where the cattle had been butchered and cut the spleens—called melts—from the remaining entrails. "I have never before heard of eating such trumpery as melts, but necessity drives us to sample this disgustingly filthy mess. Shame on a government that treats its defenders this way."[46]

Often the safest way to ingest these all-too-inadequate ingredients was to mingle them all together into stews, hashes, and soups, where the unpalatability of one might be mitigated by equally unsavory—but different—tastes from the others. "One of our dishes was composed of anything that we could get hold of," said Bellard. "Pork or beef, salt or fresh, was cut up with potatoes, tomatoes, crackers, and garlic, seasoned with pepper and salt, and stewed. This we called Hish and Hash or Hell fired stew."[47] In Virginia in 1865, Maine soldiers scavenged for bones thrown away by other soldiers after eating their beef ration and boiled them for soup. "We try to fill up on slops, but call it *soup* because that title makes it seem more filling—besides, it sounds more genteel," wrote one Down-Easter. "We boiled the bones in juice flavored with salt, bog onion, and pepper."[48]

Desserts existed almost solely in the imagination, especially with the scarcity of sugar. "If we wanted something extra, we pounded our crackers into fine pieces, mixed it up with sugar, raisons and water, and boiled it in our tin cups," said Bellard. "This we called a pudding."[49] Some Yankees bought meal at a local mill and made flapjacks and puddings in what Fisk said was "a style of simplicity such as only soldiers would think of adopting."[50] For Confederates, a final "course" could be even less appetizing. Fruit and berries were often baked into pies that for want of sugar and proper flour, could be fearsome to the taste and digestion. Some Kentucky Confederates made a sugarless fried pie, "this having all the tough elasticity of a rubber suspender."[51] Once in a while, when there was a little sugar, soldiers with Lee made blackberry pies.[52] Often the only sweetener available was watermelon juice, not easy to obtain when by 1863 a single watermelon sold for $40 in the camps.[53]

"I think the government did well, under the circumstances, to furnish the soldiers with so good a quality of food as they averaged to receive," Billings recalled with forgiving memory twenty years after the war. "Unwholesome rations were not the rule, they were the exception, and it was not the fault of the government that these were furnished, but very often the intent of the rascally, thieving contractors who supplied them, for which they received the price of good rations; or, perhaps, of the inspectors, who were in league with the contractors."[54]

Nevertheless, and perhaps not surprisingly, on both sides authorities tried to discourage the men from experimenting too much or straying too widely from traditional army dishes, for fear of illness. For a start, the soldiers ubiquitously preferred to fry everything they could and usually swimming in pork fat. A Union surgeon, reflecting on the propensity of the men to cook everything in a sea of grease, lamented that he was struggling to save the men from "death from the frying pan."[55] Some men actually became sick of meat for this very reason, even Confederates, one of whom complained that he had been "Worshipping at the Frying Pan of King Hog."[56] In June 1862 during the advance on Richmond, Union authorities frowned on the men trying to modify the flavor of their food by mixing it all together and frying it, as with hardtack and beef hash. Fisk mused that "doubtless these restrictions are made out of a wholesome solicitude for our physical welfare, so while we are all prohibited from making our rations more palatable . . . no doubt many of the imprudent are prohibited from enjoying the luxury of a sick headache quite too often to make it profitable for Uncle Sam."[57]

Neither was there much joy in the liquid mainstay for soldiers, especially in the North. Coffee was issued to Yankees rather steadily, in the form of raw beans that the men first had to roast without burning and then crack with their rifle butts or somehow grind before boiling with water. At every meal the coffee came out, and if there was a halt of more than a few minutes on a march, some men were bound to start a fire and begin making the brew, often merely to be told to throw it out unfinished as they resumed the march. While the coffee's caffeine may have been stimulating to their spirits, the boiling also providentially killed much of what inhabited the poor water usually to be had. Confederates, by comparison, cut off from sources of importation, usually had to substitute chicory, burnt corn and peas, and even potatoes and peanuts, with far less satisfactory results.[58] "Our coffee when we first went out was issued to us green, so that we had to roast and grind it, which was not always a success, some of it being burnt, while some would be almost green," said Bellard. "In roasting it we put a quantity of it in a mess pan, and placing the pan over the fire would have to keep stirring it round with a stick in order to have it roasted as evenly as possible."[59] They could never properly grind the beans, cracking them instead, and inadequate roasting could turn the beverage awful.

The officers, of course, had a cash allowance when in camp and could generally afford to furnish themselves with whatever they might buy, so they ate better than the men and often had the advantage of a "contraband," or runaway slave, experienced at cooking to make their meals.[60] In October 1862 in Maryland, Connecticut officers had detailed a man to cook for them, but he fell sick and they had to forage and cook for themselves. "We have been obliged to take to the basting ladle and toasting forks ourselves," reported Lt. Samuel Fiske. At 3 A.M. every morning, he went out with canteens to get water at a spring. Meanwhile, a captain in his overcoat, his eyes only half open, kindled the fire and then buried sweet potatoes in the ashes before returning to bed while they cooked. Another lieutenant arose later to make tea and skewer a mackerel that had soaked overnight to broil on two bent ramrods. Then Fiske went to borrow a loaf of bread from a neighboring tent and returned with half a loaf, which he said he "has found frequently in his recent experiences to be a great deal better than no bread." The three ate their handiwork, seated Turkish style over a low box for a table, spread with a newspaper for a tablecloth. They had salt and pepper, a jar of pickles, a little butter, some sugar, and condensed milk, with tin cups for tea. The potatoes disappeared first, then the mackerel fried in butter, and then the bread. Then they negotiated over who should wash the dishes. One did the job while another went into a nearby town to buy provisions for dinner—taking with him the mess's order for chicken, beef, ham, or oysters; a quart of milk; grapes or other fruit; and vinegar for a cabbage they had already. "I am not proud, personally, of cooking my own dinner or washing dishes," confessed Fiske, regarding it all as an example of "what the soldiers of the people's grand army can do in case of an emergency."[61]

Confederate officers, too, generally ate better than their men, though often not by much, and some like General Lee set an example by rarely enjoying a lavish table. But once in February 1865, when he had been sent a turkey by a well-wisher, Lee spent several days fattening the bird on soldier rice in expectation of sharing it with President Davis when he came to visit. When Davis did not come, Lee had it cooked for a dinner in his headquarters with several members of his staff. They dined first on a thick hotchpotch soup full of vegetables, and Lee enjoined every diner to help himself twice, saying "always 2 turns of soup in camp & a third if you like it." The turkey then appeared served with rice and vegetables. "That dish was a splendid one," a visitor recorded the same day. "The largest Turkey I ever saw which fed us all off one side."[62]

It was a far cry from the lot of Confederate soldiers. Eighteen months earlier, in relatively flush times, one of Lee's soldiers in northern Virginia wrote to a friend to say that "sometimes they give us bacon and sometimes beef; sometimes meal and sometimes flour; sometimes salt and sometimes none." But the only thing they could count on was a daily ration of two ears of corn, and green corn at that.[63] Even those on the relatively abundant South Carolina coast were subsisting in the summer of 1864 on a pint of cornmeal and a gill of sorghum daily, with half a plug of tobacco every Saturday. They traded the tobacco with Negroes for potatoes and other vegetables to supplement their diet. For two months, some did not receive meat at all and had to catch fish and shoot alligators in the swamps or catch a calf secretly in the fields.[64]

Still, faced with the paucity of available ingredients and limited knowledge and utensils, some soldiers managed to make the best of it, and a few even boasted of their meals. Dayton Flint of the 15th New Jersey spoke proudly of the "choice dishes" he had learned to make. "I am thinking seriously of writing a cookbook when I get home," he said in February 1863. How sad it is that he did not.[65]

CHAPTER THREE

HARD CRACKERS, COME AGAIN NO MORE

"Only bread and newspapers we must have," declared Yankee officer Oliver Wendell Holmes during the war. "Everything else we can do without."[1] General Casey agreed when he averred that bread was one of the great staples of the soldier's diet. Indeed, few if any other edible articles generated so much interest and comment during the war as did bread, both when the volunteers had it and when they did not. The soft bread—wheat bread in the North and more often corn or rice bread in the South—that came out of the soldiers' rude camp ovens and the great bakeries of the permanent installations became an integral center of the world around which their diet revolved, while the hard bread or hardtack generated a mythology all its own, one that only grew in later years.

As in so many other things, neither Washington nor Richmond was prepared to provide baked products to soldiers on the massive scale that each army would need. From a peacetime army of barely more than 13,000 men under arms in early April 1861, the Union war machine would find itself having to provide loaves for hundreds of thousands by the end of that summer, while the Confederacy, of course, started virtually from nothing. At first both sides contracted with civilian bakers for all they could supply, a source outstripped overnight, for large-scale commercial fresh bakeries did not yet exist due to the inability to preserve freshness. Fortunately, in the very early days, the chief concentrations of volunteers in Washington, Cincinnati, and St. Louis in the North, and Richmond, Nashville, and New Orleans in the South, meant that city bakeries could just about cope, while the military authorities grappled with the coming problem of providing for armies on the move. Nevertheless, it was apparent to men like Sanderson and Chapman that bread made by soldiers themselves in the camp, and perhaps even on the march, was going to quickly become a reality.

There was one factor working in their favor at the outset. As Sanderson noted, "it generally happens that every regiment numbers among its men one or more bakers."[2] Even outfits raised in rural regions usually had at least one company from a more populous county with a town substantial enough to have several bakeries, while the units from cities like New York and Charleston had many, and bakers' sons proved just as anxious to enlist as anyone else. Thus, almost every training camp in the North could expect to have at least a few men skilled in making yeast and baking loaves, men who could be used to pass on the basic skills to others. For Confederates, it would be a rather different story. Many bakers came from its cities and towns, too, but like their Yankee counterparts, they were accustomed to making bread flour from wheat, a crop grown predominantly in the Union states, except for Virginia, Maryland, and Georgia. With Maryland denied to the Confederacy and Virginia increasingly overrun as the war progressed, sources of wheat in the South were either cut off or rather quickly diminished as farmers and planters were encouraged, and then required, to plant their fields with corn. Georgia continued to produce wheat, but the endemic problems of inadequate and inefficient rail transport made it difficult to distribute grain on a wide basis.

In the main, Rebel soldiers got wheat bread when they made it themselves while campaigning in an area immediately adjacent to where the crop was grown, as with the Shenandoah Valley command of then-Col. Thomas J. Jackson, the future "Stonewall," in 1861. Even there, in the so-called Granary of the Confederacy, his Virginians could not depend on their local commissary or Richmond to bake bread for them. When Jackson issued an order to the commissary in Harpers Ferry for loaves for his men, the commissary refused, having no capacity for baking. "Flower is offered instead," complained one of Jackson's officers, but the men were "totally unprovided with means of baking it." Jackson passed the problem up to his immediate commander, Gen. Joseph E. Johnston, with the request that "Hard Bread or corn meal may be issued, if fresh wheat bread can not be."[3]

In the summer of 1862, Berry Benson's South Carolina regiment marched from Richmond to join with Jackson in the west, and he got the task of cooking marching rations for his mess, "a duty I shunned whenever possible." At least there was an abundance of bacon and flour this early in the war, and he got to work, baking some ninety-six biscuits and using the remaining flour to make small, flat wafers without salt. "The others of the mess rejected them to a man," he remembered. "To prove that it was the fault of their own depraved tastes, I ate the last one of them—and was glad when I had done so. I never made any more."[4]

The scarcity of wheat bread in Confederate camps became general knowledge in the North, and one plucky Southerner capitalized on it to mislead the foe. Captured behind Yankee lines while scouting, Berry Benson happened to have a rare loaf of soft wheat bread that he had purchased the day before in return for his own daily ration while he was away. When his captors asked, during interrogation, how the Confederates were doing for food, Benson thought to pull out his loaf and offer a piece of it, knowing that the Federals who captured him were more likely eating hardtack while campaigning. While a Union colonel savored Benson's hard-purchased bread, declaring it excellent, Benson nonchalantly led him to believe that "we got plenty of that."[5]

Benson's was a rare loaf. "Corn-bread, in homeopathic doses, cooked either with or without grease, according to the ability of the commissary to furnish his quarter pound chunk of fat, was the staple," recalled one Kentucky Confederate.[6] The predominantly rural Southern population, especially in the Deep South, were long accustomed to using corn flour for their bread baked in the home, and of necessity, after 1861 that became the staple in the army, meaning that even bakers, like the raw privates, needed to learn new skills to work with a different ingredient in supplying the men's daily rations. Overwhelmingly, the soldiers simply made their own, mixing rough cornmeal with water and salt and then baking it in a frying pan over the campfire, or even placing it in the coals and ashes and then brushing away the charred bits. Unfortunately, in the general absence of any leavening or rising agent, the result was too often a rubbery substance that was eaten under only the grimmest of circumstances. Hard, tough biscuits or bread, sometimes called corn dodgers, almost defied chewing as ably as the Yankee hardtack. "The dodgers, with age added to their actually adamantine character," lamented one Confederate civilian, "were simply indestructible."[7] Cream of tartar, soda, yeast, and even bicarbonate agents made from potassium and other sources—generally called saleratus—became increasingly scarce, even in the cities, and all but nonexistent in the soldier camps. Some actually turned to using ashes to achieve a very modest leavening to relieve the granite texture of their breads. And if they got government-issue corn bread, it might have been around so long or so ill-cared for that it was moldy or full of cobwebs when bitten into.[8]

Other expedients included so-called Indian meal—really just a coarsely ground corn—that when mixed with molasses or brown sugar and baked over a fire, became something the soldiers called sagamite. "It not only appeases hunger but allays thirst, and is therefore useful to soldiers on a scout," observed the only cookery guide to appear in the South during the war, the nonofficial *Confederate Receipt Book*, published in Richmond in 1863. But it also warned that sagamite ought to be eaten "in small quantities."[9] Soldiers who came from Georgia and South Carolina often had at least some exposure to rice and rice flour produced in the tidewater areas of those states and found it an acceptable substitute if necessary. Many a loaf of rice bread came from camp ovens, though again, without a rising agent like yeast, all too often it came out as a pudding or mush if undercooked and a brick if baked too long. Benson actually picked walnuts in the Shenandoah Valley in 1862 and ground them with flour to make a walnut bread, but after three bites it proved awful. Nevertheless, he smacked his lips gleefully, seducing others in his mess to try it—but only after buying their pieces with proper bread of their own. "After that," he said, "I ate my walnuts in the usual way."[10]

At the beginning of the siege of Vicksburg in May 1863, the Confederates in the works around the city had plenty to eat, but by mid-June, corn and meal were scarce, and as Pvt. W. O. Dodd noted, "having but little flour at any time in the Western armies, the question of bread became serious." They turned to the cow pea as a substitute but had to abandon it when several soldiers became sick.[11] A North Carolina Confederate wrote home that he was issued cow peas full of weevils, "but all the better for that as they give the pease a fine flavor."[12] In the Shenandoah, men made bread from what they called "sick flour" because the bread made them feel seasick.[13]

Such ersatz substitutes for bread also reflected another pressing scarcity in Confederate camps—ovens. "Not a cooking utensil of any kind could be had, high or low," lamented Benson of one of his campaigns. They could broil meat on sticks over an open fire, "but how to cook flour without oven, frying pan, or something, how even to make it into dough?" Some soldiers used their shirts or an old handkerchief to hold wheat or corn flour and water while mixing and then made an approximation of baking by placing the dirty dough on stones heated in a fire. Those who had rubber, waterproof blankets dumped flour and water into them to make their dough. Others just put their dough in the ashes and took their chances. Benson once baked on an abandoned rusty plow blade he found in a field. Many Confederates eventually learned to roll their dough into long thin strips or ropes, wrap it around their rifles' ramrods, and roast it as on a spit over the fire. As the ends of the dough were baked done, the soldiers broke them off and ate them while the next bit cooked, and thus "it then miraculously disappeared." One Yankee told of nailing such dough to a tree beside a fire and swearing at it to augment the heat of the coals.[14]

As the war progressed, the only soft bread a Confederate soldier was likely to experience was that in a major city like Atlanta or Richmond, but by 1865, in the capital what had once been penny loaves sold for many times that price. One wag noted hyperbolically that he found them in three sizes, when available at all in the markets. A dollar bought a loaf "only visible by microscopick [sic] aid." Two dollars bought one that at least could be seen with the naked eye. Three dollars actually got a loaf discernable "with outline and shape intact."[15]

Meanwhile in the Union, and not surprisingly after his experiments in the camps, Sanderson paid special attention in his handbook to instructions for baking fresh wheat bread. In fact, over one-fourth of *Camp Fires and Camp Cooking* contains details on producing yeast and baking bread, as well as an illustration of both a simple field oven that could be built by soldiers and the operation of the relatively small and portable government-issue "Shiras oven," which could produce 300 loaves a day, meaning that three of them could feed a regiment. It was a simple oven of tin, easily dismantled to be moved with the army, although the complex operation of bread baking required far more specialized accessories than any other branch of field cooking—dough troughs, wooden peels for putting dough into an oven and taking out the loaves, sieves, brushes, yeast tubs, and tents to provide a warm environment for dough to rise even in cold weather. A few men, properly trained, could provide for many; each regiment produced its own bread when time, locality, and issues of flour allowed.

First the cooks must make a yeast, "without which all efforts are in vain." Every implement from fermenting tubs to spoons and kettles must be spotless, for any impurities could spoil a whole batch, and ideally such containers ought to be used for no other purpose. During his experimental time with the 23rd New York, Sanderson met Frank Lockwood, a baker whose product won the universal approbation of the men and officers of his regiment, and Sanderson was sufficiently impressed that he incorporated Lockwood's methods and recipe into his handbook. Lockwood boiled hops in clear water and then poured the strained water over flour in a tub, turning it first into a paste and eventually into a thick liquid. When it had cooled to room temperature, he added malt and stock yeast from a commercial baker and then set the mixture in a warm spot for at least fifteen hours. Afterwards, it could be strained to remove any hops or lumps of flour, and it was ready for use. But the best part was that in addition to making yeast for immediate baking purposes, this was not itself a "stock yeast"; it could be used to start the fermentation process in new batches, and they on in their turn, indefinitely. No wonder Sanderson emphasized that "care must be taken *always* to keep enough on hand for stock for the next making," for "after making the first essay, you can always be independent."

Lockwood's next step was to make what bakers called a "ferment," by boiling potatoes, skin on, with flour and then mashing all of it together. Next, water and the yeast were thoroughly mixed in, and the whole was set aside in a warm tent or hut overnight. The next morning, the strained ferment was to be added to salt, flour, and water in the bread trough and kneaded into dough. Two hours' rising made it ready to throw out on the table for cutting into pieces to be shaped into loaves and set in pans for the final "proving," or rising. Forty minutes later, it was ready to go into the oven. The Shiras, meanwhile, had been filled with stove wood and heated to the proper temperature, and then the ashes were cleaned out and the interior swabbed to prevent any charred matter from falling onto the bread. When the loaf pans went in, there would be sufficient heat stored in the oven for it to cook them thoroughly in about fifty minutes, and if the cooks followed the Lockwood/Sanderson instructions carefully, they could make three batches of 288 loaves each in a period of eight hours, meaning that baking bread for a regiment of up to 900 men was an all-day job for the three men engaged.[16]

Interestingly enough, in his heavily plagiarized version of the Sanderson recipe, General Casey—or the staff officer who prepared his guidelines—managed to condense the instructions rather effectively. Still, both versions only addressed the responsibilities of a regimental baker. As the war progressed, the Union War Department came to realize the inevitability of economies of scale as it had to feed hundreds of thousands and, in many cases, in largely stationary garrisons of tens of thousands at Washington and Chattanooga, or wherever the major armies went into winter quarters to wait for spring and the return of campaigning weather. In those circumstances, as around Richmond and Petersburg, Virginia, in 1864–65, when Lee's army was essentially immobile and under siege, it simply was not practical to have hundreds of commands each making its own bread every day. The same was the case for the large military hospitals with thousands of inmates, as at Chimborazo in Richmond or the scores of tent and barrack wards around Washington, not to mention the prison camps, like those at Elmira, New York, and Salisbury, North Carolina. For these places and times, economy and efficiency argued in favor of massive centralized bakeries run by experienced staff. Not surprisingly, abundant raw materials saw the majority of them appear in the North or behind Union lines in occupied portions of the Confederacy. Early in the war, the War Department actually installed ovens in the bowels of the Capitol for a time. The War Department in Washington was also able to devote considerable time to a systematic analysis of the baking process from mill to loaf, and in true bureaucratic fashion, it produced a densely packed fifty-two-page government document on the subject that provided vastly more information than any army baker was ever likely to need or want to know. The document also contained a virtual state-of-the-art analysis of everything that went into bread making and categorical warnings of the pitfalls to avoid, whether making one loaf or thousands.

Bread and Bread Making came off the Government Printing Office press in 1864, about two years late to meet the needs that arose as early as late 1861—yet one more example of the unpreparedness of Washington for the scale of the crisis. The manual's anonymous authors attempted to make up for the government's tardiness by a rigorous attention to detail, beginning with an analysis of the prime ingredient, making it quite clear that there was flour, and then there was flour. The report concluded that nutritious bread came from wheat with a high degree of gluten and a low proportion of starch, and experiments found "southern wheat possesses this to a greater degree than any other." The fields of Virginia and Maryland produced much finer grain for bread making than Ohio or Iowa. Southern wheat was fuller and rounder in the kernel, stronger, and with more "body."[17] Indeed, the report went on to analyze English wheat, Scotch oatmeal, Indian corn meal, and the wheat produced in several of the states, North and South, to isolate gluten and starch content, as well as water and fat; to every test, Southern wheat emerged superior, making quicker rising and springier soft bread than the "starchy, sluggish Flour of the west." It also produced more loaves per barrel than Yankee wheat. The finest flour tested came from the Haxhall & Brothers Mill in Richmond, most likely captured by the Union army then encircling the Confederate capital.

The guide provided instructions for government inspectors on how to judge the quality of flour being purchased, even down to gradients of whiteness, and whereas taking the "high ground" meant seizing commanding defensive positions for fighting soldiers in action, for bakers it denoted the best flour for light bread, with a texture like fine sand. The book provided tests based on touch, workability when mixed with water, and even water content based on the season of the year. And in an admonition not to be taken in by purely self-serving marketing by millers, the authors warned inspectors that "in purchasing Flour, all brands should be disregarded, and the quality determined by reliable inspection." Even the method of transportation of the flour from mill to baker was important; that shipped by water was especially prone to unsatisfactory rising when made into dough, as much as 10 percent less than that with flour transported by rail.[18]

The authors of the report then reprised the results of their research into bread-making guides and even scientific studies, going back as far as the 1825 Army Regulations, the only previous official military cooking guide, and its recipe commonly called "General Scott's Method," after Winfield Scott. They excerpted a *Dictionary of Art and Mines* for its scientific explanation of the chemical processes that turned the ingredients into bread, including how many loaves English bakers commonly produced from a 280-pound sack of flour. From *Theory and Art of Bread Making* and *Johnson's Chemistry of Common Life* came lessons on yeast production and why it worked the miracle it did; Johnson passed on at least confirmation, if not the origin, of the assumption that fresh-baked bread, though tasty, was "generally considered less digestible." Johnson even explained that bread going stale was not because of loss of water content, but rather a molecular change. The *Baker's London Gazette* for 1849 revealed that the finer and better the flour, the more loaves it would produce, and it even engaged in some of the mathematical punditry so beloved of bureaucrats by pointing out that 56 pounds of fine flour would produce 72 pounds of "good, sound, well-baked bread." That represented an increase in finished product over raw ingredient of 28.57 percent thanks to the weight of the water and yeast added. Even then, no government inspector could resist crowing over the potential for a profit, and Union quartermasters used the goal of turning a 196-pound barrel of flour into 265 pounds of finished bread, a gain of 33.5 percent over the weight of the original flour.

The pitfalls of underbaking, overly acidic dough, and producing too thick a crust all received fair attention, and in the end, the report's author could not do better than look back to 1825 for General Scott's definition of the proper feel and appearance of a properly baked loaf. "The quality of Bread will be judged by color, smell, and still more by taste," the old Army Regulations declared. "It should not be burnt, but baked to an equal brown color. The crust ought not to be detached from the crumb. On opening it, when fresh, one ought to smell a sweet and balsamic odour."[19]

Taking advantage of three years' experience at major government bakeries in Washington and across the Potomac at Alexandria, Virginia, the report outlined steps for making yeast, renewing old stock yeast, making dough, and baking the finished loaves. From the United States Bakery at Alexandria came a version that turned four barrels of flour into 932 eighteen-ounce rations of soft bread. The recipe of the G Street Bakery in Washington would produce 1,392 similar-size rations from six barrels of flour; interestingly, that meant one less loaf per barrel. Both methods assumed that one oven, properly operated, could handle six or more batches in a twelve-hour period; thus, just one oven could bake thousands of loaves a day, and these government bakeries contained several ovens each. The reporters also conducted multiple experiments on the old Scott method, providing warnings about pitfalls of waste and inefficiency of manpower and facility required for large-scale baking. The Scott method took ten and a half hours to produce 720 loaves of bread from the same ingredients that the G Street process required to produce 696 rations in just eight hours. In other words, G Street saved two and a half hours of time at the expense of twenty-four loaves. The Scott method produced 65.57 loaves per hour; the G Street process produced 87 in the same time. Moreover, Scott bread dried out at a dramatically faster rate during the three days after baking, the time during which a batch would normally be consumed.[20]

Not content with this much information, the reporters studied average moisture loss at hourly intervals, the number of loaves that could be extracted from differing flours depending on their gluten content, the influence of using potatoes to make yeast, and the expedient of introducing soap suds to dough to arrest overfermentation. They also conveyed European chemists' warnings against using chemical fermenting agents like juristic acid and carbonate of soda in place of naturally made yeast. "Chemists, generally speaking, should never recommend the use of chemicals for culinary preparations,"—seemingly sound advice at any time, but especially in an age when, they found, such acids often contained arsenic. "After all," the reporters added waggishly, "a bake-house is not a chemical laboratory." Then came a discussion of the change in physical characteristics caused by toasting, and the authors even discussed a German scientist's investigation into the chemical change that took place when bread contacted the saliva of a consumer during chewing, noting that it aided in the digestion of the starch.[21]

In an attention to detail that presaged the mountainous government reports of later generations, Bread and Bread Making also discussed ovens, even mentioning the 64,376 five-and-a-half-pound bricks, 64 barrels of lime, and

960 bushels of sand needed to build a six-chamber oven. The merits of different kinds of brick had to be considered, as well as proper mortar mixes. Designs and specifications for large-scale ovens used by the office of the commissary general of subsistence followed, with details of construction for versions using both wood and coal, and even the introduction of an interior gas lamp to provide light for the bakers to judge when a batch was done. Once the oven was in operation, of course, its performance was entirely dependent upon the critical function of internal temperature, so naturally there had to be experiments to determine heat loss in ten-minute increments from different starting temperatures, along with an evaluation of the recommended oven temperatures from several authorities, ranging from 320 to 450 degrees. The report itself concluded that a properly baked loaf carried an internal temperature of 240 degrees after one hour in the oven. To achieve that, sufficient wood should be burned inside the oven to raise its heat to between 550 and 580 degrees before the coals were swept out and the loaf pans inserted. At the end of an hour, the oven temperature would fall off to 400 degrees, at which point the bread would be done. Naturally, the report reduced all this to a formula of one-eighth of a cord of wood to heat a cold oven to bake 1,000 loaves. If the oven was worked all day with repeated heatings, then wood consumption fell by half and hot-burning pine was the best to use. It might have seemed statistical overkill, but these were the very calculations necessary to ensure the proper supply of fuel as well as ingredients to keep the ovens feeding the men.[22]

Nor could man-hours be left out. It took eight-hour shifts by three six-man gangs of bakers to turn out a dozen batches of bread every twenty-four hours in a two-oven shop working at full capacity. A larger operation, up to six ovens as at G Street or the Alexandria bakery, needed up to sixty men, producing about 700 loaves a day per man on average. For each oven, they needed seventy bread pans, fire rakes, peels, tables, troughs, sieves, scales, shovels and scrub brushes, brooms, hatchets, axes and saws for wood, cauldrons and buckets, and brushes. The report also specified the proper dimensions of all that paraphernalia and outlined the specific duties of the oven foreman, the bakers, and the yeast makers. Leaving nothing to chance or imagination, it suggested that the internal temperature of the bake house containing the ovens should never go below 75 degrees, while sometimes it would rise to 90 or even 100. "Such a temperature is too exhausting to the Bakers, and should not be allowed," it added charitably.[23]

Finally came the matter of handling the loaves once out of the oven. Bread ought to be issued to the troops about twenty hours after baking, the report suggested, and only "in extreme cases" should it be distributed within as little as ten or twelve hours, further confirming the prejudice against eating bread fresh from the oven. This may have been partially a practical matter for transportation, however. A government wagon, fully loaded, could carry between 1,400 and 1,800 loaves. If they were too soft, the weight of those on top would crush those beneath. Letting the loaves get a bit stale made them firmer, and even then the report stipulated that loaves ought always to be stacked for shipment on their ends or sides.[24]

No wonder soldiers applauded the abundance of soft bread when they were in an extended camp. "We get verry good soft bread here," Colonel Alvin Voris of Ohio boasted from his garrison in South Carolina in 1862. "The entire command is fed with it now. The hard bread is saved for marches and camp away from baking facilities."[25] The fondness of the soldiers for soft bread resembling what their mothers had made was manifest in the expedients they found on their own for turning flour into something edible when on the march and no portable ovens could be employed, or when they were too far from established army bakeries for edible bread to reach them. They found that mixing flour, water, and a little salt and sugar produced a dough that could be fried in hot lard or fat to make fritters. Much the same mixture, boiled in water, made dumplings to add to a stew, and if enough flour and eggs could be found, flapjacks very occasionally made a small feast, especially if butter and maple syrup or sorghum were to be had.

In the 15th New Jersey one private boasted of his apple dumplings, made with apples, sugar, flour, and melted butter or pork fat. "First you get an old mess pan just like ours, to mix the dough in; then put in the flour, make a hole in the center, and pour some pork gravy in; stir it in the flour with a stick, then add some cream of tartar, and salads, and pour in enough muddy water to mix the whole," he began his recipe. "We put in muddy water because we can't get any that is clear;" he advised his sister at home that "perhaps you had better do so too, maybe that helps to make them better." Then he set the pan in the middle of the floor, and he and his mates took off their coats and caps to keep them free of the messy dough, rolled up their sleeves, and "pitch[ed] in with both hands up to [their] elbows." They rolled the dough into little balls around a piece of apple at the center and then boiled them until done. "We boys I think had the best part of the fun in eating them," he concluded, adding that "some of the dumplings were light, too."[26]

And all such chewy expedients were a wonderful break from the real staple of their diet, something that only an army bureaucrat could call bread, a product of reputedly ancient origins—and equally ancient manufacture to the soldiers' minds—that so-called "army bread" or "hard bread" that Voris mentioned, universally known after 1861 as hardtack. Its precise birth is obscure, but it had been used in European armies for generations and in the United States Army before the war. The cracker—for such it was—was simplicity itself, just wheat flour and water in a rough proportion of six to one, mixed and rolled out to a thickness of about three-eighths of an inch, then cut into roughly three-inch squares. Perforated with a few holes to speed baking, the crackers went into ovens at standard bread-baking heat, and after twenty to thirty minutes, they emerged as hardtack, imperishable, indestructible, and practically inedible, too hard to chew, too small for shoeing mules, and too big to use as bullets, though one Illinois private assured friends that "we live on crackers so hard that if we had of loaded our guns with them we could of killed secesh in a hurry." Soldiers often quipped that their ration had been in storage in commissary vaults at least since the war with Mexico in 1846-1848. One maintained that they had been to Japan with Commodore Matthew Perry for use as cannonballs, while others asserted that the initials B.C. on the cracker boxes, standing for "Brigade Commissary," really meant that it had been baked "Before Christ."[27] Yet somehow they ate it and used it in puddings, stews, and bizarre dishes of their own invention. They also cursed it and threw it away and damned all who made it, and still the richest body of mythology produced by any article of the war evolved around it. Perversely, the soldiers became almost fond of it, so long as they did not have to eat it, and thousands of Billy Yanks went to their graves in after years with a souvenir cracker in their box of war mementoes. One even dedicated a book to hardtack.[28]

Even more so than with soft bread, Washington was ill-prepared to meet its hardtack needs at the beginning of the war. It had always been made for the army on contract with civilian bakers, like the G. H. Bent Company of Milton, Massachusetts, which would remain one of the principal producers throughout the war.[29] But prior to April 1861 it had only been needed to supply companies on frontier service when away from their forts and garrisons, and their numbers were small. By the late summer of 1861, however, with close to a half million men in training or under arms all across the North, a dramatic escalation in production was needed. On the march or when soft bread was not available, the standard daily ration of hardtack was nine or ten crackers per man according to the whim of his commissary. Thus, when Gen. Irvin McDowell led his 35,000-man army out of the Washington defenses on July 16 for the five-day march that resulted in the first battle of Bull Run, his commissaries had to bring with them over one and a half million crackers, and this campaign was modest by later measure. In 1864, the Union would have 100,000 men on the march in northern Virginia under Gen. Ulysses S. Grant and another 80,000 or more commanded by William T. Sherman in Georgia, in addition to scores of thousands in other smaller commands reaching as far as the Pacific. That meant as many as three or four million hardtack being consumed every day, clearly too big a demand for any one baker to supply, and thus companies all across the North received contracts that kept their ovens at baking heat around the clock.

Capt. J. J. Scroggs, a white officer with the 5th United States Colored Troops, was curious enough about the origins of hardtack in 1864 to visit one of the bakeries employed. Five barrels of flour at a time went into a huge tray, and then salt and water were introduced in the proper proportion. That done, the baker then thrust his arms into the trap up to the elbows and worked the ingredients into a dough before lumping it into a kneading machine. The dough then fell from the machine in large rolls that reminded Scroggs, as he discretely put it, of "an animal performance on a large scale." Then the rolls slid into a basement where three more machines rolled them into the required thickness of half an inch, cut each roll into twenty-four square crackers, punctured each with sixteen holes, and then placed them on a canvass conveyor belt to the six ovens, each baking 1,000 at a time. After baking, he watched the crackers being packed by women and girls into wooden boxes, each holding fifty pounds ready for shipment to the army.[30]

The problems with hardtack commenced almost from the moment they cooled after baking and were packed into wooden crates for shipment to the central commissary depots. They were already hard as bricks, but what little water content remained in them to counter the concretinous character of the baked flour soon evaporated as they sat unwrapped and unsealed for days or even weeks before being issued. The boxes, often in virtual mountains at the depots, lay exposed to the elements, meaning that heat could dry them even further or rain could soak through the boxes and turn the contents first mushy and then moldy. That was only the first hazard. Once opened for issue to the men, rare was the box of hardtack that had not been penetrated by flies or other insects, which fed off the crackers and laid eggs whose hatch bored networks of tunnels into each cracker in which the maggots and larval worms thrived. "It was a severe trial and it tested the temper of the men," a Union chaplain wrote in 1864 when his regiment received infested hardtack. Soldiers often had to use their rifle butts to break the crackers apart, only to find them teeming with worms, and then in disgust, they threw them away on the bottom of the earthen trenches they occupied while besieging Richmond and Petersburg. An officer of the day, outraged at the mess they created, shouted at them to remove the discarded fragments and leave them elsewhere. "Don't you know that you've no business to throw hardtack in the trenches?" he howled at them. "Haven't you been told that often enough?" The inevitable company comedian replied that "we've thrown it out two or three times, sir, but it crawls back."[31]

The soldiers soon dubbed hardtack "worm castles," telling exaggerated stories of the only meat in their ration being the worms in the crackers and how they toasted their ration as they preferred not to eat their meat raw. A New England soldier advised that the crackers be soaked in coffee first—some said six weeks was long enough—and then laid on a plate, taking care not to shake the worms out. "They eat better than they look," he said, "and are so much clear gain in the way of fresh meat."[32] They even combined this growing worm lore with the other legendary characteristic of hardtack, its impenetrability. Calling the crackers "tooth dullers" and "sheet-iron crackers," volunteers told jokes about a soldier who actually found something soft inside his hardtack one morning. Asked if it was a worm, he incredulously replied, "No by G-d, it was a ten penny nail." One artillery battery derisively used its hardtack as paving stones to decorate the ground around its quarters.[33] "Who dares say it is not hard, should be condemned to eat it for a fortnight," complained Colonel Voris.[34] Wilbur Fisk concluded that when it came to hardtack "a man with poor teeth is certainly an object of pity on these occasions."[35]

It was that much worse when on the march, and the soldiers often outdistanced the ability of their commissary to keep up with them. Even in the generally better supplied Union Army, all too often soldiers on campaign found themselves limited for several days at a time to nothing but the daily ration of hardtack, and sometimes only a half ration at that. In such circumstances "a well man can easily devour his day's ration at one meal and not exert himself dangerously," John Haley of Maine sarcastically complained. "Some men do eat all at one meal, saying they much prefer one *meal* to three *aggravations*."[36] It was "positively unsuitable fodder for anything that claims to be human," said Fisk. His captain's horse refused to eat one, "and I think it no exaggeration to say that any intelligent pig possessing the least spark of pride would have considered it a pure insult to have them put into his swill."[37]

Often the only way to get the hardtack down was first to soak it in water and then to fry it in a pan in bacon fat or lard, making a glutinous dish the soldiers called "skillygalee." One soldier promised that it would "make the hair curl."[38] Using a hammer or rifle butt to crumble the crackers, they soaked them and mixed them with anything else at hand to create "hellfire stew." Hardtack even went into soup; it was added to salt pork and any miscellaneous available ingredients to produce "lobscouse," a soup with ancient origins in the British navy.[39] If a can of condensed milk was available—it cost seventy-five cents, a healthy chunk of a private's $13 a month—they soaked hardtack in it to make a sort of milk toast. Confederates, whose commissary-issue or self-made corn dodgers could be just as hard as Yankee hardtack, often crumbled their hard bread into a frying pan and cooked it in grease, adding whatever communal oddments of bacon, salt pork, or beef they could find at hand, making a dish they called "cush" or "slosh," most probably so named because of the explosive noise made by steam escaping from the gelatinous mass as it cooked.[40]

No wonder the men cursed the crackers, even embedding their imprecations in song and verse like this one, composed in 1861 in Missouri by a disgruntled Yankee:

> There's a hungry, thirsty soldier, who wears his life away,
> With torn clothes, whose better days are o'er;
> He is sighing now for whiskey, and, with throat as dry as hay,
> Sings, "Hard crackers, come again no more!"

However, when a Union general heeded the grumbling song and tried to relieve his command from hardtack by substituting corn mush, suddenly the old worm castles did not seem so bad after all, and a new chorus appeared:

> It is the dying wail of the starving,
> Hard crackers, hard crackers, come again once more;
> You were old and very wormy, but we pass your failings o'er.
> O hard crackers, come again once more![41]

And so they did come again, to remain an ever-present companion in the camp, on the march, and in the soldier' dreams to the end of their days.

CHAPTER FOUR

Visions of
Fat and Savory
Beefsteaks

"An army is a big thing, and it takes a great many eatables and not a few drinkables to carry it along," Samuel Fiske observed in 1863.[1] To that end, Surgeon General William Hammond maintained that the Union soldier was the best-fed fighting man in the world, and visiting European observers tended to agree.[2] In 1861, the standard daily ration in the Union army was based on the assumption that not all required ingredients would be available at all times and places. As a result, it operated on an equivalent or what some called the "lieu thereof" or the "or" system. "We all know that Government gives us besides our bread, meat, and coffee, sundry articles such as hominy, meal, peas, vegetables, and so forth, but which we seldom ever see. The army regulations allows us these, or something in 'lieu thereof,'" complained a Vermont soldier. "We sometimes feel it no impudence to inquire in what shape the 'lieu thereof' is coming."[3]

Each day a soldier ought to be issued three-fourths of a pound of pork "or" bacon "or" one and one quarter pounds of fresh "or" salt beef. His bread ration was to be eighteen ounces of fresh bread or flour or three-fourths of a pound of hardtack or one and one quarter pounds of cornmeal. Additionally, each 100-man company was to share eight quarts of peas or beans or ten pounds of rice, ten pounds of coffee or one and a half pounds of tea, fifteen pounds of sugar, four quarts of vinegar, and two quarts of salt.[4] In 1861, the Confederate War Department adopted precisely the same ration allowance as the old United

States prewar, excepting that it recognized the scarcity of coffee and sugar by reducing those from ten pounds of coffee to six and from fifteen pounds of sugar to twelve. In any event, the Southern commissary was rarely able to provide either those items or those quantities after 1861, or at any distance from principal commissary and transport centers.[5]

In 1863, responding to the rigors of campaigning, the Union War Department revised the ration to three-fourths pound of pork or bacon or one and one fourth pounds of salt or fresh beef, one pound six ounces of soft bread or flour or one pound of hardtack or one and one fourth pounds of cornmeal, fifteen pounds of beans or peas and ten pounds rice or hominy for every 100 rations, ten pounds of green coffee beans or eight pounds of roasted beans, or one and a half pounds of tea, fifteen pounds of sugar, four quarts of vinegar, three pounds ten ounces of salt, four ounces of pepper, thirty pounds of potatoes when available, and one quart of molasses.[6] But then the next year, this time to loud protest from the soldiers, it was reduced again, to its pre-1861 level, as genuine "bean counters" in Washington and in Congress determined that soldiers were wasting too much.

Whatever the government provided, it seemed never to be enough. Certainly the soldiers did sometimes waste food through bad cooking or improper keeping. Some of it also came to them in inedible condition to begin with, and being improvident like all young men, they also tended to eat more than a day's ration at a time if they had it available; thus, on the march they often suddenly found themselves with an empty haversack and several days to go before the next issue of rations. Sutlers, licensed merchants allowed to vend things from pies to writing paper, operated with or near most of the camps, at least in the Union army, but they soon became suspect for selling shoddy goods at inflated prices and would end the war as objects of derision and loathing. Besides, few soldiers had enough money to pay sutler prices. In that event, and given all that their commissaries were authorized to provide, the men in the ranks were left with no alternative, whether in camp or on the march, but to forage for themselves. Of course, while in friendly loyal territory, officers from army commanders on down to regimental colonels issued orders strictly prohibiting soldiers from appropriating or stealing—which is what foraging largely came to mean—goods from local civilians. All too often, even in the face of stiff penalties, such orders became hard to remember on an empty stomach, North and South alike, and when on the march, especially in enemy country, anything edible within reach became fair game.

Indeed, even when on campaign in Confederate territory, most Union commanders early in the war tried to keep their men from depredating on civilian foodstuffs, not so much out of humanitarian concern as practical political policy. Outraging civilians only risked making them more confirmed Rebels. Policy did, however, allow men to purchase goods from civilians, and it generally allowed the confiscation of property of outspoken Confederates or those who refused to take an oath of allegiance to the Union. Very quickly, Yankee soldiers applied their wit and ingenuity to profit by such distinctions. When they stole a pig they would later explain to their captain that they left the payment—which could be a bullet or an insulting note—on a fence post, and the captain, who likely shared in the ensuing meal, could rest easy that the proprieties had been observed. Far more customary, however, was for a soldier simply to address a hog or a chicken directly and demand that it take the oath. If it refused, which seemed invariably the case, then the animal was a traitor and subject to forfeiture of all its property, which in such cases tended to be its chops and hams and drumsticks.

"We have been here just one week and have lived well for we have had plenty of contraband goods such as fat cattle, sheep, hogs and occasionally a Nigger," an Iowa soldier boasted of his stay in Missouri in October 1861, the Negro presumably being for cooking and not eating like the rest of his list of goods.[7] In Sedalia, Missouri, a few months later foraging soldiers wrote home that they "had the good luck to come across a fine hog which refused to take the oath of allegiance, so they were compelled by law to shoot it. After taking its hams, putting them into their knapsacks, they started for Camp and you may bet we had a good mess of fresh pork for breakfast."[18] After the battle of Shiloh, in the summer of 1862, Yankees in Mississippi spent the Fourth of July in camp near Holly Springs. "Our dinner consisted of one hard cracker each and a piece of a Secesh sheep which we knocked in the head for entering our lines and then refusing to take the oath," wrote one Federal. "I don't think there was a hog, sheep, goose or chicken left within 5 miles of where our Division camped. Our officers told us to take what we could get to eat and not pay for it unless the owners proved themselves to be loyal to the Government."[9] Sam Merrill of the 70th Indiana recalled foragers coming in Georgia in 1864, one with a stolen carriage pulled by a goat and a cow, followed by a sheep and a cow, and loaded with "pumpkins, chickens, cabbages, guinea fowls, carrots, turkeys, onions, squashes, a shoat, sorghum . . . sweetmeats, a peacock . . . sweet potatoes . . . dried peaches, honey . . . peach brandy, and every other imaginable thing a lot of fool soldiers could take in their heads to bring away."[10]

An Ohio soldier assured his family that it was all right to take Southern chickens because "they are always sure to cackle at the Stars and Stripes" and must forfeit their lives for their impudence.[11] A Yankee near Suffolk, Virginia, in 1862 noted that "the country is so cleaned out that one can forage to no purpose now." All of the chickens had left the country in disgust, he complained—"I should say, of disgust of the Union Army."[12] In the Shenandoah Valley that summer, Ohio soldiers helped themselves. "Beef, mutton, ham, bacon, bread, honey, onions, chickens, ducks, geese, turkeys, eggs, butter, milk, sausages &c &c &c, right loyally contributed to their wants, without the formality of drawing rations," observed their colonel. "Our western boys are shifty animals and well adapted to looking out for themselves."[13] In South Carolina in 1863, a Union officer observed that "every thing here has a thorn on it or some other pointed peculiarity," but especially, it seemed, the chickens. "The boys say the chickens have sharp bills which the boys say they use with a vengeance. To punish them for this peculiarity, they kill all they find. They predicate their acts upon the necessity to retaliate to protect themselves. I tell them that biting hens are poisonous, that their flesh will beget the same biting propensity. In this game, the biter is sure to get bitten."[14]

Indeed, chickens were the almost universal favorite of the forager, easy to catch, light to transport, and versatile in the pot. "We are luxuriating on Secesh chickens," boasted a Yankee in the Shenandoah in March 1862. "I got one for 2/c yesterday. It was a chicken indeed. An old she hen of almost a centuries growth. After broiling it long enough to tan sole leather it made a chicken soup for five persons for supper and breakfast. With a little rice and pilot bread, it made, as the boys say, a bully good dish for us." He also had a rooster and some potatoes "and expect to live like a prince for the next few days. These chicken fixins are awful good."[15] It was the same west of the Appalachians. "It did not cost Uncle Sam much to board us, for our officers let us take anything we wanted to eat from the citizens," wrote a Northern forager in November 1862 near Germantown, Tennessee. "It would have done your soul good to see the boys yesterday and last night bringing in geese, chickens, hogs, turkeys, ducks, sheep, potatoes, honey and everything else that you could think of from a goose quill up to a thrashing machine, whether it done them any good or not." One fellow stole a goose, only to have the farm wife come after him with a club, yelling "You g. d. Yankee."[16]

Indeed, civilians defending their property would often be a real danger to foraging soldiers and showed no little ingenuity themselves. When Yankee foragers come to a Virginia woman's home and found the only can of lard she had been hoarding, they were ready to take it when she off-handedly remarked, "I just don't know what in the world I shall do about making soap now." One of the Yankee officers present expressed his surprise that she would make soap from such excellent lard. "When the hog died of cholera I knew we couldn't eat the meat," she explained, "so I cut it up and dried it down for lard, to make soap-grease." Of course the hog had not been ill at all, but the Federals decided not to confiscate this "sick" lard just to be safe.[17] In the Shenandoah Valley in 1864, Confederate general John McCausland warned a farm wife that Gen. David Hunter's invading forces were approaching and that she ought to save what she could of her bacon. Instead, she piled all of the slabs in her front yard and dusted them all with flour. When the Yankee cavalry rode up, they saw the bonanza and immediately began to grab for it until an officer asked what caused the dusty whiteness. She answered that she did not know, but that seeing the cavalry, McCausland's men put the bacon out in the yard for Hunter to find, laughing all the while. Convinced that the meat was diseased or spoiled, or even poisoned, the Federals dropped it all and rode on.[18] In Georgia that same season, when Yankees come foraging around her beehives, one Confederate woman tied a cord to a hive, and on the enemy's approach, she pulled the cord from some distance and tipped it over. The cavalry and their horses got stung repeatedly, and she never lost her hives and honey.[19]

Some enterprising Federals obtained some of the large amount of counterfeit Confederate money printed in the North in an effort to further devalue the already near-valueless scrip and used it when they could to "buy" goods from farmers. But sometimes it backfired, and Col. Alvin Voris wryly observed that "occasionally the boys get sold as well as the natives." One day one of his Ohio soldiers towed a sack of buckwheat flour into camp for which he had paid $5 in counterfeit Confederate money, having laboriously hauled it two miles. "On mixing his batter," chuckled the colonel, the soldier "had the satisfaction of learning that ground gypsum did not make verry digestable slap jacks."[20]

Certainly, there is no doubt of the hardship that Union soldiers' foraging visited on civilians in their vicinity. In January 1862, speaking of Yankee foragers, a Kentucky Confederate warned his family at home. "They will try and get all of your provisions," he admonished. "I would not let them have anything I thought I would need, for I can tell you that times are getting harder & harder every day."[21] In August 1863, one Northern woman even feared that the Yankees, including her own sons, were destroying so much in the way of Confederate crops that the Almighty might recoil in horror. One of her boys, then feeding off Mississippi under Gen. William T. Sherman, reassured her that "all the Federal Army has destroyed in the Confederacy has been used in the way of subsistence." They were not just pillaging and destroying indiscriminately. "If our cause is a just one, I don't think we have committed any sin by trying to get something to eat."[22] Yet some felt genuine guilt, among them Wilbur Fisk. At Warrenton, Virginia, in August 1863, Fisk and others went to a Rebel home to plunder the garden, but he found he could not join in. "When I saw the woman and one of her children looking in sorrowful submission from the window at the wasteful destruction going on in their own garden," he confessed later that day, "my courage failed me, and I withdrew without taking so much as a pod of peas or a handful of potatoes."[23] Hard as it is to believe, and if the soldiers who told the story are to be believed, some marching Yankees actually grew tired of eating well on Southern produce. In May 1863, while marching across Mississippi toward Vicksburg, some men of Grant's army protested that they were tired of fresh turkey and sweet potatoes, and they called out longingly for hardtack and beans, which they got.[24]

Soldiers came up with a host of euphemisms for what they took by the roadside. Hogs became "bears," sheep became "deer," chickens became "game birds," and so on. In Gen. George B. McClellan's 1862 Peninsula campaign below Richmond, foraging Yankees who took local farmer's pigs said they were hunting "Virginia rabbits."[25] A Wisconsin private playfully observed that "every hog seen is a 'wild hog' of course."[26] In June 1862, Voris explained a typical officer's attitude to what the men were doing. "I do not mean that they shall suffer from hunger in a land of plenty [and] as a consequence have verry often shut my eyes to many things resorted to by them to procure food," he told his wife. "The boys have very often eaten bear hams to the detriment of Secech swine herds, venison to the danger of their sheep folds and enjoyed the luxury of many other comforts that were purchased rather slyly, the gate post taking the pay or making the bargain with a house dog." Gen. Nathaniel Banks ordered them to cease, and one night at parade, Voris read the order to his regiment. "If I ever *catch* you stealing I will raise the devil with you boys," he warned, but then he told his wife that "tell the truth I never could catch the young rascals robbing a hen roost, nor did I ever see one, or more of our boys after a pig but I felt sure that pig was able to take care of himself."[27]

In fact, when an officer trying to enforce the orders against foraging did not get his pay on time, he turned to subsidizing foraging himself in spite of the orders, for unlike the men who had rations—such as they were—issued to them, he had to provide for his own table. "He must allow his servant to forage for him, or he must starve," confessed one officer, for if he foraged himself, then the men would follow the example, which could result in "widespread straggling and often atrocious plundering."[28] That became especially evident when an army marched through friendly territory, as during the September 1862 campaign leading to the battle of Antietam in Maryland. Despite all efforts to keep the men from ravaging the fields they passed, it was almost of no avail. "Acres and acres of soldiers, but not an acre of corn, or potatoes, or fruit, or anything else eatable within a circle of two or three miles I suppose," found Samuel Fiske. "A crop of soldiers kills out any other crop in the quickest possible time. Our orders against plundering are very strict, too, and guards generally placed over property. It seems to be impossible to keep an army from destroying everything through which it passes."[29]

Some things along the route of march proved especially pleasing, and nothing more than fruit. John Haley recalled finding a sour apple tree. "If, at the same time Mrs. Eve met the serpent, she desired apples as much as we did, and needed them as much, I don't blame her at all," he quipped. He doubted that she needed them as much as the soldiers, though, for she had not been "punished with ancient salt horse and rusty pork as we are." Fruit proved to be "a real blessing," and the soldiers felt better immediately upon eating it. "The apples were 'as manna to the hungry soul.'"[30] Even better were the pickings for those Federals stationed farther south. "My boys have been bringing into camp bushels of most beautiful oranges on the stalk," wrote an officer stationed with his regiment near St. Helena, South Carolina, in 1863. One branch alone had twenty-three oranges.[31] Occasionally, they even got pineapples from wrecked blockade runners offshore.[32] Yankees at Hilton Head Island in South Carolina could supplement their meat ration with alligators, of all things. "Aligators are not the only strange reptiles found here," Voris declared. There were lizards, vipers, and even rattlesnakes, and the men could eat them all if willing.[33]

And officers sometimes actively joined in, despite all inhibitions. "Did you ever see a brigadier general riding along on his splendid charger, with a string of sweet corn ears hanging on his left arm, and onion tops peeping out of his saddle-bags?" an amused Fiske wrote just after Antietam.

> I saw a colonel chuckling over a plate of peaches which he had in some way captured for his mess table, and a major spurring joyfully into camp with a couple of live chickens tied to his saddle bows. I can also speak from experience of the rapture of a starved and generally-used-up lieutenant over the possession of a loaf of real bread. . . . You haven't any idea of the blessings of a decent meal of victuals. You don't know the treasure you possess in a boiled potato, bursting its tight jacket and revealing its hidden mealiness as it comes smoking upon your dinner table. Such a sight would bring tears to the eyes of thousands now crunching their hard crackers and drinking their decoction of beans which Uncle Sam passes off upon us as coffee. . . . As for myself, I should faint at the very smell of a delicate chicken broth or a barley soup, and at the thought of a bowl of bread and milk.[34]

Naturally, it was more difficult all around for Confederates. They started with a less efficient supply system, spent the war constantly more strained for food sources, and when they foraged, with the exception of the few invasions of the North, they did so on home ground. In the best of times, that risked alienating their own people and creating a hardship on friends. In the worst, they were trying to live off land that the Yankees might already have cleaned out during their own campaigning. Nor was it just food that became subject to covetous eyes. Confederates camped in and around Bowling Green, Kentucky, in 1861, had already scoured the country for boilers for their coffee, leaving many forced to boil theirs in the same open kettles in which they cooked their meat, tainting the taste of the brew and at the same time allowing much of the flavor to escape with the steam—perhaps mercifully. Under strict orders not to plunder the civilians in the neighborhood, they still did so, and one man, after eying a gleaming coffee boiler that had been sitting for some days beside a farmer's smokehouse, finally went after it in the night, sequestering it in a dark place before dawn. When he and his comrades had let the hot item "cool" for some time, until it seemed safe to bring it out, they discovered that it had no bottom, having been set out for a passing tinker to repair.[35]

As for food, victorious Confederates often found a culinary bonanza in what the fleeing enemy abandoned in the initial wave of humiliating defeats of Union forces. At First Manassas or Bull Run on July 21, 1861, the victors picked up tons of food in haversacks. On April 6, 1862, during the battle of Shiloh out in western Tennessee, Confederates swept over an area known thereafter as the "Hornets' Nest," where Federal resistance had been particularly heavy. When the Yankee remnant surrendered later in the day, the Rebels entered their camps and found a feast awaiting them. "Here was a chance for a feed, such as we had not had before for months, and such as we never had again during our soldier-experience," wrote one Kentucky Confederate, "and as it was a free lunch we stood not upon ceremony but went at it in earnest." Some had ten pounds of tea in a kettle, enough to make a cistern full, clamoring for water. Others speared whole cheeses on their bayonets, and yet others pocketed canned meats and fruits. "O it was a grand feast, and washed down with oceans of beer, wine, and brandy."[36]

Even generals could profit from a battlefield capture—almost. A German pastry cook on the private staff of a general with Lee's Army of Northern Virginia never got to practice his principal art except when the army captured Yankee supply wagons. "His skill and ingenuity were often taxed to the utmost in providing dinners, from the scantiest materials," a mate recalled a few years afterward. His greatest trial came while Lee was still in his lines immediately after the battle of Antietam, when the cook had nothing to serve his general but some green corn. He determined to make a fine meal for his general all the same, thanks principally to a few slices from a cow fortuitously killed by Yankee artillery. He went into a local kitchen with an excellent stove, put a pot on to boil, and then serendipitously augmented the feast when he saw a turkey rooster, killed it, and put it in the pot, too. Just then, a Yankee shell hit the house and knocked down the chimney. Then another shell came through the house and hit the stove itself, knocking the burgeoning feast everywhere. "Py tam, turkey-rooster, corn and beef all gone," he thundered, and "Py tam, I go too."[37]

Confederates were often forced to forage for sheer nutrition, let alone variety or luxury. In the spring of 1863, the ration in the Army of Northern Virginia was down to a half pound of bacon and eighteen ounces of flour per man, with every 100 men sharing ten pounds of rice every third day, along with some peas and dried fruit as it could be obtained. "This may give existence to troops who are idle but certainly will cause them to break down when called upon for severe exertion," General Lee complained to his war department.[38] Henry C. Estill of the 5th Alabama echoed his general. "We have been fed on bacon entirely for two months, a quarter of a pound to each man per day," he wrote on April 9, 1863, when Lee's army was on the Rappahannock River. "It has caused us to take the scurvy from want of vegetables and Gen. Lee has issued an order detailing one man from each company every day, to search for wild vegetables."[39] Indeed, Lee actually did order his men to forage in the woods for sassafras buds, wild onions and garlic, poke sprouts, and lamb's quarter, in an attempt to combat scurvy, though he lamented to Richmond that "for so large an army the supply obtained is very small."[40] "They are very scarce, but to-day John Carson went to the river and found a nice lot of wild onions; you can't think how we relished them," Estill went on. "It is pretty hard, and we think we will suffer for meat before the beef crop comes in."[41] A few weeks later when Lee invaded Pennsylvania on the way to Gettysburg, his army captured Chambersburg and he demanded from its citizens twenty-five barrels of sauerkraut for his men.[42] Meanwhile, as one Rebel soldier noted on the march, "fowls and pigs and eatables don't stand much chance."[43] Sherman's soldiers marching across Georgia in 1864 had exactly the same problem, because their advance went too fast for their supply system to get fresh vegetables to them. Only when they foraged ripe blackberries and tree fruit and consumed both in substantial quantities did the scurvy outbreak in their ranks diminish.[44]

Contrary to their government's wishes, Rebel soldiers could be just as predatory on friendly civilians as their foes. Out in Arkansas, men of the 21st Texas Cavalry came to a home and asked a farmer if they could have one of his hogs. Surprised and relieved that they actually asked instead of just helping themselves, he graciously agreed and told them to go get one. "It's all right," replied a soldier, *"it's already skinned."*[45] Just like the Yankees, confessed John Casler of the 33rd Virginia, "we would not allow any man's chickens to run out in the road and bite us as we marched along."[46] Though Confederate sutlers were far fewer than in the North, they too became easy targets. An Alabama sutler got his wagon stuck in the mud and asked soldiers to help push him out. They were all too obliging, surrounding the wagon. "I thought that they were the politest and most accommodating fellows I ever saw," said the sutler, until he discovered that in the swarming they had cleaned out his wagon.[47]

Unfortunately, the boys in gray could prey on each other, too. In the winter of 1863–64, men of the First Kentucky "Orphan" Brigade were stationed with the Army of Tennessee in and around Dalton, Georgia, and a couple from Company I of the 4th Kentucky got a pass, as one recalled, "to take in the sights at Dalton and any thing else which was not too hot or too heavy to be carried off." They went to the railroad depot, through which passed all of the commissary supplies so inefficiently reaching the soldiery. They hoped to find boxes of goodies sent from home to fellow soldiers that they could steal, but there were none to be found. They did find a sleepy sentinel guarding a large beef supply, however. One Kentuckian returned to camp, got his rifle, and then came back, posing as a sentinel sent to relieve the sleepy man. As soon as the dupe was out of sight, the other Kentuckian grabbed the "fattest, largest, and best quarter of beef" he could find and tossed it on his shoulder. The other then ostentatiously arrested him and escorted him in full view of everyone "under guard" back to camp to be charged with his offense, carrying the beef as evidence. "The gallant old company 'I' lived well for two whole days as far as beef was concerned," they later recalled.[48]

Taking advantage of civilians was all right too, though it could backfire. Three men of the 1st Mississippi Cavalry in Georgia in 1864 were nosing around a farmer's pen and shot a hog; then one of the three went to stop the lady of the house as she charged at them, while the other two dragged away their plunder. He tried to buy time by protesting that they had only shot a chicken hawk, attempting to keep her from seeing the carcass being dragged away, but she pushed past him and then bullied the others into dropping the hog.[49] And any fortuitous bit of debris could lead to a meal if a soldier were prudent. After the battle of Chickamauga in September 1863, a Confederate found a needle case on the body of a fallen comrade, and though it was of no immediate use, he kept it in his pocket. Out foraging one day in north Georgia, he came upon a house from which wafted alluring odors of fried chicken, baked corn pone, and buttermilk. The lady of the house did not offer any for free, but when she learned that he had sewing needles, she gladly traded a meal and a haversack full of things for him to take back to camp in return for two of the pins. Thereafter, he lived rather well until he exhausted his "currency."[50]

Expedience forced many a Southern soldier to take what he could get and worry about orders or ethics later, if at all. What they got from their commissaries simply was not sufficient to keep them healthy enough to march and fight. One later recalled that "in the days of short rations," an order came to the troops to cook four days' rations. A private who knew from experience that such an amount as they were issued for four days would scarcely feed a man for half that time posed a question to his officer. If a man could eat three days' rations in one day—as most of them did—how long would four days' worth last? The captain had no answer.[51] In the winter of 1862, Confederate Berry Benson lamented that he would "eat my whole day's ration at one meal." "Slim, very slim. But half a loaf is better than no bread."[52] In 1864, a Virginia cavalryman testified that "the men in this command don't get as much as they can eat twice a day. Old salt beef and flour is all they got, sometimes a little bacon and crackers." Writing home to his family in disgust, he declared that "if we had the jo[w]ls and soap grease here [that] you all throw away, we would eat it."[53]

No doubt, they would have, though to their credit, soldiers of both sides were usually just as inclined to ask politely for a handout or to pay if they could, as to take from passing farms. As Wilbur Fisk told his family, "we soldiers often have but little else to think of, except what we shall eat and what we shall drink and wherewithal we shall get our rations."[54] His was a universal concern, and never more so than when the soldiers were on the march or insufficiently supplied from their commissaries. In part, it stemmed from homesickness, for the look and taste of something familiar, but also, it came down to simple health and nutrition. "All do not know how eager the boys all are when on a long march to get that to eat that will bear some resemblance to a favorite dish they were fond of at home," he continued. "In some cases it is a mere whim of the soldier, a sort of natural desire to get something different from what is provided, but in many cases it is essential to health." He knew of cases in which a lucky fellow would get a woman to bake him a haversack full of biscuits, paying twenty-five to fifty cents a dozen and even then waiting half a day for his turn from her oven.[55]

Marching rations were always short and indifferent in the Confederacy, but Yankee soldiers found it outrageous that some in their government actually thought it prudent to reduce theirs. In May 1864, Sen. Henry Wilson of Massachusetts introduced a bill to cut the soldier's marching ration to its prewar standard. "Now it is well known (to all the people that stay at home and read the newspapers) that no man can possibly eat the whole of the bountiful ration that Uncle Sam allows his soldiers," complained an outraged Samuel Fiske in facetious frame of mind. He felt outraged that Wilson and others expected men to carry twelve days' rations sometimes, or even thirty days' when driving beef cattle with them, and green corn was available by the road. Only fools in Washington who did not have to march could envision such a thing.

"How preposterous to mention the circumstance that nineteen out of twenty of the enlisted men spend their whole pay in purchasing additions to this same extravagantly liberal allowance of Uncle Sam," he grumbled in a public letter. He knew men to get so hungry that they bought each other's hardtack for a dime apiece or paid a dollar for another man's daily rations. "It is true that if the soldier had all the beans, rice, molasses, potatoes, dried apples, pickles, hominy, &c., &c., that the regulations allow him, and time and skill to cook them properly, he would be able to satisfy his appetite very reasonably, and even often have something over," said Fiske. But on a hard march, the soldier got ten hardtack crackers a day, frequently spoiled by wet and some parts of it unfit to eat by reason of bugs and worms, and three-fourths pound of pork or one and one quarter pounds of fresh beef "of the poorest and boniest kind," and nothing else except a small allowance of sugar and coffee.[56]

Beans and vegetables were not issued on the march because the soldier could not carry them, but they continued to be allocated per man on the books, and John Billings and other soldiers believed that since those supplies were not furnished to the men cumulatively at the end of a march, then most likely officers sold them and pocketed the money.[57] It was neither the first nor the last instance in which soldiers of both sides believed that others profiteered on food and their expense.

"Experience has already shown us, also, that a soldier's is sometimes a pretty hungry and thirsty life," Fiske grumbled on. For three days during the Antietam campaign, he and his men "had nothing to eat but a few hard crackers, and once a morsel of cheese and once a slice of ham served round; and for one night and part of a hot day we had no water in camp."[58] In October 1861, writing from the ironically named Pommedeterre Creek in Missouri, an Iowa soldier on the march complained that "we have had nothing to eat for the last three days but beef without salt which is poor diet to travel on."[59] Of course, on the march commanders usually ordered their men to prepare up to eleven days' rations for the trek, but a soldier's haversack would only hold three days' worth safely, and the rest of the rations issued to or cooked by them usually went bad. After eight or ten days on the road, the remaining rations cooked at the beginning of the march had gotten pretty frightening. "Why you might as well issue out the whole three years' provender at once and have done with it," the irritable Fiske went on. "It is half of it wasted, and then the last days the men are starved, and about three days before the time is up, the government is obliged in spite of itself to issue some more."

Compounding the problem, most men were simply too hungry to parcel out their rations to the allotted days. Wilbur Fisk found that six days' rations during his 1863 marching in Virginia usually disappeared in four days, and he had only forty-eight hardtack, one and a half pounds of salt pork, and some coffee when he set out. "Now I am willing to leave it to the most abstemious man in the United States, if that is sufficient sustenance for such fellows as we," he groused.[60] On one march in late 1862 in Virginia, officers issued rations in several successive small allotments of two or three days' worth at a time, but after a few such issues, the men forgot how long their latest batch was to last them and all ran out too soon. One morning before the march commenced, every haversack being empty, men began crying out "hard tack, hard tack." They created such a clamor that the colonel of the 2nd Vermont had to quell their riot by threatening to fine each soldier $2 of his pay for every shout of "hard tack," but still some yelled it out.[61] When finally an order came from Washington in November 1863 reducing the marching rations thenceforth to a maximum of five days', it was welcome news to old campaigners.[62] Ironically, given that the new black troops in the Union army were generally treated in every department in an inferior way, some of them actually had an advantage over their white brethren. When the famous black regiment the 54th Massachusetts went to war, it was issued a mobile field kitchen mounted on a wagon. "We have a new style of cooking department here," one sergeant boasted in May 1863. "It is a large wagon, covered similar to an omnibus, with a stove and all the appurtenances of a well ordered kitchen." If adopted armywide, which it was not, he felt it would be "a very handy affair."[63]

Confederates felt the same frustrations, compounded by the scarcity that dogged their commissaries almost from the outset. In August 1863, during the retreat from defeat at Gettysburg, one Rebel could not restrain himself from criticizing even the sainted General Lee. "I blame Lee very much for starting off with us on this campaign before the corn was fit to eat," Benson confessed. "He ought never to have thought of taking us into a strange and foreign land without waiting for the only means of subsistence to become fit to eat. But no, he carries us off, and the first thing we know we are without rations and no corn! Lee's usual foresight and sagacity failed him that pop, certain."[64]

For Yank and Reb alike, the roadside offered the best immediate hope of a quick supplement to rations, or of something even better, as soldiers passed farmhouses and through villages. Confederates fared best here, at least during the first half of the war, because they were usually marching through friendly territory, unlike their foe. "Sometimes passing one of those large Virginia mansions, or going through a village, we would find a group of ladies standing at the side of the road with buckets of milk or water, and maybe biscuits with ham or butter or cold chicken, which they would give over into the hands that would be thrust out to receive as the column of half famished men swept onward," Berry Benson recalled. At any halt when near houses, the inhabitants were sure to be besieged for food to buy or beg. "The earliest comers fared best," Benson said, "for they got the cooked provisions, while late comers must be content with flour, meal, and meat which they must cook themselves as best they could." One day, all he could get was a handful of parched corn and a few small sour apples.[65]

Capt. Isaac Coles of the 6th Virginia Cavalry recalled that one winter on the march, they came to a home near Monterey and asked for a meal. "The remembrance of that wonderful kitchen hospitality will ever be a green spot in my experience," he said later. Pans gleamed, crockery glistened, and everything was neat and clean. Their host fried buckwheat pancakes on her stove. "I never knew such an expert and magical cook," Coles marveled. "I can see the agile movement of her arm as she flopped those appetizing cakes over into the pan and onto the plates." She served them with real maple syrup, and as they ate, she watched and kept refilling their plates with her "ambrosia."[66] In 1863 in Virginia, one farmer invited a Confederate general to his dinner table, but before the general arrived, some of his men came first, one impersonating their commander, and they devoured the feast just as the general approached, leaving him nothing but the debris of their meal.[67]

The capture of an enemy supply base could be even more mouthwatering, as Stonewall Jackson's Confederates found when they captured Manassas Junction in August 1862. It proved to be a cornucopia, especially the contents of the officers' stores. One Rebel wondered at the sight of "a starving man eating lobster-salad and drinking Rhine wine, bare-footed and in tatters."[68] And there were a fortunate few who through accident managed to pass through those few regions of the South not despoiled by the war. Even as late as March 1865, in South Carolina some Confederates on the periphery of the war ate well and in abundance, and civilians could give them lots.[69]

Most Union soldiers passed through major Northern cities during transfer from one theater of the war to another or, as in the case of regiments like the 2nd Vermont, which were sent to New York to quell riots that broke out in the summer of 1863. In Washington and Philadelphia and elsewhere, they had opportunities to visit the Volunteer Refreshment Saloons operated by the Sanitary Commission and other relief agencies, places where the men could get hearty meals of things they only dreamed about in the camps, like good bread, butter, cheese, pickles "and all that a hungry soldier need ask," said

Wilbur Fisk after his Philadelphia visit. "It was not soldiers' living at all; it was good enough for a first class hotel."[70]

Confederates, too, sometimes had layovers in towns when being shipped by rail from one fort to another, and they also swarmed the restaurants and hotels for what was available, but generally to find less abundance. In June 1862, the 9th Kentucky passed through Canton, Mississippi, and had an hour between trains. They went to a dining hall where each had to buy a ticket and then wait his turn to yell, trying to get a waiter to bring something. The overworked waiters soon began to look fearful as the din of shouting grew ever louder, but finally, Sgt. John Jackman got his plate of beef. "Though I always considered my teeth good, yet I could not even make a print on the piece brought me," he complained. Seeing everyone else simply ignore the waiters at last and swarm the kitchen themselves, he joined the throng and found them crowded around a terrified cook who was cooking the only remaining thing in the larder, a cow's heart. *"My heart failed me,"* he lamented and gave up to return to the rail depot to eat corn bread out of his haversack.[71]

Even during hard campaigning, on the way to battle, and on the road after a fight, any community offered some hope for the soldiers. During the pursuit of Lee's army after Gettysburg, Wilbur Fisk spoke of his command passing through a place just below Hyattsville, Maryland. "Tired as the boys were they had strength enough left to ransack the village and purchase everything eatable, from a mince pie to a loaf of brown bread," he confessed. "The stores were drained of all groceries as fast as the goods could be handed out." No farmhouse was safe from being besieged, and the men happily purchased from the owners everything that extravagant prices could buy. "When all other resources became exhausted we resorted to the grist mill, where flour and corn meal could be had, out of which we made cakes and puddings in the most approved primitive style."[72]

Now and then, a special opportunity presented itself, none more welcome than what befell men in Lee's ragged army in the summer of 1864. That spring, one Rebel soldier said that for the past several days, his regiment had subsisted on four hardtack and a quarter pound of meat per man. "But now our rations have been doubled and all are jubilant," he wrote in May; "men in my company were whole days at a time without a morsel."[73] Some men had been reduced to picking kernels of corn out of the horse dung to crush into meal.[74] Then came intelligence of some 2,500 beef cattle herded beside the James River below besieged Richmond. Capt. Chiswell Dabney, a Virginian, recalled that "at this time we were living mostly on sweet potatoes," but when the Rebels heard of Grant's cattle herd, "visions of fat and savory beefsteaks, sirloins and roasts flitted in a most appetizing picture." Lee's cavalry commander, Maj. Gen. Wade Hampton, set out on September 11 on a daring raid to feed Lee's army, and pushing aside the herd guard, he managed to bring 2,486 of the beeves back inside hungry Confederate lines. In Dabney's own words, "we then proceeded to have the greatest beefsteak feast ever known in the army of Northern Virginia."[75]

The beef fed them for a few weeks, but it was not enough to stave off Grant's army or the return of hard rations. By the time Lee was forced to evacuate Richmond and Petersburg on April 2–3, 1865, some of the men later recalled that the lack of provisions had them in a virtual stupor when combined with shock and exhaustion. It is no wonder that hundreds simply wandered during the retreat toward Appomattox, and that the army simply no longer worked like an army. After the surrender and parole of the men, they started making their way home as best they could, some by transportation provided by the Yankees, who also fed them, at least during the period immediately after the surrender. Louisiana outfits started marching to Burkeville Station to get a train for their long journey home. Before they departed, the Louisiana brigade commissaries went ahead to try to find and have ready something to eat for the men as they marched. They got several hundred ears of corn from a free black who gave it, saying of the soldiers, most likely in relief, "They's the last I'll ever see." The ragged men came in single file to his corn cribs, and each man took two ears; then the black man opened a barrel of sorghum and gave each man a cupful. In one of the intriguing ironies of the Civil War, the last ration issued to Louisiana troops in Virginia thus came from a one-time slave.[76]

CHAPTER FIVE

THE GREAT TROUBLE ABOUT HOSPITALS

ANY LOOK AT THE DIETARY TREATMENT OF SOLDIERS IN THE HOSPITALS North and South has to begin with the ignorance of surgeons and nurses alike concerning nutrition, a science not yet born. Instead, tradition and superstition reigned, some of which just happened to have some useful basis. Doctors had some understanding of the necessity of minerals, though vitamins were yet to be discovered. They knew sugar and salt to be necessary in a good diet, and also that some fat content was beneficial. They pretty well understood scurvy and its root causes in poor nutrition, but otherwise, they recognized only two other dietary illnesses: drunkenness and the *delirium tremens* that it caused. As a result, besides abstention from liquor, the only real dietary regimens that physicians prescribed sought to combat scurvy with fresh vegetables and fruit, focusing on acidic ones like citrus and onions, and especially potatoes. Even then, some actually believed that too much fruit led to scurvy rather than prevented it. Beyond that, the physicians of the war regarded diet almost solely from the point of view of digestion and patient condition.

North and South, the surgeon generally wrote the patient's prescribed diet in a book every day, simply noting F for a full diet of soup, meat, and vegetables; H for a half diet of the same articles in reduced portions; and L for a low diet, also called a quarter diet. "Low diet is intended for patients requiring still less nutriment, and for whom the soup, meat and vegetables furnished those on full or half diet would be too difficult of digestion," said regulations. "The precise composition of the low diet of any hospital will be directed by the surgeon in charge."[1]

Surgeons, if they had any idea of nutrition and health at all, assumed generally that one of a few specific combinations of diet would address almost all diseases and conditions: roast beef and pudding, eggs and milk, vegetables for scurvy, milk porridge, beef tea, or gruel. For a man with chronic diarrhea, the surgeon would prescribe breakfast of coffee, steak, eggs, bread with butter, and milk punch; a dinner of roast beef, fish, radishes, boiled cabbage, bread, and tea; and a supper of oyster soup, raw cabbage, cheese, bread and butter, and coffee. For typhoid, however, the diet was to be varied. Breakfast was to include mutton, potatoes, and doughnuts; dinner, steak, potatoes, and plum pudding; and supper milk, arrowroot, cake, and pudding. Neither regiments contributed significantly to a remedy, and each would have been just as effectual if prescribed for the opposite malady.[2]

"Thousands of patients are annually starved in the midst of plenty, from want of attention to the ways which alone make it possible for them to take food," observed Florence Nightingale after her Crimean War experiences.[3] Her book was republished both in the North and in the Confederacy during the war, in the latter in a version issued in Richmond in 1861 titled *Directions for Cooking by Troops.* Her attention to food as something specifically linked to particular ailments and conditions would not have been a new idea to nurturing mothers at home, but in the armies, all too often doctors simply assumed that invalids could eat the same ration given to men in the field. Amazingly, it never occurred to some surgeons that the hardtack that a healthy soldier on the march could barely chew might be difficult for a man recovering from a wound in the jaw.

Nor did it help at the outset of the war that the cooks in the hospitals, as in the field, were just soldiers detailed without special training or experience. Not surprisingly, the inmates came to prefer the cooking of women who volunteered to cook for the wards, some of whom would in time be permanently attached to the armies by the Sanitary Commission and other relief organizations. A few women had a major impact, such as Ann Wittenmyer, who, with the United States Christian Commission, organized over 100 diet kitchens at Union army hospitals. In 1864, she authored a special cookbook, *A Collection of Recipes for the Use of Special Diet Kitchens in Military Hospitals,* designed for invalid soldiers and containing light broths and soups, puddings, lots of rice and egg dishes, and milk punch, some of them derived from Nightingale's earlier publications. She saw to its wide distribution and, in the final year and a half of the war, estimated that her system had provided more than two million meals every month.[4]

Probably of equal impact on feeding the men was Mary Bickerdyke, soon to be known to the soldiers as Mother Bickerdyke. She began after the battle of Shiloh in April 1862, distributing hot soup, tea, crackers, whiskey, and water to the wounded.[5] Two years later, she would be a force to be reckoned with, even by Gen. William T. Sherman in 1864, as she moved with his army in the Atlanta campaign, where she was always just behind the front making soup from cans of condensed beef extract for the wounded as they came from the field.[6]

These cooks and nurses found dealing with the varied specific diets prescribed by the surgeons for the wounded and the ill quite a challenge, and most hospital inmates North and South alike were not wounded, but sick from a host of camp ailments, viruses, and nutritive disorders like scurvy. Mary Safford, a nurse at Cairo, Illinois, in 1861, distributed currant jelly as an acid drink for scurvy, gum drops for cough, and salt codfish, molasses gingerbread, boiled custard, soda crackers, baked apples, canned oysters, rice pudding, and more according to men's conditions.[7] During Grant's 1863 Vicksburg campaign, Mary Livermore found that surgeons specified diets for each patient, but then had nothing to offer but army rations. Worse, there were only a couple of soup kettles and a small portable stove, while cooking in the open air on campaign made the food subject to rain, smoke, and ashes. Often, she had only condensed beef extract and desiccated vegetables to make soup.[8]

That monotony of diet could be a great enemy to a recuperating soldier, for men sick of something preferred not to eat it, even if doing so weakened their recovery. The author Louisa May Alcott, working as a nurse in 1862 in a Georgetown hospital outside Washington, found soldier meals "pretty much of a muchness," sarcastically describing beef that seemed originally to have been preserved for use in the Revolution, pork just off the street, army bread made of sawdust and aleratus, butter with salt churned by Lot's wife in biblical times, blackberries stewed to look like preserved cockroaches, mild and muddy coffee, and tea that appeared to be made from three huckleberry leaves boiled in a quart of water.[9]

It was in those diet kitchens following the plans of Wittenmyer and others that cooks tried to combat the monotony. The commissaries issued hospital supplies to the women, who then oversaw their cooking and distributed the meals from the kitchen to the wards carefully and systematically so that each patient got exactly the quantity and content the doctors ordered. In her hospital in Alexandria in 1863, Jane Woolsey also tried to keep in mind the individual soldier's preferences for more or less salt or sugar, and so on. The cooks also tried to vary a particular soldier's diet so he did not get the same thing every meal, recalling the experience of one patient served chicken stewed with rice so often that he threw it out the window one day. Woolsey and others also had the common sense to realize that meals would be more welcome—and the soldiers more likely to eat them—if they resembled what their mothers had served at home.[10] Mother Bickerdyke became famous for making varied and wholesome dishes for her patients from meager ingredients. One of her most used items was a postoperative restorer that she called "panado," prepared from hot water, brown sugar, whiskey, and crumbled hardtack mixed into a mush.[11] She once joked that "when I get home, boys, I shall publish a starvation cook-book, containing receipts for making delicious dishes out of nothing."[12]

Not that Yankee boys in hospitals did not find plenty to grouse about over their food. When an Iowa soldier's father was slow to write to him in his confinement, the boy told his mother to "feed him on hard crackers and sowbelly about a week and if he doesn't write all he knows and more too, I am no judge of small items." Boasting that after a couple of pounds of hardtack and some rusty bacon he could write with ease, the boy concluded, "well, I have not much to write today probably from the fact that we have plenty of soft bread and beef with other luxuries too numerous to mention. We get plenty of eggs for the moderate sum of 30 cents per dozen and butter for 50 cents."[13]

Wilbur Fisk found in 1863 in a hospital near Washington that "the diet prescribed was generally suited to the wants and condition of the patient." The more feeble patients got toasted bread with butter or applesauce every day, while boiled rice and milk, meal porridge, farina puddings, and almost any article of diet was readily granted by the physician if asked for. "I never was refused in a single instance what I expressed a preference for." The more able ate at mess tables in barracks and had the usual army ration, with butter or applesauce as an extra.[14]

More of these men suffered from chronic diarrhea than anything else, and it was caused largely by inadequate nutrition, and often a side effect of scurvy. Treatments for diarrhea and scurvy included lemon juice, potatoes, onions, leeks, garlic, squash, pumpkin, carrots, turnips, spinach, cabbage, tomatoes, and fresh lettuce, along with nourishing food that was easily assimilated. Milk and eggs were considered especially good, along with tender beefsteak, mutton chops, stale bread, and sweet milk.[15]

Tens of thousands of Yankees also came down with typho-malarial fevers, for which surgeons devised a varied diet. "In a disease so manifold in its nature, no fixed diet adapted to all cases can be prescribed," concluded a War Department medical authority. Most cases required a full diet, he said, though the sufferers usually had little or no appetite and often refused food. "No greater mistake can be committed than to let the patient run down by delaying the use of nutrients too long." They usually detested beef tea, little more than a watery broth, sometimes not even cooked. "To attempt to force beef tea upon these patients is apt to increase the fever and produce gastric disturbances," the expert warned, suggesting instead barley water, rice water, or "toast-water, acidulated with lemon juice, or with citric or tartaric acid." This last was just hot water with toast in it, a paltry version of milk toast no more appetizing than it sounded.[16] Even paltrier was a redundancy in a bowl called "water soup." At the hospital of the 4th Missouri Infantry at Pacific City, Missouri, the low or quarter-ration men got a daily breakfast of water soup. For dinner they got water soup. For supper, one inmate noted, it was "water soup again."[17] No wonder Yankees talked of "shadow soup," made from a chicken being hung in the sun so its shadow fell on the soup pot. When salt and pepper were added, the hospital cooks claimed it was chicken soup.[18]

It should hardly come as a surprise that some patients rebelled against their diet, sometimes with violence. Rice seemed to be especially reviled by Northern boys unaccustomed to the grain. Many a patient became absolutely sick of it and refused ever to eat it again. Lt. Irwin Miller of the 116th Illinois became so weary of his daily allowance of "two pieces of bread, one bowl milk and three glasses of ale per day" that he went absent without leave for nearly a year.[19] When a steward offered sauerkraut to Thomas Gillian of the 9th United States Infantry in the hospital at Fort Colville, Washington Territory, to treat a bad case of scurvy, Gillian refused to eat it, saying it would kill him. In fact, it would have alleviated his condition, but when the steward attempted to force-feed it to him, Gillian grabbed a rifle and shot at him.[20]

It did not help that many hospitals had problems with stewards stealing food meant for the patients. Bickerdyke dealt with one unknown thief by mixing tartar emetic with stewed peaches and leaving it out to be pinched. When cooks and stewards and others began vomiting, she identified the culprits and threatened that next time she would lace food with rat poison and let them steal it.[21] In May 1864, Pvt. Edward Mullen of the 2nd Invalid Corps went absent without leave from a Baltimore hospital and struck a male nurse after he caught the nurse eating a patient's pudding. "The nurse bit the patient," explained Mullen, "and I struck the nurse."[22] More than one surgeon went before a court-martial for such theft, as did Perkins Gordon, who ate the

Men North and South went to war with many things other than weapons and uniforms, and to every one of them knife and fork ranked high among his necessities.

Sauce-y Brigade.   Illinois Porkers.   Ohio Regulars.   Astor House Light Corps.   First Butcher.

REINFORCEMENTS FOR OUR VOLUNTEERS ON THE MARCH SOUTHWARD.

No sooner were the first regiments off to the war than wits made note of the legions that followed, the spoon-wielding cooks, the cattle and swine carrying the means of their own destruction and dismemberment, and the ever popular Worcestershire sauce. HARPER'S WEEKLY ILLUSTRATED NEWSPAPER, JUNE 1, 1861

In the training camps small armies of cooks made untold quantities of soups and stews in huge boilers like these in the kitchen at the Soldiers' Rest in Alexandria, Virginia, in July 1865. The brick oven and range, or hob, to their right baked, fried, and simmered. UNITED STATES ARMY MILITARY HISTORY INSTITUTE, CARLISLE, PENNSYLVANIA

It is symbolic of the relationship of love and hate that the Civil War soldier had with his hardtack that, next to his weapons, it was the prop he most used when he sat for the camera. COURTESY OF JOHN HESS

Soldiers in established forts and garrisons, as well as those in the better hospitals and even prisons, took their meals in mess halls like this one at Harewood Hospital in Washington. They filed up alongside the tables, pulled the benches away from the wall, and sat at their places with metal plates and cups, tableware, cruets with salt and pepper, and bottles of sauce. LIBRARY OF CONGRESS

Out in the field, services were decidedly less formal. The commissary sergeant of the 56th Massachusetts stands at his tent at Alexandria in June 1865, ready to disburse that day's ration of soft bread to a company. UNITED STATES MILITARY HISTORY INSTITUTE, CARLISLE, PENNSYLVANIA

A commissary at Camp Essex sharpens his knives and saws to disburse salted meat from the hogsheads surrounding him, as one man is ready at the scales to weigh each ration while another records every man's issue. MINNESOTA HISTORICAL SOCIETY

On Hilton Head Island, South Carolina, in 1863, the cook of Company H, 3rd New Hampshire Infantry, stands before his tent beside his army issue cook stove, a ladle in hand to issue soup or stew, while another fellow is ready beside the coffee grinder. The company cups and mess plates await in the lean-to behind them.
UNITED STATES MILITARY HISTORY INSTITUTE, CARLISLE, PENNSYLVANIA

A typical Union field kitchen, well stocked with cordwood to fire the several camp stoves and boilers, and a coffee grinder always at hand. LIBRARY OF CONGRESS

A rough camp kitchen in the field, the coffee, soup, and stew pots suspended on a crude branch over coals. The man in charge tastes the broth or brew while others line up, cups extended, to receive their share. The presence of the washerwomen testifies that these same pots may soon be used for washing clothes. UNITED STATES MILITARY HISTORY INSTITUTE, CARLISLE, PENNSYLVANIA

The officers, of course, will dine rather better, from tables in their tents, and on real china or earthenware, with perhaps an enlisted man as orderly to serve them as the fellow on the left is doing with the plump soft bread. COURTESY OF JOHN HESS

Some officers even employ "contraband" former slaves to serve them at their mess, on tables almost bulging with tableware and food. COURTESY OF JOHN HESS

And after the meal, for the officers there could always be the convivial cup of flip, or a julep, or eggnog at holidays. COURTESY OF JOHN HESS

Not surprisingly, since meal time was one of the most important moments of the day for soldiers, they delighted in posing for the camera while dining, especially in good weather, like this group of Yankees posing at letter-writing, reading, eating stew from their cups and soft bread from their table. COURTESY OF JOHN HESS

Sometimes they lined up, every man with his plate in one hand and cup or loaf of soft bread in the other, with their black orderly serving them from his skillet, though a mealtime serenade from fife and fiddle was a distinct rarity.
COURTESY OF MICHAEL J. MCAFEE

Whenever the men on the march stopped by the road for even a few minutes, the pipes and newspapers came out, a fire was built, and the boiler put on to make coffee, perhaps supplemented with some hardtack and salt meat on a plate. The sergeant standing just left of the boiler, with hardtack in one hand, generously shares something from a bottle with the other, and not likely castor oil. COURTESY OF RUDOLPH K. HAERLE

With hardtack so ubiquitous, and so unpalatable, it is no wonder that a nice loaf of reasonably fresh soft bread was so welcome. Virtually every man in the squad has one on his plate, and coffee in his cup. COURTESY OF JOHN HESS

rations due to five of his assistants. Worse, he diverted a whole barrel each of potatoes and dried apples, onions, and pickles. The inmates of a hospital in his care got about one-sixth of the food, and he ate or sold the rest. Perhaps most vile of all was Edmund Boemer, surgeon of the 4th Missouri, who misappropriated his regimental hospital stores, ate some, sold the rest, and even charged one poor invalid board for feeding him from government supplies.[23]

Thieves even got into the boxes of food sent to the hospitals by the relief agencies at home. "We have seen hard times this fall and winter and are seeing pretty rough ones now for we are very short of rations at present, our allowance of hard tack and sowbelly being limited," complained an inmate at a military hospital at Chattanooga in December 1863.

> The good people of the North, who from all accounts are doing all they can for the benefit of sick and wounded soldiers, have no idea how little good the thousands that they appropriate to Sanitary purposes do us. And what becomes of all the good things, you would ask. Well, it goes into the greedy maws of the one-horse quacks, alias Medics and Surgeons, hospital stewards, agents, etc. Often you will see shoulderstraps regaling themselves on a nice bottle of wine with the label "U. S. Sanitary Stores." It is true out of so much that is sent, the poor soldier gets a little, but the quantity is small after it passes through the hands of these unprincipled wretches who are all smiles when the donors of these articles come around.[24]

Even when the inmates were released from their hospitals to convalescent camps to continue their recuperation, they still faced culinary pitfalls, for often the men had to cook for themselves, though yet unable to stand the exertion and sometimes with little or no care provided.[25]

Happily, not all was hardship and gloom in an invalid's life. They got their holidays of sorts, just like the men in the ranks in the field. In Washington in July 1864, hospital inmates got a picnic. Those who could walked to a grove near their wards, while stewards carried those missing legs, all to be fed "every delicate viand which it was safe for the poor fellows to eat," according to Mary Livermore, including strawberries and ice cream. In fact, ladies distributed strawberries to nearly 10,000 invalids in all the hospitals in Washington that summer.[26] Walt Whitman, already a poet of note, who now nursed

Union sick and wounded, took the ice cream to those who could not come and get it, sometimes paying out of his own pocket. "I gave the inmates of Carver hospital a general ice cream treat," he noted in his diary, "going around personally through the wards to see to its distribution."[27]

In Confederate hospitals, all of the shortages and scarcities that afflicted mealtime for soldiers in the ranks were just as prevalent, though whenever possible, regulations allowed for them to receive locally available delicacies not included in soldier rations. The government in Richmond published a broadside in 1861 containing Diet Tables for Military Hospitals to be used in its soldier wards, but it quickly became increasingly obsolete in the face of supply shortages. Two years later, on July 6, 1863, the surgeon general's office specified ten different patient diets, addressing varying states of physical condition of the soldiers: tea diet, spoon diet, beef tea diet, milk diet, light meat diet, chicken diet, half diet, fish diet, roast half diet, and full diet. Thanks to lack of ingredients, most hospitals in the Confederacy abbreviated these to full, half, and low diets, just as in the Union, and sometimes it reduced them even more, to just two diets: one for the ill and another for convalescents.[28]

To address these diets, Richmond published *Regulations for the Medical Department of the Confederate States Army* in 1863, including "Directions for Cooking in Hospital." It provided fifteen recipes for making stewed mutton with soup for 100 men, beef soup, beef tea, thick beef tea, essence of beef, chicken broth, plain boiled rice, sago jelly, arrowroot milk, arrowroot water, rice water, barley water (the equivalent of the North's water soup), Crimean lemonade made with lime juice, citric acid lemonade, and toast and water (the Yankee toast soup).[29]

All of this depended upon available ingredients, of course. However, commissaries in Confederate hospitals in the Army of Tennessee, for instance, customarily provided only beef, pork, and flour. Vegetables and fruit had to be purchased or grown on hospital grounds, if possible, or else bought locally with money from a hospital fund. As in the Union, each soldier was allowed a daily ration calculated to be of a certain value. The sick and wounded often had little appetite and could not eat their whole ration, especially the standard army issue. The value of what they did not eat was to be tallied every month and paid by the commissary to the hospital fund to be spent on chickens, eggs, butter, milk cows, vegetable seeds, and the like. Sometimes the system worked, but often it did not. The medical director of the Army of Tennessee, Surgeon Samuel Stout, calculated that Confederate hospitals lost at least $1 million in the first years of the war by inadequate handling and calculation of the fund money.[30]

Lacking what could be bought with the hospital fund, the inmates faced perhaps their greatest culinary obstacle, the same monotony that confronted Yankee invalids, exacerbated by shortage. Patients in some Southern hospitals ate the same thing every day, mostly dried fruit, potatoes, rice, mush, beef and chicken soup, and bread.[31] Kate Cumming, a nurse in a Southern hospital in Chattanooga, complained in 1863 that "the great trouble about hospitals is the sameness of the diet." In the morning, the invalids got "very nice" batter cakes made of the mush left from the previous evening's meal added to a little flour and soda, but with no eggs, along with some rice and stale bread. At least they did not use possibly infected leftovers from the wards.[32] Ferdinand Daniel, when in a Confederate hospital, had seen so much rice that once when served more of it with milk, he balked. "Take it away," he roared. "I had just as soon lie down and let the moon shine in my mouth as to eat rice."[33] Sam Watkins of the 1st Tennessee complained of the monotonous hospital food that it only made him more hungry when all he got was a plate of soup and a piece of bread.[34] Cooks also prepared, when possible, hash made of soup meat, toast, mush, milk, tea, coffee, and beefsteak.

What the inmates of Southern hospital wards got varied as greatly as the ingredients and those who prepared the meals. "Our fare was not palatable to say the least of it, consisting of corn bread and beef soup and occasional sugar and rice, meted out to us on crockery ware plates and wooden spoons," said Spencer Talley of what he ate at a Macon, Georgia, hospital in the fall of 1864. "Often when our meals were brought in, we had to 'shoo' and knock for sometime before we could tell what was on our plates other than flies."[35] At the same time in a hospital in Atlanta, Sgt. John Jackman of the 9th Kentucky found that breakfast was "tough beef, old bakers bread, and coffee that had flies in it, and I longed for the hard tack and corn bread, which I had left at the front."[35] Still, sometimes Kate Cumming found that for dinner she could give her patients beef and chicken soup, potatoes, rice, and dried fruit, and for dessert, "a *luxurious* baked pudding, made of the same materials as the batter-cakes, with molasses for sweetening, with the addition of spices."[37]

Soldiers sometimes served as hospital cooks, though many convalescents would have been happy to cook for themselves. Directors would not allow it, thinking it degrading work to be done by slaves or women, but cooking for large numbers of men challenged the abilities and experience of the women who more and more came to supervise even Confederate hospital dining.[38] Viewing the hospital kitchen at Corinth, Mississippi, after the battle of Shiloh, Kate Cumming observed that "it is not the cleanest place in the world," but she and other women came in and made it tidy. They found dishes to feed the men from, hired slaves for cooks, engaged a good baker, and set up a "nice dining room, and [ate] like civilized people."[39] Phoebe Pember, a young Jewish woman from South Carolina, came to Richmond in 1862 to supervise a ward at Chimborazo, the largest military hospital of the war. She had never cooked in such quantities, but calling on her heritage, she felt confident that she knew how to make one thing, chicken soup. Reflecting ancient Hebraic custom, she added parsley, thinking the bitter herb good for the sick, but some men objected to eating the soup because of the parsley floating on top. One said he "might worry a little down if it war'n't for them weeds afloatin' round."[40]

Pember would in time learn to cook squirrel and rat for the soldiers when they caught them.[41] Whenever possible, she did as Yankee matrons and surgeons did and allowed the men to request what they wanted to eat, and if she could possibly get it, she did, even when it sounded awful. One man asked for a mixture of bread, milk, pepper, and salt. She asked if he was going to eat it or put it on his chest as a plaster, but she made it all the same.[42] Another invalid repeatedly asked for "scribbled eggs and flitters" and seemed happy with whatever she actually gave him. She never figured out what scribbled eggs and flitters was, but she concluded that it must be a generic name for any food, no matter what was served to him.[43]

Most seriously weakened or ill men refused to drink the beef tea or any other liquid on the low diet, so the hospital cooks turned to expedients and sometimes deception. Pember made a beef tea by chipping a pound of beef and adding it to a half pint of water; then she stirred it without cooking until all the blood was extracted and only a teaspoon of white fiber remained. She added salt and then served it to men in the dark so they could not see what they were drinking.[44] Kate Cumming made a milk substitute of arrowroot and eggs, but doctors told her "it was useless to prepare it as the men would not touch it." She made it very thin, heating a broth of water and arrowroot, stirring beaten eggs into the broth while very hot, seasoning with fruit preserves—acidic ones being best—and letting it stand until cool. "This makes a pleasant and nourishing drink," she thought. It eased cough and was good for pneumonia. It also turned out good when wine was used instead of preserves, and soon she served gallons every day. "I have not one man to refuse it," she boasted, "but I do not tell them of what it is made."[45]

Mealtime in a hospital depended a great deal on the wards' locality. Often locals were cleaned out by a long-standing hospital, or hospitals competed with each other for local produce. In Georgia in 1864, one hospital bought vegetables and dairy products not with Confederate scrip, which was worthless by then, but by trading hospital equipment like ceramic pots. By 1865, the hospital funds had dried up or were not being paid by the commissary, to whom unused rations were returned for credit, and in Griffin, Georgia, where there was no remaining hospital fund, the cooks could get nothing but corn bread, sorghum, and beef.[46] Conditions in the hospitals and their equipment also affected what the cooks served. At St. Mary's Hospital in Dalton, Georgia, in 1864, there was not enough tableware to feed all of the prisoners at once, so they ate in shifts without washing the plates in between, thus unknowingly spreading germs in their food.[47] As for the staff, they were exhausted much of the time. After the battle of Stone's River, Tennessee, in January 1863, the hospital cooks of the Army of Tennessee went without sleep as they dealt with the wounded, and cooked the beef, bread, and coffee, which was all they had to prepare.[48] In April 1864, Phoebe Pember simply referred to herself as being "up to her elbows in gingerbread."[49]

Any hospital could absorb mountains of supplies, and always in competition with the armies in the field. At the Madison Hospital in Montgomery, Alabama, four trained cooks and two matrons made special diets. In one month, it bought and used 27 bushels of apples, 46 bushels of Irish potatoes, 500 bunches of onions, 333 dozen eggs, 282 gallons of milk, 74 bushels of sweet potatoes, 167 pounds of butter, 7 bushels of tomatoes, 2 bushels of butter beans, 402 chickens, 147 pumpkins, 31 gallons of molasses, $6^{1}/_{2}$ barrels of flour, 55 bushels of turnip salad, 216 dozen ears of green corn, 2 bunches of red pepper, $6^{1}/_{4}$ bushels of okra, $7^{1}/_{2}$ dozen squashes, and 15 bushels of peas. This was all in addition to the army ration issue of 1,548 pounds of beef, 293 pounds of bacon, 370 pounds of flour, 3,976 pounds of corn meal, 294 pounds of rice, $88^{1}/_{2}$ pounds of coffee, 176 pounds of sugar, 132 pounds of salt, and 193 pounds of lard.[50]

Vegetables and dairy products being a special concern, Surgeon Stout in the Army of Tennessee urged all hospitals in his department to start their own vegetable gardens and keep cows for milk. Then he contracted with nearby farmers for a supply of vegetables. At Forsythe, Georgia, the surgeon in charge actually boasted of his vegetables in a four-acre garden with "smaller salads," onions, "eschallots," English peas, beets, squash, field peas, turnips, Irish potatoes, okra, tomatoes, cabbage, and sweet potatoes, in addition to eight acres of corn and peas.[51] However, hospital gardens were good only so long as advancing Yankees did not require them to move, and the Army of Tennessee hospitals had to move often, unlike those in Virginia. Between the beginning of the war and 1864, the Foard Hospital with the Army of Tennessee built and abandoned no fewer than eight bakeries in the face of enemy approach.[52]

By the summer of 1864, cooks at Chimborazo were forced to rely on just dried apples and rice for convalescents and herb tea and arrowroot for the very ill, adding whiskey to make it palatable. What bacon they could get by then had been cured in the first two years of the war when salt was abundant, but was now largely spoiled, "and bacon was one of the sinews of the war," lamented Pember. Not surprisingly, the more active patients turned to other sources of meat, especially rats. "Epicures sometimes managed to entrap them and secure a nice broil for supper," she recalled, "declaring that their flesh was superior to squirrel meat."[53] Some soldiers made their own pitiful soups, calling one 'sweet soup' when it was nothing but stirred custard. They made sour soup by boiling buttermilk and then making a dough of egg yolk and corn flour and tearing off pieces to drop in the milk like dumplings, adding salt and pepper. "The buttermilk when so tested by heat resolved itself into a sea of whey," recalled Pember, "with a hard ball of curds in the center."[54]

Yet as strained as provisions were in places like Atlanta and Richmond, there were spots in the Confederacy even as late as 1864 that the armies had hardly touched and where hospital inmates ate rather well. The same Jackman who complained of poor fare in Atlanta in the summer of 1864 found by December, when transferred to a remote north Georgia hospital, that "we are living well." They had "good fresh beef, fresh pork, flour, sorghum, rice and so on, issued in abundance." They even made the molasses into candy and had "'candy-pullings' among ourselves."[55]

And there were holiday feasts, especially for Christmas. In the hospital at Charlottesville, Virginia, on December 25, 1862, Ada Bacot and others prepared turkey, ham, mutton, rice, potatoes, bread, pies and apples and took the dinner to the wards, where they found the men "in fine spirits." Later that day, Bacot went back, "giving the men their Eggnog."[56] A hundred miles away in Lynchburg that same day ladies of the city gave the men in the hospitals quite a feed. "Basket after basket of good things—substantials and niceties—were received from the liberal donors," recalled one recipient, "and our convalescents sat down to a plentiful repast of soup, roast turkey, duck, corned round of beef, chicken pie, spare ribs, & Irish potatoes; and dessert of cake, pies, etc. I have seldom seen men enjoy anything of the sort more."[57]

For Christmas the next year, down in Georgia, Kate Cumming made eggnog all day for the soldiers in the local hospital. "Just at the peep of dawn the little gallery in front of our house was crowded with the wounded, come to get their Christmas treat," she wrote. Some of them had missing arms or legs, but all were cheerful, and the surgeon in charge made a good effort to provide turkeys, vegetables, and pies, to make "a good dinner for the convalescents and nurses."[58] Meanwhile, at Chimborazo that Christmas, the Jewish Pember and her assistants observed the holiday by making twenty-four gallons of eggnog, giving some to every invalid in the wards, along with a piece of cake. Then they roasted a dozen turkeys and seven gallons of oysters to share as well.[59]

On Christmas in 1864, a woman named Violetta tried to improve the meal of soldiers in the Confederate hospital where she worked at Lauderdale Springs, Mississippi. Everything was scarce by now. "Eggs, butter, chickens, came in such small quantities that they *must* be reserved for the very sick," she lamented. Some men were eating just corn bread softened and stirred in water, while others got mush and milk or a little chicken soup. One soldier said he would love to have a sweet potato pone, and she decided to make it for all the men as a holiday treat. In the town market, limited as it was, she bought several dozen eggs, lots of sweet potatoes, and some butter, all of which she concealed in her cabin. The night before she was to bake it all, hogs smelled the scent of the potatoes and got under her cabin and pushed up the floorboards to get at the food. Her servant thought it an earthquake at first, but then beat the pigs away. The next day, they baked the pones and served them on plates with cups of milk, probably the simplest holiday meal the invalids ever ate, yet in those circumstances, most welcome indeed.[60]

When Confederate soldiers were sent home from the hospital as convalescents, they often found that culinary conditions there were no better than in the wards they left. Returned from the Augusta Hospital in South Carolina in June 1863, Berry Benson found that "at home, our fare was extremely plain, being chiefly bread, bacon, rice, hominy, sorghum, and such vegetables as the garden afforded." For coffee, they used rye instead. Frequently, there was just breakfast and a midday meal, with only the children getting bread and milk for their suppers. "I have seen salt on the table quite brown in color, being made by boiling the earth dug up in smoke houses, and evaporating the water."[61]

Perhaps worst of all, the end of a hospital stay, or even the end of the war, was not necessarily the end of a soldier's suffering, and frequently a contributor was the diet he got in the wards. Much of it did little or nothing to bring an end to the diseases that sent him there, while some actually made his condition worse. Yet for those who survived the pure monotony of hospital fare, peace meant at least something better to eat, and more of it, and that no longer would the soldiers prefer to let "the moon shine" in their mouths.

CHAPTER SIX

GETTING IN A PICKLE

AS SERIOUSLY AS THE SOLDIERS TOOK THEIR VICTUALS, IT SHOULD HARDLY come as a surprise that they frequently got into trouble, often very serious trouble, when it came to getting what they wanted to eat or holding onto what they had. In the Union army alone, scores of men and even officers would find themselves arraigned before courts-martial charged with everything from the theft of a piece of candy to misappropriation of banquets' worth of food. Add the all-too-present effects of alcohol to an argument over a morsel, and with alarming frequency, otherwise normal men could be propelled even to murder over such a minor article as a pickle.

The most modest infractions of military law, and thus probably the most numerous, largely went unreported and unpunished, at least officially, as sergeants and officers simply dealt with them on an ad hoc basis without permanent damage to a soldier's record. Dereliction of duty inspired or assisted by good food and bad was surely epidemic North and South, and for all who got away with a dressing down, there were those that paid a sometimes heavy price. Like many another soldier excited at the availability of a surfeit of local produce, Pvt. John Lucy of the 2nd New York Infantry ate too many green apples and watermelons one day in the fall of 1861 at Newport News, Virginia. When his turn came for guard duty, he suffered a severe stomachache that distracted his attention, during which he allowed people to pass through the lines without challenge or countersign and then compounded his problem by falling asleep and being caught. A sentence of five months at hard labor wearing a twenty-four-pound ball and chain attached to his leg would give him time to think about the consequences of green fruit gluttony. Three years later in Pennsylvania, a private in the 16th Veterans Reserve got six months at labor for letting a pile of fresh oysters distract him from his duty at the guardhouse while a prisoner escaped.[1]

Rather more serious were those men moved to disobedience of orders by their stomachs. Victor Monier of the Regular army talked back to his officer and refused to go on guard duty at Vicksburg, Mississippi, in 1864, because he had not yet had his evening meal. "I wanted to get supper before I went," he complained, but a court put him in a military prison without pay for nine months as penance for putting dinner before duty. Edward Hubby of the 14th Iowa, complaining that "the company was short of provisions; the hard bread and meat were both unsound," thought that an excuse to refuse camp police duty at Corinth, Mississippi, in 1862, but it cost him two months' reduced pay. And in the camps around Washington, in 1865, 1st Sgt. Walter Delastatius of the 9th Veteran Reserve took for himself soft, fresh-baked bread from his commissary, when orders were for the men to have hardtack instead. When his lieutenant—who happened to be out of uniform—reprimanded him and ordered him to go to his quarters under arrest, the sergeant refused. "I don't take orders from men in civilian dress," he replied impudently. It cost him his stripes and a dishonorable discharge.[2]

Carelessness inspired by the proximity to a serendipitous feast got many a Yankee in trouble. Joseph Delevan of the 4th New York Artillery, on duty near Rockville, Maryland, in 1862, thought to augment his rations with some local produce. "I thought I would walk out a ways," he explained, "to see if we could buy any apples or cider." He walked more than a mile and, when he got back, found he had been missed and his officers were in an uncharitable mood that led to a court-martial. Sherman Streeter, a private in the 104th New York, lay in a military hospital in the winter of 1864 but felt well enough to leave without permission to go to a local oyster house, only to be charged with desertion on his return and fined $1 of his pay for two months, a leniency no doubt impelled by his having been twice wounded in action. Sgt. Charles Hill of the 4th Rhode Island also apparently excited some sympathy when he left his regiment without leave in 1863. "I went home to get a set of teeth, my others having given out," he protested in his defense. His dentist averred that his old teeth had been worn out by the attempt to chew army hardtack and was at work on replacements. "The dentist was late," pled Hill. Every soldier, and even officers on a court-martial, knew the truth of hardtack's impenetrability, so Hill got off with a reprimand. If those "sheet-iron teeth-dullers" were hard to swallow, how much more so was the excuse of William Pool of the 111th Illinois, who got two weeks' hard labor and forfeiture of eight months' pay for leaving his command for nine months in 1863, when he offered in his defense that he left to get a skillet to bake his own fresh bread.[3]

Many soldiers found themselves suddenly prisoners of war after a simple forage from camp. James Stinson of the 84th Illinois lost three months' pay for leaving his lines near Atlanta in 1864 in search of apples, only to be captured and held for two weeks by enemy scouts. A private of the 59th Indiana was captured in 1864 when he left camp at Vicksburg to gather wild berries and ran into Confederates.[4] Several privates of the 114th Ohio, 7th Kentucky, and 26th Iowa, riding the steamboat *Tecumseh* on the Mississippi in 1864, saw a group of hogs on the Arkansas bank near Napoleon. Thinking the area safely in Union hands, they managed to get ashore, apparently leaving their boat to go its way without them and thus making themselves liable at least to charges of absence without leave. They had killed and were just cooking several of the porkers when Confederate Texans disguised in Union uniform took them by surprise and made them prisoners. One of their companions, meanwhile, was plundering a local turnip patch when the enemy caught him, while another enterprising fellow brazenly went into Napoleon to get a local to bake a supply of flour into fresh bread, only to meet the rifles of Rebel captors. Somehow, in the fact of their being captured, the Ohioans escaped conviction when brought up months later on charges of desertion. The Iowans, however, had less forgiving officers, and their court found them guilty, made them extend their terms of enlistment by the sixteen months they were absent as prisoners, and fined them their pay for the same term. Kentucky officers must have been especially stern, for one of their men, even when he protested that he had been given permission to go ashore, found himself convicted and ordered to be shot before the sentence was suspended.[5]

Far greater were the number of soldiers who got themselves into trouble within their own lines, thanks to wanting something extra to eat. Theft of provisions became a common offense, as men thought they could sneak something into their haversacks without being caught. Sometimes they stole from each other, as with Nathan Kotchland of the 91st Pennsylvania, who stole half a ham, some bologna, and a roast chicken. Worse, he stole it from a sergeant. At least he knew well enough not to deny his misdemeanor, though he spent the rest of his enlistment at hard labor. The men especially prized fresh eggs, but when James Downs of the 6th Kentucky stole several in 1862, he took from the wrong larder, the headquarters mess. As punishment, he spent six days on bread and water and was forced to march once at dress parade carrying a ball and chain and a sign with the words "for stealing." The commissaries and quartermasters were always likely targets, and sometimes the temptation was just too great. "All I had for dinner and supper was hard bread," protested Lewellyn Dearing of the 9th Maine in 1861. "A barrel of sugar broke open and I had some, about a pint." Apparently suspicious of just how the barrel happened to break open, a court sentenced him to eight days of camp police duty wearing twenty-five pounds of weight in his knapsack. A Pennsylvania private walked away with a whole quarter of beef, explaining at his trial that he had been hungry, did not have a knife to cut off a more modest piece of meat, and thus had to take the whole thing.[6]

One New York private even forged his lieutenant's signature in order to get potatoes and onions from the commissary. "I wanted onions for my severe cold," he explained, but sniffling or not, he still had to spend four hours every day for ten days standing on a barrel holding a sign that proclaimed him a forger. Black soldiers were no less subject to the same temptations. Pvt. Abram Franklin of the 5th Heavy Artillery United States Colored Troops left his guard post at Vicksburg in 1865 and was caught stealing vegetables from his own regimental garden. Musician Louis Williams of the 78th United States Colored Troops took a dozen loaves of bread from the commissary at Port Hudson, Louisiana, in 1864 and forfeited virtually all of his pay for the three months that he spent at hard labor. Still, that was better than the sentence meted out to Thomas Stockwell of the 13th Missouri, who stole a government ham at Corinth. His head was shaved, the buttons cut from his uniform, and he was drummed out of the army wearing a placard proclaiming "thief." Almost as bad were the men on guard duty who turned blind eyes to the virtual pillage of stores by their comrades, as when an inebriated corporal in the 9th Veteran Reserve with the inapposite name—for a soldier—of Commodore Jackson allowed $200 worth of apples, ale, canned fruit, and oysters to be plundered from goods he was assigned to guard at Huntsville, Alabama, in 1865.[7]

Going that one better, a Kentucky Confederate on duty guarding a supply depot was dipping into the bottom of a barrel of sugar, helping himself, with only his feet protruding from the top, when a passing guard saw the feet sticking out of the barrel and thought to investigate. Marched to headquarters and charged with stealing government property, he pled guilty, but then added that "I do not think you ought to punish me, colonel, as I always give you part of every thing I *find*." He got off with a light arrest.[8]

Nor were officers immune to such larcenous temptations, and in fact, most had much easier access to government foodstuffs, under less supervision. It may not be coincidental that they also had easier access to alcohol, especially the physicians, for drinking and misappropriation frequently went hand in hand. Some just transgressed by joining the soldiers in their meals, breaking regulations about fraternization, as when Confederate captain Thomas Stokes of the 2nd Tennessee was caught late after lights-out at a drunken party with privates in his command, all of them "sucking eggs" no doubt pilfered from a local Kentucky farmer. Assistant Surgeon Nelson Isham of the 97th New York also outraged army protocol by eating his meals with his hospital cook and patients and then stealing the soft bread rations designated for those very same inmates. "I saw the doctors eat soft bread while the patients were eating hard bread," he argued, and presumed that if they could, then he could too, even if it meant stealing patients' rations.[9]

Far worse was Surgeon H. T. Shaw of the 6th Iowa, who amassed a whole litany of charges after the battle of Shiloh, starting with cowardice on the field during the fight. Then he got drunk and stole rations, including vital fresh fruit and liquor from hospital stores, thus denying them to the sick. He then refused to treat the sick and wounded while he appropriated ambulances to haul his pilfered supplies to a nearby boarding house run by his wife and to which he had assigned privates to act as cooks for his family enterprise. He even threw away hospital bedding on the march, in order to make room in a wagon for his private cook stove, and then while drunk, he refused even to prescribe for or treat the patients in his care. At least he had the good grace to plead guilty when charged. Of course, the supply officers themselves enjoyed the easiest opportunity of all, and some took it, as did Lt. James P. Shallcross, quartermaster of the 2nd District of Columbia Infantry. Late in 1864, stationed at Fairfax Courthouse, Virginia, he stole apples, eighty-five pounds of sugar, two barrels of flour, potatoes, coffee, and two wagon loads of stove wood, sending it all to his home near Alexandria. A court quickly convicted and cashiered him from the service.[10]

Most numerous of all, however, were the cases of individual soldiers who got into fights, sometimes fatal altercations, with their fellow soldiers and even friends, all over a morsel of food. Unfortunately, any food left unattended was fair game if the thief was willing to risk the consequences. They would even steal from officers, as a Maine captain discovered when he received a home-cooked ham. His tent was so small that either his feet or his ham had to pass the night outside, and he kept his feet warm at the expense of finding his ham missing the next morning. "The resulting remarks from Captain Hobson were exceedingly voluminous as well as rugged," noted one of his privates, "and he expressed a burning desire to crush the villain to indescribable atoms."[11] Some men did just that, and they would fight over any stolen food, especially if they had been drinking. A Regular in the 7th Infantry, already in the guardhouse for being absent from his post, got into a fight with another prisoner over a cup of coffee, and in a fight over the same beverage, a private in the 2nd Arkansas Union Cavalry stabbed another soldier near the heart. John Meigs, a Cherokee private in the 3rd Indian Home Guards west of the Mississippi, shot and killed another native private after they argued over which of them was to carry a bucket of cider, from which Meigs at least had already consumed a surfeit and from which he no doubt hoped to drink the rest. Even vinegar could sour soldier relations, as in 1865, when a private in the 149th Illinois shot and killed his sergeant in a squabble over a canteen full.[12]

A civilian employee in the quartermaster's department in Union-occupied Florida stabbed another employee in 1864 in a dispute over some eggs. George Flake, a black private in the 55th United States Colored Troops, shot and severely wounded a fellow private in Memphis in an argument about some sugar.[13] Stolen sauerkraut and preserved fruit landed a Maryland private in the stockade with three months' hard labor, and any threat to a soldier's sweet tooth could be especially dangerous. During an alcoholic altercation over oysters in Lebanon, Missouri, in 1863, a corporal hit Pvt. William Bush of the 8th Missouri Militia Cavalry over the head with a pistol, whereupon Bush shot and killed him. Thomas Tewhoy of the 45th Kentucky stabbed and killed another private in a fight over a pie, and Missourian Abraham Allen of the 6th Cavalry attempted to shoot and kill three other soldiers after accusing them of stealing two candy kisses from him.[14]

There were four presumed staples that led to more altercations than anything else, and in more than a third of cases, alcohol helped escalate the argument into violence. A soldier coveted another's bread at certain peril. A musician in the VI Corps, Adam Serr, assaulted and hospitalized another musician in Virginia in 1864 after a bread disagreement. Pvt. Thomas McEvoy of the 1st Louisiana Union Infantry got into a fight with his captain over a few biscuits, called him a "bastard," and threatened first to bayonet him and then to shoot him before he was subdued. He would spend the rest of the war at hard labor, and a private in the 7th New York Artillery would do three months' similar time for stabbing another private in a fight over a loaf.[15]

The meat ration, of course, could arouse tempers, especially since it could be infrequent and was often so bad when received that the occasional bit of fresh beef or pork was prized all the more. Certainly, it was one way to get even in an argument. At Yorktown, Virginia, during the Peninsular campaign in March 1862, John Sullivan of the 5th United States Artillery argued with his corporal at breakfast over the distribution of rations for the meal. First, there was a physical struggle, and then in his anger, Sullivan took the corporal's own meat ration and threw it into the coffee boiler. He got off lightly with a $10 fine. Not so for the inaptly named Smiley Craig of the 65th Indiana. At Henderson, Kentucky, in the summer of 1863, he fought with another private over a piece of meat and then took a rifle and shot him dead. Only court leniency due to Craig's presumed feeble-mindedness got him off with hard labor for the duration of his enlistment.[16]

Then there were apples. Many a soldier discovered that they could not keep the doctor away when another soldier felt angry—or drunk—enough to fight for possession. In the summer of 1862, Joseph Mason of the 48th Illinois went before a military court-martial charged with striking his sergeant during a fight over the fruit. Two years later, near Nashville, Alexander Plunkett, a civilian employee, quarreled with a soldier over an apple while riding the Nashville & Northwest Railroad in Tennessee and beat him "in an inhuman manner." When Reuben Shroat of the 100th United States Colored Troops got in a fight with another black soldier over an apple, he simply shot him.[17]

And right in contention with bread, meat, and apples in its ability to incite mayhem stood the lowly pickle. Some thought they were effective in quickly sobering a man who had imbibed too much, and perhaps that explains some of their seemingly universal desirability. Soldiers in the occupied Confederacy regularly pillaged civilian homes to loot the briny gherkins, and Lt. John Williams of the 9th Missouri Militia Cavalry shot and killed one of his own privates in a squabble over a pickle. Considering that Williams himself was "pickled" at the time, he may have been after a cure as much as a snack.[18]

The mere subject of rations in general could explode into blows or worse. Sgt. Samuel Barr of the 84th Pennsylvania got into a fight with Cpl. David Barr, probably his own brother, when they quarreled over rations and a mess pan. Shouting at the corporal to "come out and fight," the sergeant found himself in the end facing a court martial instead, stripped of his rank, and reprimanded in front of his company. In 1864, when Ruben Wilson of the 15th United States Colored Troops got into a row over a meal with another private in his company at Nashville, Wilson shot and killed the man. Since he shot him in the thigh, a court decided there was no intent to kill, gave a finding of manslaughter without criminal intent, and let Wilson go free. Also found guilty of manslaughter was Thomas Bentley, a civilian teamster working for the army, who stabbed another wagon driver to death in 1864 when they quarreled over whether they had been given enough rations. He would be sentenced to eight years. Not so for Cpl. Alfred Chapman of the 27th United States Colored Troops, however. After he had been drinking, he shot and killed a private in 1864 when the man merely asked for rations that Chapman claimed he had already been given. Chapman would hang.[19]

Of course, not just the food itself could lead to altercations. Men, in the time-honored tradition of all soldiers everywhere, complained about their cooks, and the grousing could get carried away. A private in the 9th New York Artillery found himself court-martialed simply for refusing to eat somewhat burned soup that he believed to be unfit. Pvt. Leopold Weishar of the 21st Missouri fought with his company cook over the quality of the breakfast meat one morning in 1865, and the company sergeant intervened, only to be struck by Weishar—unwisely as it happened, for the sergeant was also the cook's son. In the end, it only cost him a $5 fine and a reprimand. A hot-tempered Irishman, Edward Donohoe of the 1st United States Infantry, was serving in Texas when the state seceded and war broke out and narrowly missed being surrendered with other U.S. troops in the state in February. That was frustration enough, but then to have to eat bad soup proved too much. He threw it away while shouting at the cook, "this is what we get for marching 40 miles a day"! For ninety days after his trial he would march with a twenty-four-pound ball and chain. Hermann Temps of the 45th New York took his argument over badly cooked meat a step further by hitting the cook in the face with a piece of his own ill-prepared pork. The court-martial, applying almost biblical justice, freed Temps of the problem of meat by sentencing him to five days on bread and water, demonstrating that food could be a punishment, too. On hapless victim threw his supper into the fire after it moved on his plate, and on closer inspection, he found it covered with maggots. He was brought before a court on charges of destroying "government property."[20]

Surely that is what Sgt. R. E. Looker and Pvt. John Snow thought. At Mowrer Hospital in Pennsylvania, Looker of the 190th Pennsylvania, suffering the effects of several wounds, and with three inches of his right arm gone from one injury, still aroused himself to violence over his food. Shouting that his breakfast "stank," he threw it on the ground, berated a sergeant, and called his surgeon a "god damned son of a bitch," while the two threw him out of his bed and bound and gagged him. Snow, of the 3rd Maine Artillery, became so frustrated that he made a one-man attack on the battery cookhouse, demanded more food, threw some of it out the door, hit the cook, and then when a sergeant attempted to restrain him, Snow sank his teeth into the noncommissioned officer—presumably from anger and not hunger.[21]

More general mayhem sometimes resulted from disgruntlement over camp food, both rations themselves and their preparation, and half of the time, the problem started when the soldiers had been drinking. Alcohol was no part of the soldier's official diet, though sailors in the navies intermittently got a grog ration. Away from the restraints of home and family, many a man indulged himself a tipple when he could, but with restrictions on access to whiskey in the Union and enacted legal prohibition in the Confederacy, soldiers often had to use their wits to get a drink, and at some risk. One Confederate officer boasted that he had not had a drink in three days, as if it was something unusual, though when whiskey went at $15 a quart, few in the ranks could afford it.[22] Not surprisingly, the men resorted to every stratagem to fill the liquid void.

A detachment of the 15th Connecticut Infantry, stationed at a bridge crossing the Potomac River at Washington, stopped one poor farmer's wagon and confiscated a barrel of his cider until he could get proper papers to bring it into the city. By the time he returned, the soldiers had drained the barrel into their bellies and refilled it with river water; they loaded it back on his wagon full of smiles.[23] Out in Missouri in 1861, the commissary in one Confederate division asked for food supplies, but through a bureaucratic bungle received instead forty-six barrels of Kentucky bourbon. He left all but one under guard and took the other toward the front to deliver it to a surgeon who spoke of an officer needing it for snakebite. Apparently Missouri was full of hungry serpents just then, for soon hundreds of soldiers came to his wagon with their canteens, all pleading they also had been sent by their officers for "medicine."[24]

Even more resourceful were those who broke rules and risked punishment by making their own. In Virginia in 1862, one Rebel managed to get some whiskey and put it in an old vinegar barrel for safekeeping, even though he saw a suspicious chemical-looking substance in the bottom of the keg. The whiskey seemed unaffected, but when water was added, a chemical reaction took place that had it almost exploding as it foamed out of the glass.[25] Most adventurous were the Rebels who in 1864 built their own still out of brass fixtures and gas pipes taken from a demolished house. Taking apples from a nearby orchard, they mashed them in a cattle trough and then boiled the mash in a kettle, watching the evaporated steam rise through a condenser of twisted copper tube on which they poured cold water to make the steam condense again and drip into another kettle. "High wine" one called it, though another regarded the applejack as more like a "powerful emetic," and so it proved to be. "'It nearly turned their insides out," recalled D. E. Henderson, their officer. "Some stood resting their backs against the trees and leaning forward; others, with their hands to their heads and elbows on their knees, sat on old logs, stones, and stumps, hanging down their heads, with haggard faces and woe-begone looks."[26]

No wonder they got into trouble when they combined the effects of drink with their constant craving for more to eat. A private in the 153rd New York, who admitted he was drunk, took ten rations of tea from another soldier and poured them over the cook fire out of pure spite. Lt. Benjamin R. Helmes of the 1st Indian Heavy Artillery provided liquor to enlisted men at Port Hudson, Louisiana, and then got drunk with them in their quarters. Worse, he next loaned his officer's coat to one of them so he could go to get more alcohol, and then after a feast of stewed oysters, he encouraged a general riot that cost him his rank and his pay for three months.[27]

In late 1862, men of the 1st Connecticut Artillery in Virginia found what one called "a secessionist beef critter" not far from their camp, killed it, and were dividing the meat and celebrating the impending feast with too much alcohol when a quarrel broke out between two of them. One was knocked through a neighboring tent, and Cpl. George Blinn, whose duty it would have been as senior man present to quell the riot, simply watched, drunk himself. Then their captain arrived and upbraided Blinn; the corporal punched him, shouting, "I'll be goddemned [sic] if any officer will shit on me." He was so drunk that afterward he pled that "I didn't know I'd insulted the captain." A drunken private at Vicksburg approached John Spanhake, a saddler in the 5th Illinois Cavalry, and accidentally or playfully knocked Spanhake's holiday dinner plate on the ground; Spanhake grabbed a butcher knife and sank it in the private's back, killing him instantly.[28]

Even without being drunk, the men in the ranks sometimes came to riot over their victuals. Pvt. William Thompson of the 2nd California Cavalry, at Camp Union, California, in 1865, took part in a general melee as messmates fought over bread at breakfast, punching and shoving his way to the table, ignored an order to stop, and then punched his corporal, and later threw him out a window, a performance that got Thompson six months at hard labor with a ball and chain at the foreboding prison on Alcatraz Island in San Francisco Bay. A food fight in a Virginia mess hall in 1864 saw Thomas Hastie of the 1st Massachusetts Heavy Artillery live up to his surname by losing his patience and severely beating another private. Seven privates in the 4th Iowa Cavalry, who had not been drinking, went to trial for a riot at Benton Barracks at St. Louis in 1864, when they made off with 800 bread rations during a raid on the camp bakery. The year before, when a soldier threw an apple at Pvt. Martin Vann of the 1st Tennessee Union Infantry, Vann simply drew his pistol and shot him dead, getting off lightly with a verdict of manslaughter and a sentence of two years' imprisonment.[29]

Occasionally, the food even became the weapon, like the pork chop in the hand of Private Temps. Here again, alcohol could be an item on the violent menu, as when Thomas Flynn of the 9th United States Infantry stood drunk on the corner of Davis and Jackson Streets in San Francisco in late 1863 and made suggestive remarks about a young woman's clothing as she walked past. When her mother remonstrated with him, he hit her in the face with an apple and later tried to defend himself by pleading that he had been unconscious of what he was doing. "You were conscious enough to know that my daughter was going out without hoops and spoke of it," testified the mother, and Flynn got four months at hard labor with a ball and chain to contemplate the shortcomings in his deportment. Throwing food knew no boundaries of rank, either, as a captain in the 82nd Illinois found out in late 1864 when Lt. William Loeb became angry with him, called him a liar, and threw a plate of food in his face, followed by a fist. Surprisingly, Loeb got the charges dismissed when he pled guilty.[30]

Confederates could use food as a weapon, too, as Pvt. Charles Wakeman of the 1st California found out in 1862, when he was guarding three Rebel prisoners at Mesilla in the New Mexico Territory. A prisoner approached him innocently enough, produced an ear of corn, and then proceeded to beat Wakeman's face bloody before seizing his rifle and escaping in company with two others. On at least one occasion in Baltimore in 1865, with neither anger nor malice, food still proved to be a deadly accomplice when Pvt. Frank Biliol of the 22nd Veteran Reserve had innocently enough skewered a loaf of bread on his bayonet at the end of his rifle. When he tried to shake the loaf off, the gun accidentally fired, and a nearby soldier fell dead.[31]

Of all of the culinary avenues leading soldiers into trouble, however, it was the one that put them in conflict with the civilians in an occupied land that could cause the most trouble. By virtue of the war being fought almost entirely on Confederate soil, such incidents therefore involved overwhelmingly—and perhaps exclusively—Yankee soldiers. Not surprisingly, in a war in which Congress had passed statutes declaring the property of those in rebellion to be contraband or forfeit, it naturally followed that common soldiers felt free to "liberate" some of that property themselves and appropriate it for their own use, especially the contents of hen houses, root cellars, smokehouses, and stores. A New Hampshire soldier said it succinctly in 1862 when tried for stealing fruit from a Maryland citizen—though Marylanders, still living in a loyal state, were not subject to the confiscation laws. "The owner was a Rebel," he protested; "his apples were free plunder."[32]

Even in the face of repeatedly promulgated orders from army headquarters on down to respect private property of citizens in the occupied South, many Union soldiers simply felt too much temptation and too much animosity to restrain themselves. Lt. Emanuel Faust of the 46th Illinois refused even to attempt to restrain his men in the occupying force around Vicksburg in 1864. When they plundered the market wagon of a city woman of seven heads of cabbage, and he came up on charges of disobedience of orders, he replied that she was "a damned Rebel and I don't care." Storekeepers had to be wary. When a Brownsville, Texas, merchant threw Pvt. Edward Davis of Illinois out of his store for being disorderly and stealing preserved pears, Davis came back and threw brickbats through the windows. Cpl. Frederick Reimers of the 54th New York attempted to pass counterfeit notes for merchandise at a store in Charleston, South Carolina, and when he was caught, he simply pocketed some cigars and tobacco and then grabbed apples, vegetables, and one egg, eating it all right in front of the shopkeeper. In Fredericksburg, Virginia, in 1865, two soldiers of the 61st Pennsylvania ate cherries and took cigars from the store of George Miller, and when he demanded that they pay for what they had taken, one of them hit him on the head with a brick and killed him. They both got three years at hard labor for their modest feast, and the one who actually wielded the brick received an added, and appropriate, penance for those deadly cherries by being put on bread and water for ten days of every month for the first year of his sentence. When George Weaver of the 5th Connecticut shot a civilian's hog, he found himself brought before a military court on charges of destruction of private property. Only the fact that he had eaten all the evidence got him an acquittal.[33]

However much the vast majority of Union soldiers behaved honorably as occupiers, there were those few who badly took advantage of the weakness of civilians and their frequent lack of resort to justice. In the Railroad Eating

House in Macon, Missouri, Charles Call of the 9th Missouri Militia Cavalry got into an argument with a woman over pumpkin pie, abused her verbally, and then threw her onto the floor while he continued his rant. Sometimes, especially if the man had been drinking, it did not matter whether he would actually eat what he took. On the caboose of a Memphis & Little Rock Railroad train in 1864, two privates of the 62nd Illinois drove the passengers out of the car, threatened to bayonet the brakeman, and then took from the passengers eight pounds of sage, of all things. Black soldiers were just as guilty of such misconduct, with perhaps the added incentive of revenge on those who had kept them enslaved for centuries. Soldiers like George Mackley of the 59th United States Colored Troops went out from the Memphis garrison to steal melons from farmers' patches and fired at them when they objected. When a Maryland citizen protested at being robbed of pots of strawberry and blackberry preserves by Thomas Jones of the 8th New York Cavalry, Jones threatened to burn down his home. While striking the woman in Macon brought only a reprimand to Charles Call, Jones was discharged dishonorably and confined in a penitentiary for the rest of his enlistment, perhaps because Jones's victim was a citizen of a loyal state. Potatoes proved especially desired, and therefore vulnerable. Two New York privates were caught while one was still pulling up the stalks and the other had his haversack full of the tubers. The soldiers usually just admitted their guilt and swallowed the loss of some pay and a few days at hard labor.[34]

Sadly, some of the men even victimized local black civilians, who could hardly have been classed as Rebels. Talbot Williams of the 60th Indiana stole into a henhouse owned by a black man in Thibodeaux, Louisiana, and when caught stealing chickens, he threw a brick at their owner, earning himself a sentence of hard labor for the rest of his enlistment. When George May, a private in the 1st New York, stole a barrel of oysters from a Negro who ran a restaurant at Newport News, Virginia, the black diplomatically—if impishly—asked May if he couldn't be satisfied with the box of oysters he had already stolen two hours earlier. May took the barrel anyhow, to get a sentence of a month's hard labor and a fine for his misdeed.[35]

Southerners like those two blacks who challenged food thieves did so at some risk, for there were a few men who would not be deterred at any cost, and citizens lost their lives. One Tennessean, just seventeen years old, was shot five times by a man in a fight over the boy's hog. Pvt. Jasper Laster of the 3rd Missouri Militia Cavalry haggled with a civilian near Pilot Knob, Missouri, over buying a goose. When the owner stubbornly refused to sell the animal for less than a half dollar, Laster shot and killed him. In 1862, Pvt. William Dormody of the 1st Pennsylvania Artillery and others accosted Hezekiah Stokes and his wife on the road in their carriage. Dormody demanded apples and Stokes handed them over. Then Dormody demanded corn and beat and mortally stabbed Stokes. A court sentenced him to be hanged, and President Lincoln, who so often looked for reasons to mitigate any capital sentence, approved the finding. Another Missouri civilian met death at a soldier's hands in 1864 when J. C. Blair, a sergeant in the 145th New York, went to his home in St. Louis to take apples. The civilian came out with a shotgun to defend his property, and Blair simply killed him.[36]

Of course, it could have been Blair meeting death, and his experience and others' should have been a warning that some of these civilians were as willing to keep their food as some soldiers were to take it, as a few found to their eternal cost. A private in the 42nd Massachusetts went into the cabbage patch belonging to Christopher Hyde near Alexandria, Virginia, and Hyde shot and mortally wounded him, though it resulted in more than a two-year prison sentence for Hyde, as the Yankee War Department did not appreciate Southern civilians killing their own, even in defense of property. Down in Demopolis, Alabama, J. S. Ruffin caught a soldier in his apple orchard stealing fruit and shot at him, wounding but not killing the private, for which he would spend three months in prison. But Henry E. Johnson of Manchester, Virginia, near Petersburg, paid a much higher price, for which he was vociferously unrepentant—interesting for a minister reputed to be very successful at saving souls. Pvt. Stephen LaMay and others of the 98th New York came into Johnson's potato patch one night in 1865 after the fall of Petersburg and Richmond, and the minister caught them. He opened fire and killed LaMay on the spot and shot at the rest as they ran off. "They were stealing my potatoes," he told the court-martial that tried him, proudly pleading guilty. "I don't like Union soldiers. I was justified in shooting them and would do so again." The court pronounced life imprisonment, probably more for his attitude than his crime, and only the efforts and petitions of a host of his flock eventually got President Andrew Johnson to remit the sentence and send him home.[37]

Indeed, once the war came to an end, many of the men serving sentences or enduring fines and penalties for heeding their stomachs before regulations would be pardoned or just released. Except in the case of murder and serious mayhem, the authorities could afford to take the view that hunger—sometimes augmented by drink—simply drove the soldiers over a line no one had ever expected to exist in the first place. The government should have realized from the outset that men trained to fight, when not immediately confronted by a declared foe, could turn that aggression to other uses given idle hours, inadequate quantity or variety in their diet, the judgment-impairing effects of alcohol, and the ever-present hunger of youth.

CHAPTER SEVEN

HOW STRANGE A THING
IT IS TO BE HUNGRY

THERE WERE OTHER MEN IMPRISONED WHOSE ONLY "CRIME" HAD BEEN TO BE in the wrong place at the wrong time. For those men unfortunate enough to be taken in battle, the ensuing prison experience would be one that, if anything, magnified the importance of food in their lives even more than their days in camp, for in the monotony of seemingly endless days of inactivity in a stockade or converted fort or warehouse, a meal represented often the only break in the tedium of the day. Some prisoners of war, even those held in the Confederacy, would be fortunate enough to land in places where they ate almost as well as they had in the armies, and rarely even better. For most, however, entrance into the compounds signaled the beginning of a dietary and nutritional decline that would leave them perpetually hungry, malnourished, sick from scurvy and chronic diarrhea, and all too often on the road to death.

Just getting from the battlefield to the prison represented an upset in their eating schedules, for often, particularly in the South, there was no opportunity to make provisions available for men unexpectedly taken captive, and so the trip by train or road could pass for several days with either no food at all or else the most elemental issues of meal and perhaps a little beef. Union prisoners, of course, were always passing through hostile territory on their way to their new homes, but some Confederates, at least, encountered rather friendlier treatment, especially those who traveled through Union states like Kentucky or Maryland, in which Southern sympathy ran strong. "It was no uncommon sight to see men running into baker's shops and confectioneries, buying all the pies, cakes, and loaves they could carry, and then, regardless of the remonstrances of the guards, throw them in among the prisoners," said a man who watched Confederate prisoners pass through Louisville. "Baskets of fruit would also be bought up entire, and their contents emptied in a similar manner."[1]

If Union prisoners got no such aid on their journey to captivity, at least early in the war captured Yankees incarcerated in Richmond could hire black cooks if they had the money and could buy vegetables, butter, and coffee to add to the brown bread, beef, soup, and rice their captors issued to them. Officers even ate three times daily, and the enlisted men twice.[2] Those prisoners who could bought stocks of food, and one Federal officer wrote that "our closet is never without crackers, cheese, bologna, sausages,—fruit cake, plain cake—coffee, tea."[3] Such plenty would be a great rarity for Yankees before long. By contrast, Camp Douglas in Chicago actually had a grocery store to sell goods to Confederate prisoners in the early days, and milk and butter sales wagons and vendors brought milk and vegetables in daily for prisoners who had the money.[4] And at Johnson's Island, off Sandusky, Ohio, one Confederate found that "our men having plenty of money live as well in the way of eating as we ever did." Another inmate there, John Dooley, wrote that their food was "not, except at times, such as a prisoner had a right to complain of."[5]

Prisoners on either side usually came to camps or prisons without cooking utensils, which they either had never had or else did not have with them when captured. Moreover, even in the Northern camps there was often a shortage of tableware, as at Camp Douglas and probably all of the prisons. It was worse in the South. In 1864, men at Camp Sumter, Georgia, better known as Andersonville, could not draw their liquid rations like vinegar and molasses or soup because they had no containers. Their camp commandant finally managed to get 450 buckets for them and tried, usually without success, to obtain other necessary equipment for food handling.[6] In June 1864, his inmates had to get their rice ration standing out in the rain in squads of thirty or so, and those who did not have tin cups or pans had to take it on boards or in bags made from trouser legs and shirt sleeves and caps. By then, it had been handled so much that it was dirty and black, but they ate it with relish.[7] Andersonville prisoners cooked their own cornmeal by mixing it with a little water, putting it over a fire, and eating it as mush. Some made clay ovens to bake it into bread, and others rolled it into dumplings to boil in soup made of bacon, beef, and maybe beans when available. But often, only one man in a mess had a tin can or a skillet for cooking, and he could be kept going all day cooking the others' rations in turn.[8]

The manner of cooking also presented challenges and problems. The Union authorities discouraged prisoners from cooking their own food, just as it frowned on soldiers in the armies doing so at first. When the prisoners did their own cooking, they were messy and wasteful. At Camp Douglas, for instance, their garbage was all over the barrack streets. Even with good rations, there is waste when improperly cooked.[9] Union commissary general of prisons William Hoffman tried to combat this by issuing huge kettles called "Farmer's boilers" that made 30 to 120 gallons of soup or stew at a time.[10] At Elmira Prison in New York, for example, the food was cooked inside the prison. The cookhouse—called the soup house by some—held thirty-five of these huge cauldrons, in which to heat water and then add meat and vegetables to boil into a broth. The vegetables, unaccountably, were then removed, and the result was soup. Authorities employed citizen bakers and a head chef with an assistant and engaged a contractor aptly named Elisha Cook, who provided ovens to the prison capable of baking 1,000 loaves daily; they also allowed him to sell eating utensils to the inmates. Virtually all Northern prisons would have some variant of this scheme with bakeries and cookhouses, and several of the Confederate compounds did the same when possible. By July 1864, Camp Morton in Indiana had kitchens erected in which cooking was done, each capable of producing cooked rations for 300 to 400 men. Vegetables were in short supply there, but at least the beef came cooked properly in quantity and tasted better and went farther.[11]

Prisoners in Southern keeping at Andersonville suffered from the lack of cooking utensils until May 1864, when large baking pans and kettles for cooking arrived at last and the commandant enlisted cooks and bakers from among the inmates. It was partly a matter of camp security as well as efficiency, for with prisoners no longer doing their own cooking, they did not need to be taken out of the compound on wood-gathering details, during which many attempted to escape. Henceforth at Camp Sumter, any prisoner who wanted to cook for himself had to grub about in the compound for something to burn.[12] Yankees held in Savannah, Georgia, would be issued one skillet for every twenty men as well as bricks to build bake ovens in which they baked their own corn bread from the raw cornmeal issued.[13] North and South, no system for cooking would be uniform. At Camp Douglas, for instance, after a time, authorities paid little attention to cooking in camp or to cleanliness and efficiency, allowing prisoners to cook for themselves in messes of four to eight men using the farmer's boilers, but they were almost universally regarded as a failure, and even Yankee inspectors asked that regular cook ranges be provided so the men could properly prepare for themselves. Washington balked at coddling the prisoners, since by this time the horror stories coming out of Southern prisons were already creating a mood for retaliation.[14] By 1864, the superintendent at least addressed efficiency in a fundamental fashion by designating three permanent cooks for each mess.[15]

The simple physical act of getting the food to the men also posed problems on both sides, especially as prison populations rapidly outstripped facilities. In some smaller prisons, there were mess halls where prisoners could take their meal at the same time together, though it could be difficult. At Washington's Old Capitol Prison, Confederates marched to the long tables in a double line, one going to each side, and sat at plates that were already filled, "upon which all fall to," recalled Berry Benson. They sometimes tried not to close up tightly, so that two men would actually share a third plate, but it usually didn't work. Many men were already ill, though, and had not appetite to eat all their meal, and so others fell on the leftovers.[16] More typical, though, were Fort Delaware, Delaware, and Point Lookout, Maryland. Prisoners marched in a line into a long hall and then turned to face tables at which each man's ration was laid out. He picked it up and the line marched back out to eat in their barracks; then the next line came in.[17] In one Yankee prison with 5,195 men, they had to eat in mess halls in 1,800-man shifts, meaning it took three hours to complete a meal.[18]

Another prison at Rock Island, Illinois, on the Mississippi, tried to combat this by issuing ten days' rations at a time and leaving control, distribution, and cooking completely to the prisoners. Every cookhouse had a forty-gallon cauldron and made its own meals, with water from the Mississippi. The problem was that the rations rarely lasted the ten days, some men finding themselves going hungry for days at a time before the next issue. Even at many other prisons where authorities frequently issued two days' rations on Saturdays in order to give staff and prisoners release from regular routine on Sundays, the men still usually ate it all at once and went without on the Sabbath.[19]

Setting aside the Civil War soldier's natural propensity for complaint, at first the prison ration on both sides was at least adequate and not substantially different from that encountered in his regiment. "Our dinner today was very good for prisoners of war; we had beefsteak, mashed-Irish-potatoes, and a bread pudding with a nice sauce," William Barrow of Louisiana wrote in his diary in May 1862 at Camp Douglas. "The beef steak and potatoes was the ration but the sauce was not."[20] A year later, at Richmond's Libby Prison, which was already notorious, conditions were bearable for the officers held there.

Complaining humorously that his captors "don't furnish us any sugar to put in our coffee, nor yet any coffee to put sugar in," one officer still found that the daily ration of half a loaf of good bread and a half pound of bacon per man was "a pretty short allowance, but enough to sustain life." Moreover, they could purchase sugar at $1.50 a pound and eggs at $2.50 a dozen or potatoes at $12 a bushel. Indeed, they bought so much that they created a speculator's shortage, he believed, for the price of potatoes went up to $18 a bushel and eggs increased a quarter a dozen.[21] At Washington's Old Capitol Prison in 1864, Berry Benson said that the diet was chiefly bean soup, "of which I was quite fond." They also got salt pork or beef in the place of it and soft bread or hardtack. "Coffee we had until the 4th of July; then it was stopped. I suppose it was intended we should celebrate the day somehow. It was an interesting sight to see the men go in to meals."[22] Confederates at Point Lookout testified during the war that they had "very fine beef," though insufficient in quantity, but they got barrels of turnips, beans, and carrots, and thus had little problem with the scurvy that beset other camps.

Even late in the war there were a few places in the Confederacy where prisoners fared well. In the camp at Millen, Georgia, Yankee inmates actually commented on their ample, if perhaps initially unsavory, rations. Their fresh beef was the heads of cattle killed to feed the guards, but it came in wagon loads. They broke them up so that every man got a substantial piece of bone and meat and then boiled and reboiled the bone "as long as a single bubble of grease would rise to the surface of the water." They gnawed and scraped every vestige of meat from the bone and then charred it until it crumbled; they ate that, too. Sometimes they got sorghum instead of meat, barrels of it being rolled into the compound and every man getting a fourth of a pint.[23] Even at infamous Andersonville, rations seemed good at first. In February 1864, they were a quart of good meal, a sweet potato, a piece of meat the size of two fingers, and now and then some salt.[24] Isolation worked to the advance of the prisoner. At Fort Jefferson on one of the Dry Tortugas, off the Florida coast, the most isolated prison of the war, Confederate prisoners did well, getting salt pork or beef, potatoes, bread, coffee, vegetables, and fruit once a week on a supply ship. Meanwhile, they were allowed to catch fish and turtles from the moat surrounding the fort.[25]

At the same time, following the model in both armies of regimental or company funds created from excess rations uneaten and returned to the commissary for money, prisons, especially in the North, established prison funds out of deductions of small amounts from rations of beef, bread, beans, etc., not used and spent the money on extra items, including food.[26] Camp Morton at Indianapolis got its own bake house suitable to supply 5,000 men on a contract paid for partly by the prison fund. Furthermore, local vendors were contracted to act as camp sutlers in most prisons, and prisoners with money or credit at the commandant's office could buy extras like pies, cakes, sodas, and candies.[27]

Just as bread, hard or soft, formed a staple of the active soldier's diet, so was it an elemental component of prison fare, the chief difference being that however bad it may have been in the field, it was usually worse in prison. The larger Northern prisons established bakeries capable of turning out thousands of loaves of wheat bread a day, but that proved to be a hardship for Confederate inmates all the same, for many of them were entirely unused to anything but corn bread. At Indianapolis's Camp Morton, bakers' soft bread was provided, but the men complained that they wanted "good cawn pone, with drippin's." To the suggestion that the men be given cornmeal to make their own, officials concluded that it was not practical as most of the men could not cook. Citizens, meanwhile, said their guards ought to compel "these maize-loving rebels to eat Northern wheat bread," because "with every mouthful . . . the hungry rebel swallows and incorporates in his treasonable system so much loyalty and patriotism."[28] But then at Camp Douglas, there were Irish-born Confederate prisoners who did not want to eat "Yaller Hammers," as they called corn bread. They wanted to bake their own white bread, which they called "gun wadding," even petitioning to be allowed to buy stoves on their own, but it was disallowed because of the fuel use.[29]

There was no satisfying everyone, of course, though Confederate prisoners did get enough cornmeal in their rations to bake pones for themselves occasionally. Jacob Hartsfield of Virginia said in the spring of 1864 that some prisoners got ten ounces of cornmeal a day, with black moldy lumps in it.[30] Meanwhile, they ate the white bread and complained about it to their heart's content. At Elmira, some prisoners said it was so thin they could read a newspaper through it.[31] Some prisoners in Camp Douglas managed to have their own flour sent from home or purchased, and they made pancakes on coal stoves ordinarily used for heat.[32]

Meanwhile, Union prisoners had to deal, often for the first time in their lives, with cornbread when they reached their Southern prison compounds. Unfortunately for them, everything in the inadequate Confederate system conspired to make it an unpleasant experience, from the shaky transportation system and inefficient supply organization that often got the cornbread to them moldy and full of insects, to the milling that could not sift the coarse hulls and chaff from the flour. There would be some wheat bread for captured Yankees, but very quickly it all but disappeared, and cornbread dominated the prison diet for almost everyone. After 1863, at places like Andersonville, it was often their only diet.

Men made their bread by mixing dough with hoes in long troughs. The bakers sometimes cooked the loaves too hot, trying to bake them faster, but they only managed to burn the outside of the loaves while leaving the middle uncooked. Worse were the flies baked into it, which looked like crunchy specks in the bread.[33] Michael Dougherty in Camp Sumter found that "the bread was made of yellow meal and somewhat resembled fruit cake—the flies taking the place of the raisins."[34] On Belle Isle, the batter of unsifted corn-meal, with no salt, was baked in sheet-iron pans into loaves twelve by eigh-teen inches and two inches thick. Soldiers called them "half-bricks," while the Rebel bakers called them "cards," perhaps because after baking, they were simply stacked outside the bakery in the sun, uncovered.[35] In Libby Prison, Yankee officers made sieves by perforating tin plates, to try to sift the bits of cob and sharp hulls from their cornmeal ration, one lieutenant complaining that "we were hungry all the time on that fare."[36] John McElroy thought the half loaf of cornbread furnished to Andersonville prisoners actually looked, felt, and perhaps tasted like a brick. His meal, too, came badly ground, with jagged bits of hull still in it "which cut and inflamed the stomach and in-testines like handfuls of pounded glass." Even hunger failed "to render this de-testable stuff palatable." Some men simply starved rather than eat it. Dougherty himself found that he could only eat it by breaking off small bits at a time "and forcing each down as I would a pill." The meal was coarse, foul, and badly cooked, with no salt. The monotony of it was overpowering.[37]

It would not be long before overcrowding and inefficiency, especially in the Confederacy, saw rations plummet both in quantity and quality, and the impounded men began to suffer. In May 1864, having successfully made soup and rice, the new cookhouse at Andersonville tried for the first time to make boiled beef and corn bread, but either the cooks or the apparatus botched the job, and it only managed to feed half the camp, and that by cutting the ra-tion. Thus variety in the prison diet abruptly ended.[38] In the prison at Flo-rence, Alabama, early in 1864, the men got cornmeal, sweet potatoes, and a little meat once a day, but by December it was down to nothing but the corn-meal.[39] The tedious diet of cornmeal became so unending that in Anderson-ville and other prisons, men made jokes about being in the "Corn-fed-eracy" as a result of their ration.[40] Soon, the sweet potatoes disappeared from their issue and they were given cowpeas instead.[41] Before long, new potatoes in Andersonville sold for a dollar a dozen, but Michael Dougherty lamented, like so many others, that he couldn't buy any even if they were "a cent a bushel."[42] Men started performing little chores for the weak and dying to earn from them the uneaten bread that the sick could no longer swallow.[43] In the warehouse prison at Danville, Virginia, in 1864, men got bread made from ground sorghum cane and coffee derived from scorched rye. Finally, they cut splinters from the rafters of their buildings, which had been tobacco warehouses, and absorbed some of the leafy aroma, to boil into a hot drink.[44]

The meat ration, if any, could be terrifying. At Andersonville, Dougherty averred in his diary that they got only a piece of rusty bacon, and it got smaller as time went on. During the last six months he was there, he thought he got meat only a half dozen times.[45] Rebels in Camp Morton complained that they were accustomed to lean bacon, but there they were issued streaky bacon, and their beef was all bone and the bread sour. In Camp Douglas, a Kentucky cavalryman said "we draw fresh beef every other day, but it is not a number one article being mostly neck, flank, bones, and shanks."[46] Prisoners at Castle Thunder in Richmond believed they got mostly horse and mule meat and quipped that after every cavalry battle, their rations became "more liberal" as a result of the animals killed in action.[47]

Vegetables could be a rarity. At Camp Ford near Tyler, Texas, the Yankee prisoners were allowed to plant gardens.[48] At Camp Sumter, they went months without onions, potatoes, pickles, or anything green. One mess had a single stalk of green corn growing beside a tent, carefully guarded, but a mad prisoner snatched it one day and ate it, stalk and all.[49] Prison inspectors quickly identified the problems of scurvy and diarrhea caused by absence of vegetables, finding that "the men got better as soon as they got better treatment and fresh vegetables," according to one report, and they did what they could to bring them into the stockade. The trouble was that by this point in the war, even the guards were not getting enough to prevent scurvy, and simple camp diarrhea was actually made worse by fresh fruit and vegetables.[50] At Andersonville, Dr. John Bates found one boy in the hospital ward who asked for a potato, and when Bates found him one and advised him not to cook the potato but to eat it raw, it cleared up his scurvy.[51]

Soup was no better. At Belle Isle in the James River opposite Richmond, cooks boiled muddy river water in large kettles and served from wooden buckets that had absorbed uncountable tastes, smells, and vermin. The soup itself, found one diner, "contained a considerable amount of pods, leaves, stems, and dirt, with multitudes of weevil or black bugs which would rise to the top to the thickness of an inch and formed the principal ingredient of our soup." Some tried to strain them out, but gave up and just broke up and mixed in their corn bricks "and ate it bugs and all."[52]

In Andersonville and most other Confederate prisons, the inmates suspected the cookhouse managers of shorting their meals and hoarding for themselves some of the meat, flour, and particularly salt. Certainly it did happen. Moreover, the prisoners detailed to work in the bakeries and cookhouses had the opportunity to steal some for themselves, even though they already got an extra ration for working.[53] For those men, as for so many others, desperation simply led to desperate measures. At Andersonville, when a prisoner died, another man would answer his name at mess call to get his meal and then race to another place in the line to answer when his own name was called. On one occasion, the authorities found that they had been called upon for 2,000 more rations than there were living men in the camp.[54] The practice apparently started at Andersonville, and men spread it elsewhere when they were transferred, as at Florence, where camp authorities severely punished men caught "flanking."[55] The situation became so bad that at least seven Union officers held in the prisons at Andersonville, Savannah, and Florence, Alabama, took the oath of allegiance to the Confederacy to get out of prison because they had no clothing or food.[56]

Still, deprivation was never a conscious policy of Confederate prisons. It was simply a tragic artifact of the war, disorganization, and disintegration. Confederate law required that prisoners be fed the same ration as their guards: one and one-quarter pounds of meal, a pound of beef or one-third pound of bacon, and some vinegar, molasses, and salt, supplemented with black-eyed peas or beans. Supplies came through generally all right, even though, as in the North, some arrived rancid or moldy. After 1862, however, the population of the prisons soared and the supplies became rapidly inadequate.[57] Even at the infamous Andersonville, despite all lurid later rumors to the contrary, on only two days was the garrison denied rations, both of them because bad weather interfered with the issue. In fact, one day the prisoners actually got a better ration than they had in their own army, but only due to vagaries of the Confederate transportation system.[58]

Nevertheless, thousands were dying all across the Confederate prison system, and the Union knew about it, with exaggeration and rumor doing much to inflame Northern public opinion to a conviction that such inhumanity came on direct orders from Richmond. It was inevitable that someone would

A mess of Company K, 11th Rhode Island stops in the field in Virginia for coffee and bread with a little spread from a jar, perhaps cheese, and maybe a bit of sugar from a tin. Very few such poses were truly candid, as evidenced by the rather unnecessary candlestick in this daytime view. COURTESY OF LES JENSEN

"Today our mess had their ambrotype taken representing us as taking a meal on picket," wrote the man on the right of this January 7, 1862 image, and giving evidence of the fact that such was a popular pose with hardtack and coffee in hand. COURTESY OF B. N. MILLER

The soldiers came to the outdoor field "studios" of the photographers following the armies, bringing their mess pans and cups and the ubiquitous hardtack. COURTESY OF RICHARD F. CARLILE

And they came to the indoor tent studios with the same gear for even less natural poses, though at least these men give proof that it was possible to take a bite out of an army cracker. COURTESY OF JOHN HESS

Everything that was important in the world to the Civil War soldier was in his haversack, and many a man kept those things with him—his mess plate and cup, a spoon and knife, and even bits of hardtack—long after he became a civilian once more. COURTESY OF LES JENSEN

There was little difference between Yank and Reb at mealtime other than what went on his plate. The more established Rebel camps, like this one near Pensacola, Florida, in 1861, had their company kitchens, here in the two lean-tos in the right distance. UNITED STATES ARMY MILITARY HISTORY INSTITUTE, CARLISLE, PENNSYLVANIA

Louisiana Confederates of the Washington Artillery of New Orleans stand with cups and plates in hand in front of their company kitchen in 1861, their black cook at the left. UNITED STATES ARMY MILITARY HISTORY INSTITUTE, CARLISLE, PENNSYLVANIA

Interestingly enough, Confederate soldiers were more likely to pose at reading or playing cards than at eating like their foemen, perhaps because they were less fond of their diet. Still, the tin ware lined up on a rude shelf beneath the "shebang" made of shady branches betrays a company kitchen for these men of the 9th Mississippi in 1861. COURTESY OF RONN PALM

The Lexington mess of the Washington Artillery display their plates stacked on the table before the seated man in the tent, and ready to be filled at the company kitchen in the distance. UNITED STATES ARMY MILITARY HISTORY INSTITUTE, CARLISLE, PENNSYLVANIA

As in the North, the officers lived better, like these leaders of the Washington Light Infantry of South Carolina in 1861, with their two black servants about to serve wine and food from the picnic hampers in front of them. COURTESY OF THE WASHINGTON LIGHT INFANTRY, CHARLESTON, SOUTH CAROLINA

A Confederate meal actually on the plate appears on the floor of the tent of the Washington Artillery's Carondelet mess. Perhaps it is nothing more than a chunk of soft bread or a slab of salt beef, but the cups betoken coffee, and the urn-handled bowl may mean they even had sugar or cream. COURTESY OF THE CONFEDERATE MUSEUM, NEW ORLEANS, LOUSIANA

In winter quarters Confederates, like Yankees, cooked and ate their meals in log huts like this one in Virginia in the winter of 1861–62. These Texas soldiers seem equipped in the pose for every aspect of the soldier's life, including the man at far right with cook pan and spoon in hand. UNITED STATES ARMY MILITARY HISTORY INSTITUTE, CARLISLE, PENNSYLVANIA

Hard as it was to eat in the camps, it was worse in the prisons, where despite mess halls and issues of food from their captors, many soldiers still had to fend largely for themselves, and nowhere more so than here at Camp Sumter at Andersonville, Georgia. The presence of a few cooking pots and mess plates testifies to their struggle to eat and stay alive. UNITED STATES ARMY MILITARY HISTORY INSTITUTE, CARLISLE, PENNSYLVANIA

Even Andersonville had its bakeries, using the coarse, unsifted corn meal that so irritated the stomachs of the men who ate the bread baked in the prison bakeries located southeast of the stockade, at far right. NATIONAL ARCHIVES

Even in prison, however, some men could make at least a pretense of dining well. These Kentucky Confederate cavalrymen, captured in 1863 and incarcerated in the Western Penitentiary at Allegheny City, Pennsylvania, have managed to make quite a pose of a prison meal. COURTESY OF RONN PALM

THE FOOD QUESTION SETTLED FOR THE CAMPAIGN—1865.

In spite of hardship at the mess tent, Confederates proved wonderfully resourceful, and tolerant. This crude 1865 woodcut shows two Johnnies declaring they can fight forever as long as blackberries and huckleberries last, and they can even live on the persimmons in their hands, food that most Southerners once thought fit only for opossums. LAND WE LOVE, VI, MARCH 1869 think of retaliating on Southern prisoners held in Northern camps. Even before then, inefficiency and inexperience in the Union prison system were doing their parts under the pressure of a rapidly growing prison population to impose growing hardship on the men in its care. At Fort Delaware, Henry Rudasill of North Carolina "found the fare not good, two meals a day, bread the size of an ordinary loaf, half a loaf each meal, and I judged it to be made of corn meal and flour; about eight ounces of beef per day; soup or beef water, in summer too thick with flies for use."[59] Another man at Fort Delaware spoke of soup "too weak *to drown* the rice worms and pea bugs, which, however, came to their death by starvation," and at Camp Douglas, one Rebel prisoner swore he had been issued a chunk of mule neck with the hair and hide still on it.[60]

Soon their descriptions would become dramatic, mixing soldier wit with the desperation of the case. Rations in Elmira were "characterized by disappointed 'rebs' in language not to be found in the prayer-book," said Anthony Keiley.[61] At Point Lookout in February 1864, the Rebel inmates were fed codfish balls and soup, which one described as "a very mean bill of fare, even to a hungry soldier." The smell of the fish did at least kill their appetites, "and so made one better ready for light rations."[62] In prison on Hilton Head, Capt. Isaac Coles of Virginia in October 1864 said he and others fed largely on meal and pickles, eating it off of long planks in their barracks "where starvation rations mocked us." Coles and his fellow prisoners had a kettle and a little pan for cooking, "one vessel too many for our modest needs." They cooked outside the building in the wind amid blowing sand, where the cook made "one grim dish," cornmeal. The meal was a good three years old, he suspected, and the pickles had been preserved "in some devilish acid, a terrible chemical that took all the skin off the tongue." It required experience to eat them, for they had "some sensitive points and had to be approached in a delicate manner." Only by persistence and wariness could one be consumed, "but hungry men's gulps it stingingly rebuked." He believed that at least the acid might counter the effects of the wormy meal they were issued, and "as time was no consideration, we finally got on the outside of it some way."[63]

Meanwhile in the camps with cookhouses, the farmer's kettles boiled everything to a glop. "There was no more nutritious matter in it than an old dish cloth," one Rebel wrote of his soup. "For dinner one pint of bean soup and five ounces of bread, this was our living!"[64] A Northern visitor to Elmira wrote glowingly that the prison soup "looked rich and savory" and the bread was "as good as can be found in any bakery of our city." In the fall of 1864 a new commander there averred that the daily ration of eight ounces of bread and eight ounces of meat for breakfast, and eight ounces of bread and a pint and a half of soup for dinner, were all "of excellent quality," the soup made from meat, potatoes, onions, and beans. There was no third meal of the day, and an inmate saw the case rather differently. "I only get two meals a day, breakfast and supper," he complained. For breakfast, there was a third of a pound of bread and a small piece of meat, and for supper the same bread and no meat, "but a small plate of warm water called soup."[65] The men called it "quasi soup" and "nothing more than hot salty water," joking that they could see through it "to the bottom of the pan." They also trotted out the standard complaint of bean soup in their own armies, that there was only one bean to a quart of water.

Then came the retaliation. Some were isolated, like the moving of 600 Confederate officers to a stockade on Morris Island, South Carolina, in 1864, putting them in direct line of fire from Confederate batteries around Charleston as a result of reports that Confederate authorities had done the same with Union prisoners, using them as a shield to try to stop the Yankee bombardment of the city. There the unfortunate so-called "Immortal 600" got a supper of "a scrap of bacon and a pint of mush made of spoiled cornmeal," complained Capt. Thomas Martin, who counted and removed from the mush 365 worms and 14 other insects. He promised that he "could have counted more, but felt he could not afford to lose more of one meal."[66] Others of the 600 said their sour cornmeal "would stand alone when the barrel was knocked from it," and their only other issue was sometimes some salt pork and pickles. "Our rations was a menu for wooden gods," one complained. "It consisted of four hardtack army crackers, often rotten and green with mold, and one ounce of fat meat, issued to us at morning roll call." Dinner was one-half pint of bean or rice soup, and for supper "we were allowed all the wind we could inhale."[67]

More systematic, and infinitely more cynical, was the institutional retaliation imposed by General Hoffman and Secretary of War Edwin M. Stanton. Late in 1863, Stanton cut off without explanation the privilege of buying extra edibles from sutlers to supplement prisoner rations, and with it their right to receive food in boxes sent across the lines by friends and relatives. Two months later, he relaxed the order, but it was a bad portent.[68] Before long, Hoffman began a program of reducing rations in his prisons, the theory being that Confederates in the North should be fed no better than Federals in Southern hands. There was a certain grim logic to it, of course, but it could only work if the Confederacy was actually capable of feeding its charges any better, whereas unknown to Hoffman and Stanton, Confederate soldiers in the field were not eating a lot better than Yankees in their prisons. Judging by his subsequent conduct, however, the reduction also appealed to the bureaucrat in Hoffman.

Just one of his prisons, Camp Morton, in 1864 issued substantial quantities of rations to an average of 3,550 prisoners that year: 13,957 pounds of pork, 262,799 pounds of bacon, 11,473 pounds of salt beef, 826,447 pounds of fresh beef, 1,146,540 pounds of flour, 188,533 pounds of hardtack, 50,216 pounds of cornmeal, 91,817 pounds of beans, 100,649 pounds of potatoes, 34,805 pounds of rice, 38,901 pounds of hominy, 26,176 pounds of roasted coffee, 1,009 pounds of tea, 60,597 pounds of sugar, 10,738 gallons of vinegar, 48,547 pounds of salt, 972 pounds of black pepper, and 1,020 gallons of molasses.[69] Multiply those quantities by the tens of thousands of Confederates being held all across the North, and the total—and the potential for savings through even modest reduction—was enormous.

And so again and again Hoffman instituted ration reductions in May and June. At Camp Douglas in May 1864, after the cuts, a mess of eight got 24 cups of meal, 22 pounds of pickled pork, 4 quarts of hominy, 18 pounds of fresh beef, 24 loaves of bread, 4 pints of coffee, 3 pints of molasses, 5 quarts of sugar, and 1 peck potatoes, all to last them ten days. At least the beef and bread were not issued all at once for the ten days—some of it would have gone bad or stale—but instead came three times during the period, so they were usually fresh.[70] Then in July rations improved again; the men at Camp Douglas, for instance, got corn bread, pork, sour hash, beef, and pot liquor, enough for two full meals a day. But then in August came another retaliation for Andersonville, and rations were reduced to boiled beef and sour bread six days of ten, with boiled pickled pork and light sour bread the other four and an issue of hominy at dinner.[71] Hoffman again made cuts in February 1865, by as much as half sometimes, his justification being that he did so partly in retaliation for Southern treatment of prisoners and partly because the prisoners' sedentary life required fewer calories.[72] He also rationalized that prisoners' rations ought to approximate those issued to Confederate soldiers in the field, thereby unknowingly acknowledging that he knew how hard-pressed the South was to feed its own men, and thus, logically, the hardships in Southern prisons were due to scarcity and not spite. Small luxuries like candy and molasses were already gone from Union camps, and now sugar and coffee and tea went only to the sick, while Hoffman cut the potato ration, promoting an increase in scurvy. At Camp Morton, the prisoners actually revolted, stockpiling rocks to throw at guards and destroying some of their cooking utensils in protest.[73] By August, in response to the scurvy outbreak, onions were being purchased from the prison fund, and Hoffman allowed the regular issue of antiscorbutics like potatoes and onions throughout the prison system.[74]

The prisons established different ration issues for men who were doing work and those not working because of illness or disinclination, and the allocation for both would be reduced over the course of the last year of the war. Ration allowances at Camp Morton for working men in April 1864 were 14 ounces of hard bread or 18 of soft bread or 18 of cornmeal; 14 ounces of beef or 10 of bacon or pork; and for each 100 men, 6 quarts of peas or beans or 8 quarts of hominy or rice, with 14 pounds of sugar, 7 pounds of coffee beans or 5 of grounds, 18 ounces of tea, 2 quarts of salt, 1 quart of molasses, 3 quarts of vinegar, and 30 pounds of potatoes.[75] Two months later, working men saw their hard bread reduced, but their meat, hominy, and rice increased, while nonworking men got reduced measures of soft bread or meal, beans, sugar, tea, and salt, and the potato ration cut in half.[76] The nonworker ration went down again in January 1865, with less hard bread and salt, and potatoes eliminated entirely. Men performing labor got an increase in their ration of beans, which some might have quipped meant bean soup with two beans per quart now.[77]

Meanwhile, in August Hoffman again restricted the delivery of boxes with food from home and prohibited sutlers from selling goods to the prisoners, this time a pointed retaliation for the stories coming out of Andersonville. The latter restriction may have been a blessing in disguise, for the sutlers were charging usurious rates in many cases, like one who peddled two-cent ginger cakes for eleven to a dollar to prisoner agents, and then the agents charged the prisoners themselves fifteen to twenty-five cents each. Some sutlers were also getting away with requiring that prisoners spend at least thirty cents at a time, or no change would be returned from a $1 chit used as currency.[78] Then in February 1865, the nonworkers' ration was cut yet again, their hardtack reduced, but since they still had fresh bread from their bakery, they did not much mind. Orders reduced their salt and vinegar, too, but at least Hoffman allowed them to augment that by purchases from the prison funds, just so long as the total available to any prisoner did not exceed the standard Union soldier ration. The rationale was simply that no enemy prisoner should be allowed through gift, chance, or purchase, to be eating better than a Yankee soldier in the field. But sutlers were allowed to sell vegetables again, and soon afterward other extra food items came back on the allowed list.[79] Yet the application of the quotas was haphazard, showing that system and efficiency could fail in the North as well as in the South. Prisoners at Point Lookout by this time found that dinner was a cup of soup, usually bean or vegetable, and a piece of meat with vinegar poured on it for scurvy. Breakfast was coffee and a loaf of bread that was to last all day, but they usually ate it all at once.[80] Nor was retaliation limited to the Yankees. Black soldiers captured on Morris Island in 1863 were kept in squalid conditions and fed only a piece of corn bread each day as punishment for rising against their white betters.[81] Of course, Confederate policy was not to hold onto Negroes as prisoners of war, but to treat them as runaway slaves and thus return them to slavery if masters could be found. Consequently, most of them did not remain prisoners for long, or rather their military imprisonment was soon exchanged for another sort of confinement, but at least one in which they were better fed. As a result, retaliatory underfeeding of black soldiers such as happened on Morris Island was idiosyncratic, the consequence of immediate local circumstance—and perhaps emotion—rather than a conscious government policy.

Through it all, the Southern boys in those prisons made do just as their counterparts in Dixie did. Men in Elmira, which was every bit as bad as Andersonville for disease and death, called it "Hellmira" or "Sheolmira," and one of them recalled that at breakfast, the prisoners formed in a line and marched to the soup house, where they found several long tables with rations of one-fifth of a loaf of bread and a half-inch-thick, three-inch-square piece of pickled or salt pork or beef. They picked it up, took it back to their quarters, and ate it. For dinner, they marched back again and got "a cup of quasi soup and a slice of bread." As for the evening meal, they had none, but at dinner, the prisoners could ask for seconds on the "quasi soup."[82] By December 1864, at Camp Douglas the men ate twice a day and on Sundays got a bonus of two ounces of bacon. Their tableware was mostly tin cans and wooden spoons. At 8:00 A.M. in the morning, they got a third of a loaf of bread and a piece of meat boiled into what one called a "dish rag" in Hoffman's giant boiling kettles. Dinner came at 1:00 P.M. and was bread and beef soup, with no evening meal.[83]

What the prisoners did get they had to watch carefully. At Elmira, men had to watch for moldy flour supplied by unscrupulous contractors, for it produced sour bread. The prisoners got fresh beef from a local supplier who provided inferior meat, and it did not help that the commissary issued it to the men the same day it was killed without letting it age a little. An inspector also found it to be old and too lean. As an experiment, he took a ninety-two-pound quarter of the beef and boiled it down, finding it reduced in weight by half when boned.[84] Even Yankee officers and guards complained that their prisoners were sometimes given short weights and measures by unscrupulous contractors. Camp Douglas experienced scandals over misappropriation of rations. Bakers baked undersized loaves for the men and then made extra loaves from the purloined flour and sold them to the prisoners at a quarter apiece. Contractors sometimes laced their supply of beans with cheaper peas for a little extra profit.[85] Just as bad, on both sides boxes sent from home were frequently plundered by guards before the prisoners got them. Christmas provisions provided for prisoners in the North at one prison were stolen by guards.[86] Boxes sent to those Rebel prisoners who had no money were often the only source they had for things like sugar, coffee, canned milk, mustard, tomatoes, butter, flour, ham, onions, dried fruit, cakes, strawberries, sardines, and pies.[87] At Libby Prison, inmates found their Sanitary Commission parcels in 1864 delivered with letters mentioning contents of hams, coffee, sugar, butter, and tea, but the items were missing, all taken by guards who then sold the food to the prisoners.[88]

During the suspensions of sutler services, inmates still occasionally managed to circumvent Hoffman, usually with some local aid stimulated by the profit motive. In Camp Douglas, prisoners got a woman to slip whiskey to them in the milk can she daily brought into camp to sell. She peddled milk at ten cents a quart, but they encouraged her to put in the can "something more in keeping with the needs of a grown-up individual."[89] A woman named Finley established an unlawful food stand outside the Camp Douglas fence, actually cutting a hole in the fence big enough for a window, and through it she sold food to the inmates virtually under the eyes of the guards. Authorities closed her window, but she just reopened it again and again, more than a dozen times in all, and eventually, when sutlers were allowed to operate again, she obtained a license to purvey inside the prison.[90]

Not surprisingly, prisoners turned food into currency. At Camp Morton, prisoners attributed values to bread, which they called "duffers," hardtack, beef bones, bone butter, and more. Bone butter was a prime luxury. A man who happened to get the bone on his ration just scraped the meat off it and cooked it; then he split the bone in small pieces and boiled it until all the water was evaporated, leaving the fat and marrow. Straining what remained through a cloth, he allowed it to congeal, and it became "bone butter."[91]

Soldiers also foraged within the confines of their pens. At Elmira some prisoners fished in a local pond for perch and bass until authorities put disinfectants in the water because camp sewage flowed into it and made it a stagnant green mire where the fish died and floated to the top, stopping that source of protein.[92] Near the pond, Benson and others foraged for edible weeds and gathered "lamb's quarter," a popular herb.[93] But nothing in the way of scrounging for food matched the determination shown by men on both sides in their quest for rats.

It should hardly come as a surprise that in the face of such appalling inadequacy of rations and cooking, thousands of prisoners turned to expedients that would have revolted them just months earlier. No matter where the prison was, North or South, the men inside quickly developed a predatory relationship with anything that moved within their reach, and with nothing more than the lowly rat. In almost every Union prisoner-of-war camp in the South and in at least eight Confederate prison camps in the North, the inmates ate rats. At Johnson's Island at Sandusky, Ohio, one man became so adept at catching them that he gave rat feasts for his mates.[94] Confederate Joseph Ripley of Tennessee caught so many that he could afford to entertain his comrades, recalling how pleasurable it was to play host to a rat dinner.[95] "Rats are found to be very good for food," said another Johnson's Island inmate. "They are fat and gentle and easily killed."[96]

"So pressing is the want of food that nearly all who can have gone into the rat business, either selling these horrid animals or killing them and eating them," said John Dooley, a Confederate soldier in prison.[97] "A 'rat killing' was about the only real amusement we had," recalled one Rebel at Camp Chase in Ohio. "Fresh meat, regardless of the species, was too much of a rarity among these hungry men to be discarded on account of an old prejudice. When properly dressed and fried in pork grease, a rat has the exact flavor of a squirrel. The uninitiated would never know the difference." Soldiers unable to catch their own soon paid as much as a dollar each for rats caught by others.[98]

It required some stealth to trap the vermin, but the prisoners had nothing but time on their hands. At Camp Douglas in Chicago, "fried rats had been regarded as a dainty dish for several months," recalled one Confederate prisoner, "but after the barracks were raised five feet above the ground to prevent tunneling, the rats had no place to hide." They moved to the sewer, but the men watched the openings, and whenever one ventured out, it was kept under watchful eye until they could cut off its retreat, "and then it was only a question as to which mess would feast upon it." He remembered a breakfast of fried rats that he relished very much, but the meat tasted so much like squirrel that he was never afterward able to eat squirrel.[99] The consensus seemed to be that rats did taste like squirrels, which many of these men had hunted and eaten as boys. At Camp Douglas, a gourmand found them "as tender as a chicken," and some of his mates caught a number and made a rat pie.[100]

At the prison at Fort Delaware, Confederate prisoners formed themselves into "squadrons" and posted themselves at rat holes with sticks, "patiently awaiting to strike a blow for 'fresh meat and rat soup'—for dinner!" as one recalled. "When deviled or stewed, they resemble young squirrels in looks," he added. "The flesh of these rodents is quite white, and when several are on a plate with plenty of dressing, they look so appetizing one cannot help regretting his early mis-education, or prejudice." When mates protested against eating vermin, more practical friends retorted: "Why, you eat wagon loads of hogs, and everybody knows a rat is cleaner than a hog. Rats are just as dainty as squirrels or chickens."[101] At the Elmira prison in New York, the men hunted rats in the dark of the evening. The rodents gathered around the cookhouse refuse piles, and there the men trapped them, throwing stones or just clubbing them with sticks. They cooked them two ways, grilled or fried. Virginian John Opie confessed that "I ate rats, myself, several times, and found them really palatable food."[102] Sometimes they were cooked with things like hard cabbage stalk or raw potato peelings that had been thrown into the sewers to make a stew.[103]

Rodents weren't the only opportunistic additions to prisoners' diets. No living thing, it seemed, could venture into a prison compound without risk of winding up in a kettle or over a fire. At Andersonville in 1864, the men sometimes managed to catch swallows and other birds that flew too low, cooking and eating them, and sometimes just devouring them raw.[104] One of the more unusual additions to prisoner fare was at the prison camp in Millen, Georgia, when one evening in November 1864, the Yankee inmates saw a small alligator that had somehow slipped inside the compound to a stagnant pond. Risking teeth and claws, they killed and ate it.[105]

Most popular, however, were pets, especially if they belonged to their prison officials and guards or anyone else against whom the prisoners held a grudge. At Indiana's Camp Morton in 1864, some men managed to catch and eat a sutler's dog, though others could not bring themselves to share the meal.[106] At Elmira prisoners caught and ate a particularly unpopular cook's dog.[107] The dog belonging to a much-disliked lieutenant often came into Camp Douglas, but one day a Confederate cook grabbed him and killed and cooked him, making roast dog and dog soup. When the lieutenant posted a reward for the dog's return, a prisoner wrote on it, "For lack of bread the dog is

dead, For want of meat, the dog was eat." When the lieutenant caught the culprits, he cut off their rations in revenge.[108] And at Belle Isle camp in the James
River at Richmond, a chicken belonging to the commandant was caught and
eaten, followed on January 15, 1864, by the catching of the commandant's dog
in the compound, also quickly killed and eaten. Having gotten "a taste of fresh
meat," said one prisoner, "the boys contrived all manners of projects to decoy
an unwary dog across the line." Guards' pets followed the commandant's dog
into the pots, and soon there were no dogs left on Belle Isle.[109]

Even those who had not fallen afoul of the inmates took a pet inside the
gates at high risk. At Andersonville on November 28, 1864, a doctor came to
the camp, and his dog strayed into one of the tents, where a prisoner threw an
old blanket over him and killed him. "He ate part of it and said it was ele-
gant," another inmate recorded in his diary. "He buried the entrails, but one
of the other poor fellows dug them up, cooked and ate them."[110]

Perhaps the most spectacular catch—certainly the highest-ranking ca-
nine meal—came at Camp Douglas when Gov. Richard Oglesby and members of the Illinois legislature inspected the camp. One politician had a small
dog with him that wandered away from the group and ran up to a prisoner
from the 2nd Kentucky Cavalry, who quickly dropped his blanket over it and
made away to a cook house. There he and a cook quickly dispatched, cooked,
and ate the animal while the owner was still in the compound. They were
never discovered, but ever after people, on meeting the Kentuckian, asked if
he had "tried dog meat" lately.[111]

Dogs were not the only pets at risk, as Gen. John G. Foster, commanding
the prison camp for Confederates on Hilton Head Island, found in 1864. A
cat commonly believed to be his wandered inside the stockade, and hungry
Rebels saw it. "From common impulse we acted, and before the fair visitoress
knew what had happened she was a headless trophy, a prospective dish of
meat, a real meal!" said Isaac Coles. Joyfully, they skinned and dressed her,
burying the head and claws, and then parboiled and stewed her, though there
was no pepper or salt. "She was deliciously fat," said Coles. "She must have
been a notoriously fine mouser." They baked cornmeal to go with the cat
meal and could scarcely contain themselves until the feast was ready. "And it
was a king's dish indeed, a whole pan full, two whole yawning stomach fulls
and to spare!" said Coles. "We fell to and partook with relish, almost greedi-
ness, declaring the cat as an article of food was misunderstood, that it was
wholesome and delicious." The next day, General Foster had all cats and dogs

locked up, "and our hope of another cat party vanished."[112] A Rebel prisoner in New York declared that without question, "a cat, notwithstanding its proverbial nine lives, wouldn't last five months" at Elmira.[113]

Prisoners, in the face of starvation, disease, and interminable boredom and loneliness, still managed to find even little festive occasions with celebratory meals. In Fort Delaware, inmates made a kind of beer by mixing molasses, ginger, and cornmeal, and letting it ferment, pronouncing it "villainous at best," but even worse when warmed by the sun.[114] Some men in Andersonville let their cornmeal get soaked and then sour, fermenting it into a rude beer to help against scurvy.[115] In Camp Douglas, Curtis Burke of Kentucky made himself a birthday dinner on January 24, 1865, using of a pound of butter and a pound of sugar with bread to make dumplings, along with boiled beef, bean soup, and vinegar pie.[116] Nor was Christmas to be forgotten. For Christmas 1864, the Florence prison inmates made a holiday dinner on about a half pint per man of unsalted cornmeal.[117] In Andersonville that same Christmas, the holiday dinner for some was also only cornbread, with a little rice and molasses. One soldier feasted on a pint of cooked peas and a three-inch-square piece of corn bread, with two ounces of cooked beef.[118] Then, as always, mostly the prisoners talked about the sumptuous meals they remembered from home and restaurants and what they would eat if they ever saw home again.[119]

Virginian John Opie said that prison brought out the "hog" in a man's nature, and some men were so reduced in health and mental strength that they turned scavengers and attracted the contempt even of their fellow prisoners.[120] Men in prisons often fought over food and the division of rations, especially when doled out for several days at once.[121] They learned to eat it quickly before someone else filched it.[122] Worse, a few dug in hospital garbages for scraps, though authorities soon stopped that.[123] One man at Elmira saw another pick up a hospital plaster made of mush, thrown out after use on a wound, and eat it.[124] Others scavenged bones and chewed and sucked them for hours. Yankee John King recalled that "I got up many times in my bunk with a bone and after gnawing the soft ends, sucked at the bone for hours at a time."[125] In Camp Douglas, some men were caught rooting bones from the garbage to chew on, and the guards fastened the bones between their teeth and made them get on all fours and howl like dogs.[126] At Camp Chase, the guards sometimes threw their own melon rinds and apple cores into the compound and enjoyed watching the men scramble for them.[127] On February 5, 1864, at Belle Isle, Michael Dougherty saw a fellow Yankee prisoner vomit up improperly cooked sausages brought into camp by a new prisoner and watched as another man picked up the chunks and washed and ate them.[128]

No one in the war suffered more culinary deprivation than the men in the prison camps. Confederate Randolph Shotwell at Fort Delaware later reflected on his experience. "How strange a thing it is to be hungry!" he said. "Craving something to eat, and constantly thinking about it from morning till night, from day to day; for weeks and months!"[129] While still a prisoner at Elmira, another poor victim of the system simply exclaimed, "I am almost starved to death."[130]

CHAPTER EIGHT

THE "IRREPRESSIBLE" TURKEY

HOMESICKNESS BECAME A PERENNIAL PROBLEM FOR SOLDIERS DURING THE long weeks and months spent in camp or winter quarters, and very often it seemed tied to food. "A genuine case of downright home-sickness is most depressing," recalled Leander Stillwell of the 61st Illinois in May 1862 near Corinth, Mississippi. "The boys had not learned how to cook [and] the poor fellows would sit around in their tents, and whine, and talk about home, and what good things they would have there to eat, and kindred subjects, until apparently they lost every spark of energy."[1] An Iowa soldier in Missouri in late 1861 confessed to his mother that "I don't know if I've been homesick yet but I would just like to be there sometimes about meal time [for] I think I could relish your good biscuits and would not grumble if there was a little too much soda in them."[2]

It often proved to be too much. One day, one of Stillwell's camp mates lamented that "I wish I could jest be down on Coon crick today, and take dinner," adding "I'll tell you what I'd have: first a great big slice of fried ham, with plenty of rich brown gravy, with them light, fluffy hot biscuits that Bill's wife could cook so well, and then I'd want some big baked Irish 'taters, red hot, and all mealy, and then . . . I'd want with the biscuits and 'taters plenty of that rich yaller butter that Bill's wife made herself, with her own hands, and then you know Bill always had lots of honey, and I'd spread honey and butter on one of them biscuits." When the talk turned to mince pies, Stillwell left in disgust. "I wanted to say, 'Oh, Hell!' as I went out," he grumbled, but "the poor fellows were feeling bad enough"[3] In 1862, Union soldiers stationed in the backwater of occupied Florida actually invented a camp game in which they charged each other penalties for accidentally mentioning something they missed from civilian life. Accusation led to trial, and conviction led to the fine of a "muggings"—a bottle of whiskey—or a big muggings, a gallon jug. Something like "now how would you like to drop into the Astor House for a superb dinner and a glass of iced champagne?" was sure to get the offender a hefty fine.[4]

Thus the arrival of something special to eat from home became all the more welcome, and hundreds of thousands of such parcels would be sent during the war, especially from the North, where more abundant foodstuffs and better shipping services made them a frequent and practical reality. "If there was a red-letter day to be found anywhere in the army life of a soldier, it occurred when he was the recipient of a box sent to him by the dear ones and friends he left to enter the service," remembered Pvt. John Billings. The parcels were usually the size of a soap or shoe box and were filled with everything parents and friends could cram inside. Indeed, whole neighborhoods, knowing that a box was going off to a volunteer, might contribute something from each family.[5] Billings recalled such "articles for the repair and solace of the inner man" as "pudding, turkey, pickles, onions, pepper, paper, envelopes, stockings, potatoes, chocolate, condensed milk, sugar, broma, butter, sauce preservative (for the boots) . . . boiled ham, tea, cheese, cake, preserve (as jam or jelly); and sometimes (against the rules) 'intoxicating liquors'" hidden in the contents.[6]

The effect on a soldier's spirits could be magical. "I am under a thousand obligations to you all for the nice poundcake I received," a Confederate in the 5th Kentucky Infantry wrote home in January 1862.[7] Across the lines the joy was the same. "Tell Mother that I return a thousand thanks for her labor in fixing the box of provisions," wrote Iowan George Richardson to his father. "I am sure you would have laughed if you had been here when the box met my eyes. I had been out and when I came in Bill had it open so I stepped out and took a regular breakdown double shuffle after which I pitched in. The honey was upset but we got the most of it. . . . The jelly and preserves were all right, also the turkey, cake, pies and butter which was the most welcome of anything."[8] If there just happened to be some liquor within, so much the better. A Tennessean in 1863 reported his glee when he got his box "and enjoyed the contents, especially that part that was in bottles."[9]

The boxes came to camp all at once in wagon loads from the inspectors, so there was a bonanza on box days and a spirit of jubilation in the regiment.[10] But first the boxes had to get through those inspectors, and there lay a persistent source of aggravation and resentment. All boxes from home were stopped at the provost office, which is "truly paternal in the affectionate interest it displays in the boxes which are sent on by express to the dear boys, lest they should contain liquors," groused Samuel Fiske of the 14th Connecticut. "Why, every mortal box that the hand of love directs to the soldier boys is stopped at corps headquarters, and I don't know but at army headquarters too, and goes into the vast pile that is always to be seen there awaiting the pleasure of the provost marshal and his minions to wrench off the cover, ransack the contents and confiscate." Often boxes were delayed days and even weeks by this, often being opened and then left open and exposed to rain. "Half the content of the boxes and packages get broken, spoiled, lost, injured or stolen in the opening process; everything is turned topsy-turvy, the apples, eggs, and doughnuts roll out in the dirt; pickle and jam bottles coming to pieces mingle their contents with silk handkerchiefs, flannel shirts and quires of writing paper, more than the taste of the donors would probably choose; the packages of tea, and the pepper boxes, and the saleratus, and the tiny ink-bottle got into one well-mangled compound, and it becomes difficult to tell which is cow-hide boots and which is mince pies, by the time the lid is finally pressed back to its place by some strong knee and fastened by nails."

In one load Fiske found two boxes from home that were entirely empty when delivered to his men. "But what are these little inconveniences to the private soldier before the working of this great moral, preventive, reformatory movement?" he asked with dripping sarcasm. When he challenged a provost officer about the unfairness of it all, the functionary could only reply, in true bureaucratic voice, "Well, it would be a great deal better if these privates didn't get any boxes from home. Uncle Sam provides for them well enough." Such sanctimonious and unfeeling sentiments were usually expressed by officers even as they themselves passed a bottle and took a slice of "that pudding" removed from some soldier's box, and then proceeded to give orders to the caterer of their mess for what things they wanted him to send for from Washington, a source denied the common soldier. "Oh, father, nail not up so grimly, with iron bands around each end, that box with Christmas turkey and mince pies and sundry comforts and luxuries that mother's hands have prepared for the boy at the war," Fiske wrote for publication in his hometown newspaper. "You cannot bind so fast that provost's axe may not loose, nor ensure that that turkey shall not be a 'gone goose.'"[11]

"It was really vexing to have one's knick-knacks and dainties overhauled by strangers," said Billings, especially since the contents got damaged, jammed back inside, and sometimes stolen.[12] The problem was almost as great in the Confederate army, though less from inspectors than foraging fellow Rebels, who, when not on duty, often hung around railroad depots where the boxes piled up on the platform. At Dalton, Georgia, in the winter of 1863–64, Kentucky Confederates, among others, frequently lurked near the station, and one confessed that "very many, of these boxes had found their way into the Kentucky camp by the aid of quick wits, elastic consciences, and strong shoulders."[13]

Not getting their boxes from home depressed the men's morale, too. "For a long time it has been a standing shame, the way this thing has been managed," complained Pvt. Wilbur Fisk of the 2nd Vermont. "Boxes sent from friends by express, and containing things that we very much need have been allowed to remain piled up in great pyramids at the landing, until their contents are spoiled." When Gen. Joseph Hooker took command of the Army of the Potomac early in 1863, he acted at once to start the process of releasing the logjam of undelivered boxes, and morale almost immediately jumped in response.[14]

Of course, friends and family did sometimes manage to get a bottle of liquor through the inspectors. "A favorite ruse was to have the bottle of alcohol introduced into a well roasted turkey," Billings found. "The bottle was introduced into the bird empty, and filled after the cooking was completed, the utmost care being taken to cover up all marks of its presence. Some could conceal (a bottle) in a tin of small cakes, others inserted it in a loaf of cake, through a hole cut in the bottom."[15]

The other special day in camp, often tied to one of those boxes, was a holiday, especially Christmas in the North and South, and Thanksgiving in the North. All too often, the war and problems of supply did not allow the men anything special for a holiday meal. "In the army we have no holidays," wrote a Yankee officer in South Carolina at Christmas 1862. "To us all days are alike."[16] Yet none could fail to miss what they had known before the war. "I should like to be home just now for I hear the cry 'Grub is ready.' I guess I shall have to close or I will lose my regular rations of beans," an Iowa boy wrote on his first war Christmas.[17] His brother, with apparent homesickness, wrote home that "I suppose you had the pleasure of satisfying your appetites on some roasted turkeys on Christmas. Our Christmas dinner was pork and beans."[18] Much to their delight, just a day or so later there came for them a Christmas box. "It was the first good grub we have had for some time," one told his parents. "All we can get here is Dutch or Irish bread, which along the railroad is not the cleanest, and pies made of buckskin and stuffed with burnt peaches and hairs. But never mind, we are coming home some of these times and then you will brag about your turkey from the other side of your mouth for I intend to make up for lost time."[19]

A year later in December 1862, campaigning in Mississippi, the same Iowans found the holiday much more Spartan. "I should like to be at home today to get my dinner for, to tell the truth, we have but little here," complained William Richardson. "We have been living on one third rations for over two weeks which is three crackers and two small pieces of rusty bacon each day with about one half pint of coffee twice a day. Well, I hear the greasy cook yelling Company G dinner, so I shall close until I eat my dirty bite." When he finished eating, he took up his pen again. "I have finished my dinner which consisted of some black beans the boys got yesterday while out on a foraging expedition, which did not go so bad when cooked with our bacon. I sometimes feel when marching over the hills of this God forsaken country that if I could only have as good fare as our dogs at home I would be well satisfied." Sometimes the men got only parched corn. "I don't know who is to blame for all this," he added. "The Division Quartermaster says that he issues full rations to each Regiment but if he does our Regimental Quartermaster cheats us out of it."[20] In no time at all, most soldiers North and South alike would become convinced that their commissary and quartermaster officers were withholding rations and delicacies, either to eat themselves or to sell for profit.

Officers fared far better, of course, so long as they got their pay on time. With the occupying troops on Hilton Head Island in South Carolina, Colonel Voris looked forward to "a splendid dinner" for Christmas in 1863: roast mutton, peach pie, green peas, bread and butter, and sweet potatoes, all cooked on a little oven in his officers' tent that could make a dinner for four. Just as preliminaries for the holiday, that oven poured forth buckwheat pancakes and roast beef. The officers could even bake raised biscuits, and they had plenty of the condensed milk canned by Gail Borden's new company for their tea and coffee. "As long as we stay here, we can have as good living as men need to keep them in good plight," he assured his wife. The only real problem was their local black servants and cooks, who fed them too extravagantly.[21] Two days before Christmas, they began feasting on bread and butter, roast sheep, baked sweet potatoes, boiled peas, canned peaches, peach pie, and coffee with white sugar and condensed milk. "This magnificent array of food was well cooked and served up in grand style for the field," he boasted. They even ate from tea cups and saucers, white plates, and metal cutlery.[22]

And yet some officers made it their business to ensure that the men had a special holiday dinner, too, without distinction of color. At Christmas 1863, on Morris Island, South Carolina, during the siege of Charleston, the officers of the 3rd United States Colored Troops treated their men to apple dumplings "equaling a young mortar shell in weight" with a rye whiskey sauce. "The boys enjoyed them notwithstanding the seeming lack of talent in the pastry cooks," observed Cpl. James Gooding of the 54th Massachusetts.[23] Farther down the ranks, other Yankees stationed on occupation duty close to the coast, such as in Savannah, Georgia, in 1865, could go to town and buy chickens, canned fruits and vegetables, eggs, and the ever-present condensed milk, and turn them over to a black cook to create what one Indiana soldier called "a Christmas Jubilee."[24] And late in 1863, volunteer agencies were able to send 5,000 roasted turkeys "with all the *etceteras*" to the camps of the Army of the Potomac to brighten their holiday.[25]

Confederates found any trifling luxury at Christmas just as much a respite, and in 1861, at least, many enjoyed as good a feast as their foe. In the camps around Centreville, Virginia, that first war Christmas, Virginians in one regiment got hearty boxes from home as well as a broken barrel of pickles. "So we had a fine dinner yesterday," reported one private. "We had quite a variety of meats and deserts and plenty of hot apply toddy to drink it down." Besides gallons of the toddy, there was a half gallon of eggnog, ham, turkey, chicken, corned beef, two varieties of pickles, and three kinds of cakes and pies. "Well may we enjoy such a dinner when we pause for a moment and think how did we happen to get it!" Indeed, unlike the Union, boxes with liquor seemed to get through rather easy in the South, at least that first holiday season, for many soldiers were delighted to find jugs of apple brandy and the like.[26]

But Confederates' treats were quickly exhausted, their expectations diminished, and feasts like that first Christmas merely a taunting memory as the war dragged on. In 1862 in Virginia, one boy was delighted with a Christmas stocking sent from home with six peanuts, nine persimmons, some dried apples, a couple of hickory nuts, a piece of hardtack, and a corn "nubbin."[27] That same day, in Lee's army camped in and around Fredericksburg, Virginia, which had just been ravaged by a terrible battle only days before, the soldiers were actually asked to share some of their rations with townspeople so that the civilians could have something to eat for Christmas.[28]

On Christmas Eve 1863, officers of the famed Louisiana Tigers made their headquarters in a dilapidated Negro cabin near Raccoon Ford, Virginia. They sent a servant out to scour the countryside for some whiskey and eggs, but by a late hour he had not returned. "We had made up our mind to go egg-nogg-less to bed, when—about 11 o'clock—the welcome sound of horses hoofs on the crisp snow outside attracted our attention; out we rushed & there we found the tardy 'Mose' with his well filled demijohn," one of them recounted gleefully. "The eggs were quickly beaten—the sugar stirred in and then the whiskey added, and we had one of the most delicious noggs that ever mortal man quaffed. Taking a couple of glasses apiece, we retired merrily to bed—to forget the hardships of a soldier's life, and dream of a joyful reunion with the dear absent one far away in Southland."[29]

Somehow most Confederates managed to get at least something for the holiday meal, though almost always it depended on the generosity of local civilians or access to a hotel or restaurant. In Lee's army quartered for the winter near Gordonsville, women of the town brought soldiers in the 16th Mississippi three kinds of meat, fresh hot bread and butter, potatoes, vegetables, pies, and cakes, leaving the men startled. "I haven't had a meal like this in over a year," one private wrote in his diary that night.[30] Out in Georgia that same holiday, Rebel soldiers on furlough from the Army of Tennessee took lodging wherever they could if unable to make it home for Christmas. A lodging housekeeper in LaGrange boasted to his gray-clad guests that he had a turkey for their dinner and spoke of it often and proudly, but on the appointed day, he informed them that the bird had died of a sore throat. He proposed to serve it anyhow, and some of the soldiers agreed, though with little enthusiasm at the idea of eating a diseased bird. "Christmas day came on and the Christmas feast was spread on the table," recalled Capt. Richard Beard. "I thought to myself that I had never seen a finer looking turkey. There he lay in that dish, stuffed with truffles to the throat, swimming in rich gravy, and garlanded with springs of green parsley; I hated to turn that turkey down, but I had to do it." When the host put a glistening slice of breast on his plate, Beard declined, as did several others except one soldier on whom they thought they would play a joke by not telling him of the turkey's recent illness. That fellow greedily ate what all the others passed up, and only later did Beard find out the landlord was only joking, meaning the turkey briefly had a sore throat when he cut off its head prior to cooking.[31] Other Confederates in north Georgia were not so fortunate. Kentuckians of the famed Orphan Brigade, with the Army of Tennessee around Dalton, got only bean soup—not even bread—for Christmas dinner.[32]

A few Rebel soldiers managed to have their eggnog, as did officers of the 13th South Carolina in Virginia, but only because they found farmers who still had eggs to sell. "We are trying to have some enjoyment for Christmas if we are out here in the woods," one of them wrote home, and the War Department commissaries did what they could to try to get a few extra things in the meager soldier ration for the day.[33] In the 3rd South Carolina, camped at Centreville, Virginia, in December 1861, soldiers managed to get three dozen eggs for their "nog." They beat the yolks in a tin bucket, but having no other receptacle large enough for the whites, they divided them among several soldiers' mess plates for beating. "You had better believe there was a rattling of plates and spoons and knives," Tally Simpson wrote later.[34]

But generally by 1864, even eggnog was a luxury unattainable. For some, even generals in the field, just coffee was a cause for celebration on the holiday. "The sad Christmas has passed away," one Confederate in Richmond lamented. "The Christmas turkey and ham were not. We had aspired to a turkey, but finding the prices range from $50 to $100 in the market on Saturday, we contented ourselves with roast beef and the various little dishes which Confederate times have made us believe are tolerable substitutes for the viands of better days." Gingerbread cakes and tea made "two very rare indulgences" to a little party, "and but for the sorghum, grown in our own fields, the cakes would be an impossible indulgence. Nothing but the well-ascertained fact that Christmas comes but once a year would make such extravagance at all excusable."[35] Out in the trenches around Petersburg that season, one North Carolina soldier made his Christmas dinner on a rat.[36] That December the merchants and women of Richmond sent word to the soldiers in the trenches that they would provide them with food for a New Year's feast, prompting one Mississippian to write in his diary, "Good! We have something to look forward to." They did not expect much, but when the meal came, all felt joyous surprise. "Our meal was sumptuous," declared Pvt. Franklin Riley: "loaf bread, apple butter, choice of meats—mutton, beef, chicken, turkey, or pork. And, of course, we had rations. Quite a repast."[37]

Easter, too, saw some observance on both sides of the line, with its special traditions observed as much as possible. "I enjoyed Easter very well this year," wrote George Richardson in 1863. "I paid 75 cents for all the eggs I could eat at one meal. You will think this expensive. It is. We don't often get such luxuries. If we did it would take more than our pay to live on." Across the lines, some lucky soldiers of the 58th North Carolina actually got Easter boxes from home, containing boiled and colored eggs with their wives' names and special sentiments written on them in wax. Capt. George Harper's wife just sent him raw eggs, which was fine with him. "You probably forgot that it was Easter so [I] will excuse you," he wrote back, "especially as I prefer to cook 'em myself & don't care much for the shells."[39]

Union soldiers celebrated two holidays a year that their enemy did not necessarily observe. One was the Fourth of July. Early in the war, Confederates, too, venerated it as the anniversary of American freedom and celebrated as they could. Even in the earthworks and forts surrounding Port Hudson, Louisiana, where a besieged Confederate garrison found itself steadily driven toward starvation, the defenders strove to make something special for the holiday. Their skimpy beef ration already exhausted, they began eating mule on July 1, 1863. "All who partook of it spoke highly of the dish," said one Rebel. "Mule meat was regularly served out in rations to the troops from and after 4th of July."[40] After the surrender of Vicksburg on that same July 4, the defeat at Gettysburg the previous day, and the surrender of Port Hudson five days later, however, the day became anathema in the South.

Yankees officers held Fourth of July banquets beneath leafy arbors in their garrisons, and when possible, the men in the ranks got a little something special, but more often than not, the day came with them all on campaign or, as in 1863, exhausted from recent battle, and it passed with only a modicum of culinary observance.

The Sanitary Commission attempted to encourage celebration of the Fourth by sending special treats to the armies, fresh vegetables in 1864, for instance, but the distribution came to little more than two or three onions and tomatoes for each man, much diluting the effect for a holiday meal. Some men actually managed to save things from their Christmas boxes for months, in order to bring them out for the Fourth, such as canned salmon and green peas that appeared on a 1st New York Infantry officer's table in 1864.[41] Rhode Island officers in the army besieging Petersburg in 1864 celebrated the day with canned stewed oysters, canned roast turkey, bread pudding, tapioca pudding, an apple pie made in camp, and lemonade.[42]

The unique holiday meal, of course, was Thanksgiving, which would become an official holiday during the war, but which Northerners, especially New Englanders, had celebrated informally in November for generations. As with the other holidays, when Yankee soldiers were on the march or in a sustained campaign, as in 1862 and 1863, its observance might be mainly in the mind. "Coarse meal, cold water and salt have been the ingredients composing many a meal for us, which a thanksgiving supper, in other circumstances, will scarcely rival," Wilbur Fisk complained in Virginia in 1862.[43] A year later, now near Warrenton, Virginia, he recalled that "we had a thanksgiving last week I suppose in common with the whole nation, although it passed without any demonstration here . . . We had not so much as an extra ration of hard tack to celebrate the day." He did have a canteen of milk foraged from the neighborhood, but by the time he went to make the flapjacks he had dreamed of having for Thanksgiving, it had turned sour. "It is of no use to mourn over milk that is spilt, and it is worse than useless to cry when milk sours," he concluded in resignation, "but to lose one's thanksgiving in that kind of a way is harrowing in the extreme."[44] Nor were officers exempt from the hardship. Col. Alvin Voris lamented in November 1862 that "Thanksgiving is almost over and I have had neither turkey or pumpkin pie."[45]

Samuel Fiske could at least show some grim humor in the face of holiday shortage. For his 1863 Thanksgiving in Virginia, he sent on November 25 a requisition to the brigade commissary "wishing to celebrate with due festivity the national Thanksgiving to-morrow." He asked to have sent to his mess 1 dressed turkey, 3 dressed chickens, 11 mince pies, 200 oysters on the half shell, 5 gallons of cider, 2 bushels of apples, 10 pounds of hard crackers, 4 pounds of pork, and a pumpkin, 8 dozen eggs, and a gallon of milk to make pumpkin pies. All that came back from the commissary was the pork and crackers.[46]

Yet sometimes Yankees did get something of a feast, as Samuel Fiske and his Connecticut officers did the year before in 1862. They began by buying several pounds of candles and then collecting a score of cracker boxes for seats and tables for what they planned as "a dinner and social entertainment on a scale of magnificence not to be surpassed," though guests were asked to bring their own plates and cutlery. Four captains pulled their rank at the commissary to get what they could in the way of salt, coffee, and sugar, which they then bartered with locals around Belle Plain, Virginia. Meanwhile, Fiske and others decorated with evergreens and flags under tents, drilled holes in hardtack to make candleholders, arranged the regimental band to provide music, and enlisted the drums and bugles and trombones for added pomp. They invited speakers to address the gala, and throughout the day, the orators practiced their panegyrics.

Alas, the appointed hour arrived and the foragers were not back, some of them the speakers, so the celebration started without them. First came prayers, and then they took their seats "to get what sort of a Thanksgiving dinner we might, mostly alas, for soldiers and officers, of the inevitable 'hard tack and salt junk,' washed down with the bean coffee." The officers had nothing at their table and postponed their dinner to the next night, when the foragers ought to be back. When they came in, they arrived with poultry and four big quarters of beef that Fiske found to be "enough for ourselves and to present a soup to a good part of the regiment." There followed "such roasting, boiling, stuffing, baking and stewing under difficult circumstances, with few condiments, spices and sauces to do *with*, and scarcely any pans and dishes to do *in*, [as] perhaps you may never have seen in your varied experience." They took over a sutler's big tin oven and made a successful banquet. "Turkeys, chickens, partridges and roast beef disappeared like ghosts at break of day, even though we had no bread save hard crackers and no spices of any kind (not even pepper, save Cayenne), nor sauces and ketchups for a relish," said Fiske. "The songs and speeches needed no spices to make them relish." The foragers told stories of the expedition, they all toasted their wives and sweethearts, and then "we separated very well satisfied with our two days' Thanksgiving celebration."[47]

The better funded officers' messes, especially in the New England regiments, managed to set a good table for the day. The 1st New York's field officers managed to get champagne and canvasback ducks "cooked to a turn and served up hot," along with soup and boiled mutton. One colonel even contributed his sherry for the soup and currant jelly to garnish the fowl. The whole meal was presided over by a major who once had run the restaurant at a New York City hotel, and on this occasion, he "came fully up to his reputation as a caterer," thought Lt. Col. Charles Wainwright. He even managed to furnish a printed bill of fare for the occasion:

Fresh oysters, not on the shell.
Green turtle soup, a la tin can.
Leg of mutton, cut in capers
Roast turkey, a la "Hard Tack," and cranberry sauce.

Sweet potatoes, aux cendres
Haricots, farcis aux vents
Riz, a la Dixie
Pommes de terre, a la Smash

Canvasback ducks, au feu d'enfer, and currant jelly.
Lobster salad, rather doubtful.

Mince pies, a l'essence de pommes.
Pumpkin pies, au New England rum.
Almonds—no raisins-apples.
Ginger, "hot in the mouth."
Fruit cake.

Coffee and whiskey

The imaginative menu flourishes could not conceal that the sweet potatoes were cooked in the fire ashes, the "haricots, farcis aux vents" were just green beans, the "riz" was rice, and the "Pommes de terre, a la Smash" were just mashed potatoes. As for the duck "au fer d'enfer," the suggestion was that they came from the fire of the infernal regions, while the "pommes" in the pies were apples.[48]

By late 1864, now thoroughly in control of the war and on the road to certain victory, the Union was better able to meet at least some of the holiday wants of its men in the ranks. In the Shenandoah Valley of Virginia, Wilbur Fisk enjoyed some recompense for what he had missed in earlier years. "Yesterday our Thanksgiving consisted of turkeys, sent us by the Sanitary Commission, from New York," he wrote home, and in the camps he heard it reported that 50,000 pounds of turkeys had been sent to the armies by the Sanitary. That may or may not have been true, but Gen. Philip H. Sheridan's command in the Shenandoah got 6,000 turkeys that his commissaries doled out to his men. "Out there on the picket line it was a rare luxury, and seemed all the better being sent us through the kindness of the people at home," wrote Fisk on a full stomach, and with morale boosted. "We ate it thankfully, and hoped that when another Thanksgiving day should roll around, there would be no picket lines in these Re-United States."[49]

Even close to the firing line some Yankees found the day equally delightful, thanks to their pocketbooks and their commissary. The anticipation was everything. "Thanksgiving is only a week from today, just think of it," Colonel Voris wrote his wife in 1864 from the besieging works surrounding Richmond and Petersburg. "But what are we going to have for Thanksgiving? That is what is the matter," he added.[50] When the day came he mused: "Here I am quietly waiting for Thanksgiving. Not an old fashioned New England Thanksgiving—with turkey, pumpkin pie, hard cider and all the family at the same table, but an army Thanksgiving with reveille at 5 1/2 A.M. and all hands, under arms, and drum and fife, and shoulder arms, and hard tack—perhaps a turkey for the men cooked in a camp kettle stew style." He heard a rumor that 1,300 turkeys had arrived in camp for the enlisted men of his brigade and hoped it was true: "It will be a splendid treat for them."[51]

In fact, almost all of the men in Grant's army besieging Richmond and Petersburg got a good dinner. Several supply vessels laden with turkeys and other victuals contributed by Northern relief agencies arrived at the City Point quartermaster depot the night before the holiday, and then the men and officers charged with getting the meal to the soldiers worked all through the night and the next morning to get it distributed. "Everybody seemed to be jubilant over Turkey & in a good humor generally," found Florance Grugan of the 2nd Pennsylvania Heavy Artillery, attached to the chief quartermaster's office at City Point. "Thanksgiving passed off joyously enough, there being Turkies for all who needed them," he wrote that evening. "It seemed more of a Holiday here than any other that we have had." After the distribution of the birds he discovered that "we have had Turkey in every variety of shape & form," adding that "the Turkey question," or what he called "the 'irrepressible' Turkey," had been a very important question on the minds of all.[52]

The enlisted men got turkey, geese, chickens, pies, cakes, and fruits, some furnished by the Sanitary Commission, but much no doubt purchased from sutlers and the rest scavenged from the already exhausted Virginia countryside. The officers held their own Thanksgiving meal on the last afternoon of the month, and ate well enough on turkey, pumpkin pie, and cake.[53] One corps of the Army of the Potomac alone received from relief organizations in New York seven tons of turkey, 100 barrels of apples, and a similar quantity of cranberry sauce and pies, meaning that each man in the 24,000 corps would get about a half pound of turkey, one apple, and perhaps two bites of pie.[54] In the 2nd Rhode Island Infantry, there was one turkey for every three men, and the regiment actually shared its bounty with a neighboring camp of men from

Connecticut.[55] In the II Corps outside Petersburg that day, two privates in a Pennsylvania regiment shared a goose leg and a chicken leg cooked in a one-quart tin cup, with dumplings made from flour and water. Still, one wrote in his diary that evening, "I enjoyed that dinner as well as the good old home dinners."[56]

Now and then there was even something out of the ordinary like a wedding. Everything was too scarce for much celebration in the Confederacy, of course. There would be no ducks or terrapins or pâtés at a winter nuptial, for instance, but still celebrants could usually find turkeys, hams, pickles, deviled or "stuffed" eggs, sausages, and some kind of bread and butter, with apple toddy boasting floating roasted pippins.[57] Those sorts of wedding feasts would be reserved mostly for civilians and officers, however, as when Confederate general George E. Pickett and LaSalle Corbell were married in September 1863. They went to Richmond where well-wishers provide a wedding feast of stew, turkey salad, beaten biscuits, and roasted sora, a small wading bird. There being no sugar, they had no sweets, but General Lee's wife, Mary, made a fruitcake for them, while another older woman sent a "blackcake" preserved in liquor that she had been saving for her golden anniversary. "So we even had sweets at our wedding-supper," Mrs. Pickett could recall.[58] If an enlisted man got married, it was usually when on leave or furlough. In the North, he could expect a celebratory feast almost as if there were no war. In the Confederacy, he would be fortunate to find a few oysters if his bride lived near the coast, and perhaps some ice cream.[59]

Special groups managed somehow to observe their own special holidays, too. The number of Jews serving in either army was small, though usually concentrated in companies from urban areas, and mostly from the North. In 1862, a number of men in the 23rd Ohio Infantry ordered several barrels of matzo from Cincinnati at the beginning of a Seder celebration and then foraged in the western Virginia countryside for cider in place of wine, chickens, eggs, and a lamb. They needed bitter herbs but had neither horseradish nor parsley, but someone located an unnamed bitter weed that they concluded outdid anything the ancient Hebrews ever encountered.[60] Confederate Jews were much smaller in number in the army, and their special dietary requirements for holidays made them suffer all the more with a commissary hardpressed to acquire just bread and meat. Kosher food was all but impossible to find, and the unleavened matzo nearly so. When available in one of the major cities like Charleston, it could cost $2 a pound. One group of Jewish soldiers in the 46th Virginia celebrated Passover in 1864, telling relatives that "we are observing the festival in a truly orthodox style." They began on the first day with a vegetable soup of onions, parsley, carrots, turnips, cauliflower, and a pound and a half of rare available fresh beef, with smoked meat for the days following.[61]

Then there were the Irish and their St. Patrick's day, and there were plenty on both sides of the firing line. Liquor—it did not matter what kind— was the principle comestible ingredient required for that holiday, often the only one. In 1863, the Irish Brigade in the Army of the Potomac consumed twenty-two gallons of whiskey, ten gallons of rum, and eight buckets of champagne, for which the thirty-five hams, half an ox, and assorted fowl were just an amusing accompaniment.[62]

In after years, the men who served fondly recalled those holiday meals in camp and field. With the exaggeration typical of old soldiers, their hardships and scarcities became greater in recollection, the dishes they invented more imaginative, and even the flavors enhanced. What they did not need to embellish, however, was the comfort of companionship over any festive morsel during the most trying days of their lives.

CONCLUSION

ONCE THE SOLDIERS WENT BACK HOME, PERHAPS THE GREATEST RELIEF TO all, next to being alive and seeing loved ones again, was the chance to eat home cooked meals once more. Even in the war-ravaged South starvation had been isolated during the conflict, and whole regions untouched by Union armies had lived in relative plenty, with the result that solders coming home experienced an immediate and dramatic enhancement in the quality and quantity of what they ate. North and South alike, what the soldiers most craved was what homecoming soldiers from all wars crave, the things they could not get in the army. For Confederates that was real coffee, fresh fruit, the fresh pork that had always been a staple of the Southern diet, and home-cooked cornbread. Yankees crossing their thresholds once more got the oysters they had done without, and the homebaked pies that could not keep up with their advancing armies during the war.

North and South alike, virtually all of the temporary expedients to which they had resorted out of necessity immediately disappeared from their plates. They might tell tall takes about hardtack and blue beef, but none cared to eat it any more. Rats, dogs, cats, pine-tip whiskey, "cush," "skillygalee," and a host of other lamented dishes went permanently off their *table d'hôte*. Nor did men who had spent four years largely cooking for themselves develop a taste for the kitchen. To the end of their generation, the cookstove remained a woman's domain, and once the necessity of cooking for themselves ceased, so did the veterans' time with spoon and pot. Occasionally, when they got together to spin their war stories, they would reminisce of their days improvising meals from ersatz ingredients, but few if any tried to relieve the experience by an encore of the entrées of yore. Like the war itself, they were happy that it was no longer on their plate.

Neither then nor later could anyone seriously argue that soldier fare played a critical or decisive role in the course of the war or in determining its outcome. The Confederacy never lost a battle from want of rations or weapons. It simply never had enough men. By 1864 it had achieved almost total statistical mobilization, meaning that virtually all able-bodied men of military age who were willing to go into service had done so, and still they were too few. Certainly some men, perhaps hundreds, deserted because of the inadequate food, but even if Johnny Reb had been fed by the young Auguste Escoffier, even then perfecting his craft in France, the war's outcome would have been the same. The biggest influence of food on the Confederate war effort, in the end, was not its poor quality, but the inability of the Confederate transportation system to get it where it was needed. Warehouses bulged with rations in Virginia and North Carolina, but the railroads and rolling stock were so worn out that they could not deliver to Lee's army efficiently. Billy Yank did not win the war because he was better fed; there were simply more of him, backed by an economic and industrial powerhouse and a population willing to stay the course.

The biggest impact of food on the war, one still elusive of precise measurements, was its negative contribution through malnutrition, and this hit both sides almost equally. As many as 700,000 men lost their lives during the war or immediately afterwards as a result of wounds or disease. Bullets and shells killed perhaps 200,000 of those. Of the remainder, the majority died of disease, and the biggest single killer was diarrhea, accounting for perhaps 100,000 or more including men who died in the prison camps.[1] Of course diagnosis was haphazard in the late 1860s, and what one surgeon defined as the cause of death might only have been a symptom of something else, and almost all of the killer diseases and viruses in the camps had diarrhea as one of their manifestations. Still, it is clear that malnutrition, particularly the lack of fresh vegetables and fruit, and the inordinately high fat content of a soldier diet usually cooked in a sea of pork grease, had to be major contributors to the universal prevalence of bowel complaints that sometimes turned deadly. Tens of thousands of soldiers were quite literally dying for a meal. To the extent that food-induced disease took men out of the Confederate lines where they were harder to replace, then rations did play an important military role, but still there is no basis to suppose that the South ever lost a battle because too many men were incapacitated in the rear suffering from what one soldier aptly misspelled as "die rear." After all, there were just as many if not more Yankees hunched over the latrines or languishing in hospital tents with the same complaint. Many would continue to suffer chronic gastric complaints years after Appomattox.

In the afterglow of later memory they might miss the camaraderie of their mess mates, the sights they had seen, the worldliness that went with travel, and even the excitement and fear of battle. But virtually none of them missed the food. Of all their constant wartime companions—fear, disease, death, insects, rain, heat, and more—what they ate was the only one that had given them at the same time relief and chagrin, the only one simultaneously welcomed and reviled. Like Napoleon's soldiers of old, they had marched on their stomachs, and for all too many of them it felt like it.

RECIPES

"I am seriously thinking of writing a cookbook when I get home."
—Dayton E. Flint,
15th New Jersey Infantry,
February 1, 1863

A WORD OF EXPLANATION IS IN ORDER. NUMEROUS "CIVIL WAR COOKbooks" have been published in recent years, and many proved useful in writing this book and in providing the basis for some of the recipes that follow. However, almost without exception, these are in fact Civil War–era compilations. That is, the recipes in them are taken from sources such as newspapers, fashion magazines, and contemporary cookbooks, virtually all originally aimed at the *civilian* population and reflecting nothing of what the *soldiers* themselves cooked and ate in the field, which is the focus of this present volume. With few exceptions, the soldiers had neither the wherewithal, the ingredients, or the equipment to make such meals, and only encountered these dishes when visiting at home or dining in a restaurant, and not even then for Confederates.

Consequently, such civilian dishes that appear in the sections that follow are chiefly those that the soldiers might have encountered in boxes from home or for which they reasonably could have acquired ingredients and prepared practically in camp. These civilian recipes are drawn from a variety of sources, most notably from the admirable Internet compilation, Civil War Interactive Civil War Cookbook (http://www.civilwarinteractive.com/cookbook.html), from Lily May and John Spaulding's *Civil War Recipes: Receipts from the Pages of Godey's Lady's Book*; the several monographs by Patricia Mitchell; and Sharon Peregrine Johnson and Byron A. Johnson's *The Authentic Guide to Drinks of the Civil War Era*. These sources and most others use contemporary recipes verbatim, taken directly from the original published cookbooks, and as a matter of

128

convenience and ease of access, those recipes used here are cited to these compilations rather than to the original sources. The balance of the recipes are drawn from original soldier sources, letters and diaries.

Readers will note that no account is given either in the text or in the recipes of Civil War naval fare. This is not because food wasn't just as important to sailors as it was to soldiers, but because, in the main, they ate almost exactly the same things. There are a few dishes distinctive to the water services, such as grog, dandyfunck, and plum duff, and numerous varieties of fresh fish of course, and recipes for those will be found in the pages that follow. Otherwise, seamen used the same ingredients and their cooks prepared virtually the same dishes. If anything, sailors ate better than their land-locked comrades because proximity to rivers and oceans made fresh fish and produce more readily available. Moreover, ships almost all had designated cooks who gained experience and at least some degree of expertise at cooking, unlike the soldier messes, in which men did for themselves. Still, monotony dogged the sailor's table, too. For an excellent brief assessment of what the seamen ate, refer to chapter six of Dennis J. Ringle's *Life in Mr. Lincoln's Navy*.

All of these recipes have been adapted to some degree, either by filling in what was missing from often sparse soldier accounts, or by simplifying contemporary descriptions. Most have been adjusted to call for modern weights and measures. Where possible and necessary, oven temperatures are suggested for baked items, though virtually all soldier cooking other than breads was done over or beside an open fire. Necessarily, anyone trying these recipes in the open will have to do a fair bit of experimenting with fires and times to achieve favorable results. Just as even *cordon bleu* chefs prepare dishes several times until they feel they are getting them right, so it would be wise to make these items once or twice before actually attempting to serve and eat many of them, for several of the old recipes are approximate and require some experimentation. It may be well to remember that overwhelmingly, the soldiers of both sides erred on the side of overcooking.

Similarly, even though some items involve processes for preservation of food that our ancestors found efficacious, readers would be wise not to attempt to keep any of the so-called preserved dishes for too long. Make only enough to use immediately, and any sauces to be kept should be refrigerated at once and checked carefully if reused more than a week or two after making. While all of these dishes are quite safe if properly cooked and preserved, needless to say, readers who prepare and eat any of the dishes contained herein do so at their own risk.

BREADS, BISCUITS, AND YEASTS

G STREET GOVERNMENT BAKERY BREAD

In a large bowl, place 1³/4 pounds of flour. Add ³/4 cup plus 4 tablespoonfuls of warm water. Mix in ¹/2 cup of prepared liquid yeast and 2 teaspoons of salt. Knead for several minutes until a firm dough is formed; then cover and allow to rise for 2 hours. Punch down the dough, divide in half and place in 2 loaf pans. Cover and allow to rise for 1 hour. Then bake in a 400° oven for 1 hour or until the top is well browned.[1]

FRANK LOCKWOOD'S 23RD NEW YORK INFANTRY BREAD

Mix one package of slow-acting yeast in a ¹/4 cup of lukewarm water and set aside. Add 2 teaspoons of salt to 1 cup of boiling water, and allow it to cool to room temperature; then add the mixture to the yeast in a large bowl. Place 6 cups of white or brown bread flour in the bowl, and knead it thoroughly for about 5 minutes, adding flour if it sticks to the hands. Cover and set in a warm place for 2 hours for it to rise. Knead it for an additional minute, and then shape it into 2 loaves and place in greased loaf pans. Cover and let rise for another 90 minutes, then bake in a 400° oven for twenty minutes. Reduce heat to 350° and bake an additional 30 minutes. (This is, of course, an adaptation, as Lockwood's recipe makes 864 loaves at a time!)[2]

HARDTACK

Mix 5 cups of flour to 1 cup of water containing a ¹/2 tablespoon of salt. Knead into a dough, and roll out to a ³/8-inch thickness. Cut into approximately 3-inch squares, and pierce each with a fork or ice pick several times. Bake in a 400° oven for 30 minutes or until slightly brown.

WHEAT-MEAL CRACKERS

Mix quantities as for hardtack to form a stiff dough. Roll out to about ¹/4-inch thickness and cut into 3-inch squares. Bake at 400° for 30 minutes or until slightly browned but not burnt.[3]

RICE BREAD

Drain and cool 1 cup of boiled rice, add 2 cups of flour and mix well and then add three eggs and beat thoroughly. Bake in a skillet over hot coals until a toothpick inserted in the center comes out clean.[4]

MR. GRAHAM'S BREAKFAST ROLLS

Mash 2 pounds of boiled and peeled potatoes through a colander, add 1 pint of water, $1/2$ cup of sugar, 1 teaspoonful of salt, and two packets of dry yeast. Mix in enough whole wheat flour to make a stiff dough and let stand in a warm place overnight. In the morning, punch down the dough and separate into breakfast roll–size pieces, allow to rise for 1 hour, and then bake in a 400° oven for about 30 minutes or until browned.[5]

SKILLET HOECAKE

Mix a batter of $1/2$ cup of white cornmeal, $1/4$ teaspoon of salt, and a $1/2$ cup of water. The batter should be rather thin, and more water can be added if necessary. Grease a skillet with pork fat or bacon fat and heat over a high flame; then pour in the batter. Immediately reduce to a low flame and cook for about 10 minutes; then turn and cook the other side for an additional 10 minutes.[6]

MRS. H. W. HAYES WISCONSIN CORN CAKE

Mix 2 quarts of cornmeal and 1 quart of whole wheat flour with 1 cup of molasses or brown sugar. Add a $1/2$ teaspoon of salt and a $1/2$ teaspoon of baking soda. Add 1 package of liquid yeast and sufficient water to make a firm dough. Let stand covered in a warm place for 1 hour, and then place in a greased baking pan and bake at 350° for 1 hour or until a toothpick comes out of the center dry.[7]

INDIAN CAKE

Into 1 quart of sifted cornmeal, thoroughly mix 2 tablespoonfuls of molasses, 2 teaspoons of salt, and 2 tablespoons of shortening, and then moisten thoroughly with very hot water. Pour the batter it into a well-greased pan, smooth over the surface with a spoon, and place before a blazing fire until brown, turning it to brown equally on all sides. A little stewed pumpkin can be added to flavor the cake.[8]

MRS. CORNELIUS' 1863 CORN CAKE

Mix 2 cups of cornmeal, 1 cup of white flour, 1 egg, 2 tablespoons of molasses, a teaspoon of salt, and 1 teaspoon of baking powder. Pour in and mix thoroughly 1 pint of buttermilk. Bake 25 minutes at 350° in two shallow pans, or 35 minutes in one deep pan.[9]

DAYTON FLINT'S 15TH NEW JERSEY DUMPLINGS

"First you get an old mess pan just like ours, to mix the dough in; then put in the flour, make a hole in the center, and pour some pork gravy in; stir it in the flour with a stick, then add some cream of tartar, and salads, and pour in enough muddy water to mix the whole. We put in muddy water because we can't get any that is clear. Perhaps you had better do so too, maybe that helps to make them better. Now set the pan in the middle of the floor, so you can get all around it, pull off your coat and hang it up on the floor in 1 corner and hang up your cap in the other, roll up your sleeves and pitch in with both hands up to your elbows. Perhaps the dough will stick to your hands as it did to mine, but no matter. Make up into little balls with the apples inside and boil them until they are done."[10]

SGT. DANIEL CHISHOLM'S II CORPS DROP DUMPLINGS

Make the dumplings by mixing a little flour and water in a cup and dropping small balls of it into boiling water.[11]

PONE

Beat three eggs until fluffy, and then stir in a 1/2 pint of milk. Gradually add 1 quart of cornmeal, 1 teaspoon of salt, and 1 tablespoon of softened butter, and stir into a soft dough. If too thin, like a cake batter, add more cornmeal. Beat hard for several minutes, and then pour into a greased cake pan and place in a 400° oven and bake for 90 minutes to 2 hours, increasing heat to 500° after 1 hour. If using a covered Dutch oven and cooking in coals, keep the fire as hot as possible and check frequently. The pone will be done when a toothpick inserted in the center comes out clean.[12]

CURTIS BURKE'S CAMP DOUGLAS BIRTHDAY DUMPLINGS

Mix 1 pound of butter and 1 pound of sugar with soft or stale bread to form a stiff dumpling dough, and then drop small egg-size balls into boiling water and cook until done.[13]

INDIAN DUMPLINGS

Sift 1 quart of cornmeal with 1 teaspoon of salt and 1 tablespoon of butter or 2 tablespoons of finely chopped suet; then stir in two well-beaten eggs and enough milk to make a firm bread dough. After thorough kneading, form dumplings the size of a large biscuit, dust them with flour, and drop them into a pot of boiling water. Boil them briskly until done. Serve hot with molasses or mixed with bacon or salt pork.[14]

SWEET POTATO WAFERS

"When flour is so high priced as at present, sweet potatoes can be used to great advantage in a variety of breads. Boil two large or four smaller sweet potatoes. Peel and mash them. Put in a large spoonful of lard, a little salt, and knead into them half a pound of wheat flour. Cut into small pieces and bake in a waffle iron, or roll out thin, cut into squares, and bake in an oven as biscuits. A little milk—an egg—or one or two tablespoons of sugar may be added—at will or possession, but simply made as above they are excellent tea cakes."[15]

INDIAN WATER CAKES

Sift 1 quart of cornmeal. Add enough cold water, a little at a time, to make a soft dough. Then mix well. Form the dough into soft, thin cakes about 4 inches wide and a $1/2$ inch thick and cook on a greased griddle over a hot fire until lightly browned on each side.[16]

FLORIDA JOHNNY CAKES

Combine 1 cup of cornmeal, a $1/2$ teaspoon of salt, and $1^1/2$ cups of boiling water. Add 2 tablespoons of lard of ham drippings and stir until smooth. Slowly add a $1/2$ cup of milk, and then drop silver-dollar-size dollops onto a greased skillet or griddle, and cook for 5 minutes on each side over moderate heat. The cakes may also be cooked by placing the dough on a slanted board placed close to an open fire until brown on both sides.[17]

SOUTH CAROLINA JOHNNY CAKES

Combine 1 cup of cooked rice with two eggs, 1 tablespoon of butter, a dash of salt, and sufficient flour to produce a stiff batter. Then drop by tablespoons onto a greased skillet at moderate heat, cook until brown on one side, and then turn. Boiled hominy can be substituted for the rice. The cakes can also be baked before an open fire on a board.[18]

CONFEDERATE ARTIFICIAL OYSTERS

Grate 1 pint of uncooked corn. Add one well-beaten egg, 4 ounces of flour, 3 tablespoons of butter, and a dash each of salt and pepper. Mix thoroughly, and then drop tablespoon-size balls of batter into hot fat in a skillet. Fry until light brown, and eat with butter.[19]

JOURNEY CAKES

Mix 2 cups of buttermilk into 1 cup of cornmeal. Add three slightly beaten eggs, a $1/2$ teaspoon of salt, and 1 teaspoon of baking soda. Beat vigorously for 20 minutes. Drop by tablespoons onto a greased skillet at moderate heat, cook until brown on one side, and then turn.[20]

MOTHER BICKERDYKE'S PANADA

Crumble hardtack with brown sugar and mix with hot water and whiskey into a mush.[21]

SODA BISCUITS

Melt a $1/2$ pound of butter in 1 pint of warm milk, adding a teaspoonful of baking soda. Stir in gradually a $1/2$ pound of sugar and set aside. Sift into a bowl 2 pounds of flour, make a depression in the center, and then stir in the milk mixture. Knead for at least 15 minutes into a light dough, and then roll out until a $1/2$ inch thick. Use any circular item, such as a can or a cup, to punch out small, round cakes, and then perforate the tops and set them on a cooking sheet or baking pan sprinkled with flour. Bake in a 400° oven for 10 minutes or until light brown.[22]

CREAM OF TARTAR BISCUITS

Mix 2 teaspoons of cream of tartar into 1 quart of flour, and add a $1/2$ teaspoon of salt. Mix in 2 tablespoons of thick cream, or rub in 1 tablespoon of lard or butter. Add 1 teaspoon of baking soda dissolved in a teaspoon of hot water. Add sufficient milk to form a soft batter, and then form into biscuit-size balls of dough and bake in a 400° oven until brown on top.[23]

CONFEDERATE BISCUITS

Mix 1 quart of flour and 3 teaspoons of cream of tartar. Then dissolve 2 tablespoons of shortening or lard and 1 teaspoon of baking soda in hot water, and add enough to the flour to make a stiff dough. Cut into biscuit-size pieces and bake in a 400° oven for 15 minutes or until done, or on a plank in front of a fire until brown.[24]

CONFEDERATE PUMPKIN BREAD

Boil the flesh of a pumpkin until it is very soft, and then mash into a thick pulp. Press it through a sieve to remove fibers. Measure 1 cup of the pumpkin and mix with two eggs; then mix into it 2 cups of flour. This can be baked in a 9 x 5 loaf pan at 350° for 1 hour to make a good bread. It will be tastier if $^3/_4$ a cup of sugar and a $^1/_2$ teaspoon of nutmeg are added prior to baking.[25]

JOHN INZER'S
JOHNSON'S ISLAND PRISON BREAD YEAST

Take a small Irish potato, boil it until soft, and mash it with water until texture is creamy, like buttermilk. Then stir in a spoonful of flour, and set the mixture in a dark place for 24 hours, until it has soured and started to ferment.[26]

MRS. CORNELIUS'S 1863 DRY YEAST

Boil 4 ounces of hops in 6 quarts of water and reduce by half. Strain immediately into a bowl containing 3 pints of flour, 1 tablespoon of ginger, and 1 teaspoon of salt. When cooled to lukewarm, add 1 pint of brewer's yeast and mix. When the mixture begins to froth, stir in sufficient cornmeal to make a stiff dough. Form it into loaves and then slice each loaf into thin slices, laying them out in the sun on a clear day. When the top side is dried to a crisp texture to the touch, turn over and dry the other side. Then break into small pieces and continue to dry in the sun for another 2 or 3 days, frequently stirring and crumbling by hand. When completely dry, place the yeast in a coarse bag of muslin or other porous material, and hang in a cool place to continue drying. A $^1/_2$ cup of the dried yeast, soaked in enough water to make a thick batter, will start foaming in a few minutes and will be sufficient to make five loaves of coarse bread.[27]

MRS. PUTNAM'S 1863 YEAST

Boil a $^1/_2$ cup of hops in 2 quarts of water for 30 minutes. Boil ten peeled medium-size potatoes for a $^1/_2$ hour and then mash. Strain the water from the hops and pour it into the potatoes, stirring in 2 tablespoons of salt and 1 pint of flour. Set this aside and allow to cool. When it is lukewarm, add 1 pint of brewer's yeast and let it rise for 6 hours. Strain through a colander and place in a securely sealed container. Use within 3 weeks, but in warm weather, use within 1 week.[28]

SOUPS

GENERAL SILAS CASEY'S BEEF SOUP

In a large pot, add one or two beef bones and 1 pound of cubed beefsteak, cover with water to within 1 inch of the top of the pot, and bring to a low boil until the water is reduced by one-third—about 3 hours. Add a $^1/_2$ pound of presoaked dehydrated or fresh mixed vegetables, and salt and pepper to taste. Boil for 3 hours, and add 1 cup of rice. Boil for a $^1/_2$ hour and serve.[1]

CAPTAIN SANDERSON'S
COMMISSARY BEEF SOUP WITH DESICCATED VEGETABLES

"In no form can meat and vegetables be served together more profitably and more nourishingly." Take one or two substantial beef bones and place in a large pot with 2 pounds of sirloin, tenderloin, or rump steak slices. Cover with water, add 1 tablespoon of salt, and bring to a boil. Reduce heat and simmer for 90 minutes, skimming any fat off the top. Remove the meat and add to the pot 1 pound of dehydrated mixed vegetables. Boil for another 2 hours, continuing to skim any fat from the surface; then season with salt, pepper, and 1 tablespoon of vinegar. The soup is ready to eat, or the meat may be added to the pot once again for a heartier dish.[2]

MRS. PUTNAM'S 1860 BEEF SHIN SOUP

Boil a beef shin, cut or cracked into several pieces, in 5 or 6 quarts of water for 5 or 6 hours, frequently skimming the fat and scum from the surface. Shred one-half of a cabbage, chop 2 turnips and 3 carrots, and finely dice 3 onions, and add to the pot. Salt and pepper to taste and boil for 2 hours. A $^1/_2$ hour before serving, remove the bone and gristle. Dumpling dough can be prepared and balls dropped into the soup to boil a $^1/_2$ hour before serving.[3]

BEEF OR MUTTON SOUP

Gently boil 2 pounds of cubed beef or mutton with a $^1/_2$ cup of rice or bread crumbs in 4 quarts of water in a covered pan. Skim often. Then season with salt and pepper, and slice and add 2 turnips, 2 carrots, 2 onions, and 1 head of celery. Stew for 4 hours.[4]

PVT. ISAAC LEVY'S
46TH VIRGINIA SEDER VEGETABLE SOUP

One group of Jewish soldiers in the 46th Virginia celebrated Passover in 1864, telling relatives that "we are observing the festival in a truly orthodox style." They began on the first day with a vegetable soup of onions, parsley, carrots, turnips, cauliflower, and 1 $^1/_2$ pounds of rare available fresh beef, with smoked meat for the days following.[5]

SHEEP'S HEAD SOUP

Dice one sheep's liver and lungs and stew in 1 gallon of water with a sliced onion, 2 or 3 carrots and turnips, a $^1/_2$ pound of pearl barley, and 1 teaspoon each of salt and pepper. Cook until thoroughly done, and then add a skinned sheep's head and boil until all the meat is tender. Remove the head, and strain the broth. Allow it to cool, and skim fat from the surface. Return the broth to heat, and add flour and butter sufficient to thicken it. Then stir in a $^1/_2$ cup of sherry.[6]

MULLIGATAWNY SOUP

Cut up a knuckle of veal, and put it into a stew pan with 1 tablespoon of butter, a $^1/_2$ pound of lean ham, one sliced carrot, one sliced turnip, three sliced onions, six peeled and quartered apples, and a $^1/_2$ pint of water. Stew over moderate heat until the water is reduced and a glaze begins to form on the bottom of the pan. Add 3 tablespoons of curry powder or curry paste, and stir in a $^1/_2$ pound of flour; then pour into the pan 1 gallon of water. Add 1 teaspoonful of salt and a $^1/_2$ teaspoonful of sugar, and bring to a boil. Lower heat and simmer $2^1/_2$ hours, skimming off all fat as it rises.[7]

PHOEBE PEMBER'S CHIMBORAZO CHICKEN SOUP

To any clear chicken broth, add a $^1/_2$ cup of parsley and 1 teaspoon each of salt and pepper.[8]

ANNE WITTENMYER'S DIET KITCHEN CHICKEN SOUP

Place a large chicken, skinned and jointed, in a 6-quart pot and cover with 1 gallon of water. Simmer without boiling until done and the meat is falling away from the bones—1 to 2 hours. Skim the fat from the top of the water, and add six crushed hardtack, $^2/_3$ cup of light cream, and salt and pepper to taste.[9]

ANDERSONVILLE MEAT SOUP WITH DUMPLINGS

Place 1 pound of beef, pork, or bacon in a pot, add a $^1/2$ pound of dry beans, and cover with water. Bring to a boil and then simmer for 2 hours, adding water to keep the ingredients covered. Skim the fat from the surface, and then add dumplings made of cornmeal mixed with a little water until they will compress into dough balls. Cook another $^1/2$ hour and then serve.[10]

CHICKEN BROTH

Cut one chicken into quarters and place in 3 or four quarts of water, adding in 1 cup of rice. Season with pepper and salt, and nutmeg if desired. Bring to a boil, and then reduce heat and simmer gently until the chicken falls from the bone. Shredded parsley leaves may be added, as may a sliced onion. A few pieces of cracker may be added 15 minutes before serving.[11]

CAPTAIN SANDERSON'S BOILED PORK AND BEAN SOUP

Soak a 1-pound bag of dried navy or pinto beans overnight, and then drain. Place the beans in a large pot, and add water according to the recipe on the package; bring to a boil for at least 1 hour. Add 1 pound of parboiled pork and boil for another 90 minutes. Add one onion chopped, pepper, salt, and 1 teaspoon of vinegar, and boil another 15 minutes. Mash the beans with a potato masher, and serve with a slice of pork that has been boiled for $2^1/2$ hours. A finely diced onion sautéed in fat and flour, with a few teaspoons of water, may be used to top the pork slice.[12]

CAPTAIN SANDERSON'S
COMMISSARY PORK SOUP WITH VEGETABLES

Cut 2 pounds of lean pork into 1-inch cubes. Add them to a skillet with pork fat heated very hot, and fry the pork very brown. Add the pork to a kettle of boiling salted water, and boil at medium heat for 15 minutes. Then add 1 pound of dehydrated mixed vegetables and boil for 90 minutes. Remove any fat from the surface, season with salt, pepper, and vinegar, and then add 1 quart of stale bread sliced into 2-inch cubes. Boil at low heat for another 15 minutes and serve.[13]

CATFISH SOUP

Clean two large or four small catfish, and cut each into three parts. Combine them in a large kettle with 1 pound of lean bacon, 1 large, sliced onion, a $1/2$ cup of finely chopped parsley, and pepper and salt to taste. Cover with water and bring to a boil; then reduce to a simmer until the fish is tender but not flaking. Meanwhile beat four egg yolks and add 1 tablespoon of butter, 2 tablespoons of flour, and a $1/2$ pint of half-and-half cream. Warm them in a pan until they begin to thicken, and then add to the soup. Simmer 15 minutes, and then remove the bacon and serve the soup.[14]

MRS. HASKELL'S 1861 OYSTER SOUP

Place 3 quarts of fresh oysters into 2 quarts of water and bring to a boil. Meanwhile, thoroughly mix a $1/2$ cup of butter and 1 tablespoon of flour with a $1/2$ cup of the boiling soup until the butter is melted; then pour into the soup. Bring again to a boil, and then remove from heat, taking care that the oysters boil a total of no more than 15 minutes. Pour the soup over hard crackers or toast, and salt and pepper to taste.[15]

DR. JONATHAN LETTERMAN'S
DESICCATED VEGETABLES SOUP

Desiccated vegetables should be steeped in water for 2 hours and then boiled with the soup for 3 hours and a half ration of desiccated vegetables previously soaked in cold water for 1 hour, with a few small pieces of pork. Add salt and pepper, and water to cover the ingredients, and stew slowly for 3 hours "to make an excellent dish." "The secret in using the desiccated vegetables is in having them thoroughly cooked. The want of this has given rise to a prejudice against them which is unfounded; it is the fault of the cooking, and not of the vegetables."[16]

HOTCHPOTCH

Into 3 quarts of water, add 1 cup of rice or barley and bring to a boil for a few minutes; then simply add whatever chopped vegetables are at hand—onions, carrots, turnips, parsnips, cabbage, parsley—in quantities sufficient to make a very thick soup. Salt and pepper, and add 2 tablespoons of butter. Simmer until thickened and all the vegetables are well cooked, about 1 hour.

CAPTAIN SANDERSON'S COMMISSARY PEA SOUP

Prepare Captain Sanderson's Commissary Pork Soup (page 138), but do not add dehydrated vegetables. Thoroughly wash 1 pound of dried peas, and then boil for 1 hour. When they are soft, drain the water, and add them to the pork soup. Also add one large onion, sliced, and boil for 2 hours. Season with salt, pepper, and vinegar, mash the peas to thicken the broth, and serve.[17]

DR. THRALL'S SPLIT PEA AND BARLEY SOUP

Soak 3 pints of split peas and a $1/2$ pint of pearl barley in water overnight. Drain and cover with fresh water, and then bring to a boil over high heat. Reduce heat to a simmer, and add a $1/2$ pound of crumbled stale bread, one sliced turnip, and a $1/2$ tablespoon of sugar. Simmer until all ingredients are soft; drain, reserving the liquid; and force the vegetables through a colander. Add 1 quart of the cooking liquid, stir to mix, and return to heat to boil for another 10 minutes.[18]

SPLIT PEA SOUP

Boil 1 quart of split peas, three sliced onions, and 1 teaspoon of salt and pepper for 2 hours in 3 quarts of water, until the peas are soft. Drain the water, and press the vegetables through a colander or sieve; then add the cooking liquid and return it to the pot, adding 2 tablespoons of butter and 2 tablespoons of flour, and stirring until the butter melts and the soup is thickened. Add a $1/4$ pound of diced salt pork and 1 teaspoon of crushed celery seed. Boil until the pork is cooked, and then serve over hard crackers or toast cubes fried in butter.[19]

MRS. HALE'S VEGETABLE SOUP

Dice one dozen onions, five turnips, two heads of celery, and three large carrots. Wash them and drain, and then put in a large pot with 2 ounces of butter. Cover and cook over low heat until the vegetables start to soften, and then add 1 gallon of beef broth. Simmer for 4 hours; then drain the liquid and force the vegetables through a sieve or colander. Add the cooking liquid, stir and bring to a boil, and serve.[20]

MRS. PUTNAM'S 1860 VEGETABLE SOUP

In a large pot place beef bones and 1 pound of boiled turkey; add the liquid that the turkey was boiled in; cut two or three each of carrots, turnips, and onions; and add a $^1/_2$ dozen whole cloves, 1 teaspoon each of salt and pepper, and two or three cut-up tomatoes. Add enough water to cover and bring to a boil. Simmer for 4 hours, adding water as necessary; then remove from heat and strain. Return the broth to the pot and return to a simmer. Make a paste of 2 tablespoons of flour in a little cold water, stir until smooth, and stir it into the soup and simmer another 15 minutes. Pour over slices of toast or toasted bread cubes fried brown in butter.[21]

ULEINNE SOUP

Put a piece of butter the size of an egg into a soup kettle and stir until melted. Dice three onions and sauté in the butter until brown; then add 3 quarts of beef stock, a $^1/_2$ teaspoon of ground mace, and pepper and salt to taste. Bring to a boil for 1 hour, and then add three sliced carrots and three sliced turnips, a stalk of chopped celery, 1 pint of string beans, and 1 pint of green peas. Boil for 2 hours and serve.[22]

TARHEEL SOUR SOUP

Boil 2 quarts of buttermilk. Make a paste of three egg yolks and enough corn flour to form a stiff dough. Tear off pieces to drop in the milk, adding salt and pepper to taste.[23]

CONFEDERATE HOSPITAL TOAST SOUP

Toast a $^1/_4$ pound slice of bread gently until it reaches a uniform light yellow color, and then place it near an open fire. When it reaches the color of brown chocolate, put it in a pitcher and pour over it 3 pints of boiling water. Remove from heat and cover. When it is cold, strain; it is now ready for use. A piece of apple, slowly toasted until it is black, can be added to make a refreshing drink.[24]

CONFEDERATE BREAD SOUP

Bring 1 pint of water to a boil in a pan, and then add one beaten egg, two slices of toasted bread, a $^1/_2$ cup of milk, and 1 teaspoon of butter. Reduce heat and simmer a few minutes, and add salt and pepper to taste.[25]

PIGEON SOUP

Pluck, clean, and cut up two pigeons, and place in a pot with 4 quarts of water. Bring to a boil, and then simmer for 2 hours. Remove from heat and strain, reserving the liquid. Then season six pigeons with mixed spices and salt; bind them with string. In a frying pan, combine $^1/_4$ cup of chopped parsley or onions, a $^1/_2$ pound of spinach, and a $^1/_2$ pound of butter; heat until the butter melts and the vegetables sizzle. Add half a cup of bread crumbs, and stir until all are thoroughly browned. Then add the trussed pigeons and the fried herbs and crumbs, and boil for 1 hour or until the birds are done.[26]

MRS. PUTNAM'S 1860 GUMBO

In a large pot, place one plucked and cleaned chicken and one veal shin with two sliced carrots, two sliced turnips, a whole peeled onion, and 6 quarts of water. Boil for 5 hours, and then remove the chicken and cut into small pieces. In a skillet, sauté two sliced onions in 2 or 3 tablespoons of butter until browned. Remove the onion, and fry the chicken in the seasoned butter until browned. Then remove the chicken, and return the onions to the pan; shake a little flour over them and stir. Then add the onions and the chicken to the liquid in the pot, and boil for a $^1/_2$ hour. Wash 3 quarts of oysters, and add them to the soup; bring it to a boil, stirring in 3 tablespoons of gumbo file. Reduce to simmer for no more than 10 minutes, and then serve with a spoonful of boiled rice in each serving.[27]

STEWS AND HASHES

GEN. SILAS CASEY'S BEEF STEW

"This will make an excellent dish," said the general. Using 1 pound of steak or stewing beef, cut into cubes the size of a hen's egg; add two potatoes, peeled and quartered, and a small sliced onion; and place in a pot. Add 1 pound of soaked dehydrated mixed vegetables and a 1/4 pound of finely cubed pork. Salt and pepper to taste, and cover with water. Simmer for 3 hours.[1]

CAPTAIN SANDERSON'S COMMISSARY BEEF STEW

Cut 2 pounds of beef roast into cubes 2 inches square and 1 inch thick, sprinkle with salt and pepper, and put in frying pan with a little pork fat or lard. Put them over a fire until well browned but not fully cooked, and then empty the pan into a kettle and add enough water to cover the meat. Add a handful of flour, two quartered onions, and four peeled and quartered potatoes. Cover and simmer slowly over a moderate heat for 3 1/2 hours, skimming any fat that rises to the top. Then stir in 1 tablespoon of vinegar and serve. Other vegetables available, such as leeks, turnips, carrots, parsnips, and salsify, will make excellent additions.[2]

CAPTAIN SANDERSON'S COMMISSARY BRAZILIAN STEW

Take 2 pounds of any common stewing or soup beef and cut into cubes the size of an egg. Then dip them in vinegar and place in a kettle with two sliced onions. Do not add water. Cover and heat this over very low heat for 3 or 4 hours, and then add salt and pepper and serve. Sliced or quartered boiled potatoes may be added before cooking.[3]

VIRGINIA STEW

Cut up two chickens and parboil. Then boil 1 quart of peeled potatoes. Peel and chop 1 dozen large tomatoes. Shell the corn from a dozen ears and mash, adding one large diced onion. Add all of the ingredients to the chicken in a large pot, and barely cover with water, simmering for about 2 hours or until the chicken is falling off the bone. Remove all bones, add salt and pepper to taste, and serve hot.[4]

ALFRED BELLARD'S
5TH NEW JERSEY HELL-FIRED STEW

Anything left over makes this dish: bits of beef and salt pork; potatoes, tomatoes, garlic, onion, or any other vegetable at hand; and hardtack. Cut it all up, salt and pepper, and stew in a pot until cooked.[5]

LOBSCOUSE

In a large pot, combine 4 cups of cubed bottom-round beef, a $1/2$ cup of salt pork, 4 cups of cubed raw potatoes, and 2 cups of sliced onions. Cover with water and bring to a boil; then simmer for 1 hour covered. Add 4 cups of pre-cooked corned beef in cubes, and simmer another $1/2$ hour. Two or three crumbled hardtack may be added with the corned beef if desired.[6]

WILBUR FISK'S 2ND VERMONT BEEF HASH

To make "a dish good enough for anybody,—a super-excellent one for soldiers," pound eight or ten hardtack until finely ground. Boil a $1/2$ pound of stewing beef and two or three small potatoes in water until thoroughly cooked. Then cut the beef into small cubes. In a pot, mix 1 cup each of the broth from the stewing beef—or else beef broth—and water and bring to a boil. Add the meat and hardtack flour. Smash the potatoes and add, and then simmer until thickened to a hashlike consistency. "I have heard unimpeachable critics pronounce it bully," said Fisk in May 1863, "and as that is the most expressive word in the soldier's vernacular, it precludes the necessity of further comment."[7]

RED FLANNEL HASH

Boil four or five beets and four or five potatoes, and then drain. Brown 1 pound of 1-inch beef cubes and three small chopped onions in pork fat. Dice the beets and potatoes, and mix into the meat mixture in a skillet; then sprinkle with salt and pepper. Pour in enough water or milk to moisten the hash slightly, and then mash it down into the pan with a spoon or spatula and fry on each side until browned.[8]

CORNED BEEF HASH

Boil a $^1/_2$ cup of corned beef, allow it to cool, and then dice. Boil two potatoes in the liquid used to boil the corned beef, allow them to cool, and then peel and dice. Stir the potatoes gradually into the meat in a ratio of four parts potato to one part beef, until the whole is mixed. Allow the mixture to cool completely; then melt a teaspoon of butter in a skillet, stir in 4 tablespoons of water, add and thoroughly mix in the hash, and heat thoroughly, adding salt and pepper to taste. Turn over a few times as it browns, and then reduce heat, cover, and simmer.[9]

FORT SNELLING HASH

Brown 1 pound of cubed beef and a diced onion in pork fat in a skillet. Boil four potatoes, drain and dice, and add to the meat. Add salt and pepper and vinegar to taste, and enough water to moisten the mixture. Then press down into the pan with a spoon or spatula, and fry on each side until brown.[10]

PORK AND PARSNIP HASH

Boil 2 pounds of parsnips; then allow them to cook. Dice a $^1/_2$ pound of boiled or roasted pork. Mix the whole together and press into patties. Fry the patties in a hot skillet with 1 teaspoon of butter.[11]

GEN. BASIL DUKE'S KENTUCKY CAVALRY BURGOO

"As for the 'burgoo,' no description can give one who has never tasted it an idea of its luscious excellence, when it has been made by a real expert." In a large pot, place a $^1/_2$ dozen chopped tomatoes and the kernels cut from a $^1/_2$ dozen ears of corn. Other vegetables such as onions, okra, or green beans may be added if desired. Add 1 pound of beef, 1 pound of mutton or lamb, a $^1/_2$ pound of pork, and one whole chicken, all cut into pieces about $1^1/_2$ inches thick. If available, one or two squirrels—or a rabbit—are desirable additions. Cover with water and bring to a boil. Continue to boil, adding water as necessary, until the meat is falling apart and the ingredients are blended into a very thick soup. Salt and pepper heavily. Serve, ideally, in a new tin cup. "Gastronomic authorities averred that its taste was impaired, if served in any other way."[12]

CAPTAIN SANDERSON'S
COMMISSARY CORNED BEEF AND CABBAGE

Captain Sanderson was working with salt beef, of course. Now just take a standard chunk of corned beef, place it in a pot covered with water, and cook over a moderate fire for 2 hours or more, skimming any fat that may cook out of it. Add as much cabbage as will fill the pot, removing some of the water if necessary, and boil gently for 90 minutes.[13]

CAPTAIN SANDERSON'S
COMMISSARY BUBBLE AND SQUEAK

Take up to a $^1/_2$ pound of leftover corned beef, slice it thin, and sprinkle with pepper. Then fry it in a pan with a little grease or pork fat. Boil a head of cabbage until soft, dry it thoroughly, and then chop finely and season with salt, pepper, and vinegar. Serve a piece of beef with a good helping of cabbage.[14]

SKILLYGALEE

Soak several hardtack in cold water, and then fry them in pork fat in a hot skillet, adding salt to taste.

USS *HARTFORD* DANDYFUNCK

Soak a $^1/_2$ dozen hardtack in water. Then mix with a $^1/_2$ pound of salt pork and a $^1/_2$ cup of molasses and bake.[15]

MEATS

GEN. SILAS CASEY'S ROASTED BEEF

Taking 2-inch cubes of steak or stewing beef, place on a stick or fork and roast over hot coals until done. Do not salt or pepper before cooking, which would make the meat less tender.[1]

ROAST BEEF

Place a fresh rump roast on a spit over hot coals or beside a blazing fire and roast for 15 minutes for every pound of meat, turning frequently and basting with salt water.[2]

STEWING A RUMP ROAST

Remove the bone from a large rump roast and fill the cavity with a stuffing of butter, bread crumbs, and diced onion. Tie the end, and set the roast in a pan with 2 quarts of water, 1 pint of red wine, a $1/2$ dozen carrots and turnips cut small, and a head of celery chopped. Add a $1/2$ dozen cloves of garlic, 1 dozen smashed cloves, and 1 teaspoon each of pepper and salt. Bring to a simmer and stew about 15 minutes for each pound or until done to preference. Remove from the pot and let stand for 5 minutes; skim the fat from the broth and use flour to thicken it into gravy, adding broth as needed. Grate horseradish over the roast and serve.[3]

MRS. HASKELL'S 1861 FRIED BEEFSTEAK

Trim the fat from a large steak, season the fat with salt and pepper, and fry it in a hot skillet until enough melts to allow placing the steak itself in the pan. Fry the steak at high heat, turning and dusting it with salt and pepper. In a teacup, mix $1/4$ cup of water and a $1/2$ teaspoon of flour until smooth, remove the steak and fat from the skillet, and pour in the flour and water, stirring and scraping the bottom rapidly to make a brown gravy. Pour over the steak and serve.[4]

STEWED BEEFSTEAK

Melt 1 tablespoon of butter in a hot pan and fry the steak until just brown on each side. Then pour in 2 cups of beef stock or water, salt and pepper to taste, and 1 tablespoon of vinegar, and stew over moderate heat until the meat is done. Remove the steak and mix the broth with flour to make a thick gravy.[5]

BEEFSTEAK PIE

Take partially stewed steaks (see above) and cut into 1-inch cubes. Place into a baking dish lined with pie crust (see chapter on desserts), cover with a slice of ham or with chopped onions and carrots, and then take the stewing gravy or beef stock, salt, and pepper and fill the pie shell to cover the ingredients. Cover with a lid of pastry and bake at 400° for 1 hour.

MRS. CORNELIUS'S 1863 VEAL PIE

Take any pieces of veal or beef available, including the shank and neck, and boil for 1 hour or more, skimming off all scum that rises. Cut the boiled meat into 1-inch cubes and place a layer in a pie or baking dish lined with pie pastry (see chapter on desserts). Salt and pepper the meat, and place a $1/2$ dozen thin slices of butter over it; then lay on thin slices of salt pork. Repeat the process until the dish is full, and then pour in liquid from the boiled meat and cover with another crust, crimping the rim to seal. Puncture the top with a knife to allow steam to escape. Bake in an oven for 1 hour at 400° or place in a pot with water rising to just below the rim of the dish and boil for 90 minutes.[6]

BOILED CORNED BEEF

Bring the unsliced corned beef nearly to a boil, drain, and cover with cold water, bringing once more to a boil. Simmer covered until the meat is tender, skimming off any fat that rises to the surface.[7]

BEEF JERKY

Slice $1^1/2$ pounds of beef brisket into strips about 6 inches long and $1/8$ inch thick, cutting away all fat. Marinate overnight in a mixture of $1/4$ cup each of Worcestershire sauce and soy sauce (see chapter on sauces), 2 teaspoons of salt, and a $1/2$ teaspoon each of ground pepper, onion powder, and garlic salt. Place the strips on an oven rack and dry at 150° for 8 hours or more, turning occasionally for complete drying, and leaving the oven door ajar.[8]

GEN. SILAS CASEY'S "EXCELLENT LUNCH" OF PORK

Boil a pork roast for 3 hours, and then slice and accompany with a slice of raw onion and a piece of soft bread. The pork may also be sliced and toasted over coals on a stick or fork, making a dish that is "sweet and good."[9]

MRS. CORNELIUS'S 1863 ROAST PIG

Ideally, a 1-month-old suckling pig should be used, killed on the morning of the day it is to be roasted. Remove the feet at the first joint, remove the internal organs, scrape the skin to remove any bristles, and then wash carefully and dust liberally inside and out with salt. Fill the cavity with a stuffing made of bread crumbs, milk, melted butter, marjoram, sage, and salt and pepper. Pack the cavity tightly, and then sew closed. Run a spit through the carcass lengthwise; then baste with melted oil, dust with flour, and place over the fire. Turn frequently, about every 4 minutes, and when the outside begins to brown, dust more liberally with flour and keep dusting if it falls off. When all of the flour on the skin has turned a dark, deep brown, scrape it off and set aside. Collect the drippings from the pig in a pan, and add a large lump of butter. After removing the flour from the pig, begin basting frequently with this gravy. After about 2^1/$_2$ hours, the pig will be thoroughly roasted. A gravy can be made from the remaining pan drippings, and the liver and feet can be boiled, the meat removed and cut up, and the liquid and meat added to the pan drippings, and then thickened with flour.[10]

PORK STEAKS

Cut 1-inch-thick steaks from a pork loin, trim the fat from the edges, and dust well with salt and pepper. Then place on a gridiron over hot coals or a low fire. Broil for about 10 minutes on a side, turning at least once. Then dust again with salt, and add a small pat of butter on top when served.[11]

MRS. HASKELL'S 1861 SALT PORK

Cover the bottom of a barrel or stoneware crock with 1^1/$_2$ inches of salt, and then place chunks of pork that has had as much lean meat removed from it as possible, but with fat and rind remaining, on their cut edges in the salt. Pack tightly, and then cover with another 1^1/$_2$ inch layer of salt. Repeat until all the pork is laid down. Cover with a final layer of salt. Make a brine of water with as much salt as will dissolve in it and still leave the brine liquid, and pour it into the container to a level several inches above the top layer. Allow to stand and soak for several days, and then remove pieces as needed, keeping the container tightly covered at all times.[12]

MRS. HASKELL'S 1861 BOILED SALT PORK

Place a chunk of salt pork in a kettle and just cover with water. Bring to a boil, and then drain the water immediately. Instantly add more boiling water. Reduce to a simmer and continue cooking until the meat is done and tender. Remove from the pot and cut off any skin—which should peel away easily— and dust with pepper. Boil potatoes, turnips, carrots, or other root vegetables, or cabbage, in their own water, and serve with the pork.[13]

CAPTAIN SANDERSON'S COMMISSARY FRIED BACON

"The great secret in frying is to have the fat as hot as the fire will make it before putting the article to be cooked into it." If using salt pork or salted bacon, soak it well to draw out the salt first, and then cut it into thin slices and fry it until crisp. Another option is to slice the bacon into a pan and cover it with stale bread crumbs, adding a little fat to make the crumbs adhere. Then fry the bacon for 4 or 5 minutes on each side.[14]

CAPTAIN SANDERSON'S COMMISSARY GERMAN-STYLE BACON

Parboil bacon first and clean it, removing any rind, and then slice it into thin strips and place in a pan with enough water to cover. Put it in an oven at 325° to bake until the bacon on top is browned. Baste frequently as the water evaporates.[15]

CAPTAIN SANDERSON'S COMMISSARY BOILED BACON

Wash raw bacon carefully and soak overnight. Then bring to a simmer over a low fire until it comes to a slow boil. Drain and refill with fresh water, and simmer for 3 hours. It is done when the rind comes off easily and the meat is soft, yet firm.[16]

USS *HARTFORD* SEA PIE

Make a pie crust pastry and line the bottom of a 9-inch pie pan. Then alternately place layers of thinly sliced fresh or salt pork or beef with layers of pastry, until about 2 inches thick. Bake in an oven at 375° for about 45 minutes.[17]

SAUSAGE CAKES

Into 1 pound of chopped or ground pork, mix a $1/2$ teaspoon of pepper, a $1/2$ teaspoon of whole cloves, a $1/2$ teaspoon of ground coriander, and 4 tablespoons of cold water. Mix well, form into small patties, and fry in a hot pan.[18]

MRS. HASKELL'S 1861 PICKLED PIG'S FEET

Place pig's feet in a pan and cover with water and a teaspoon of salt. Boil until the meat is soft enough that a broom straw can be run through it, and then remove and pack while still hot into jars and cover with vinegar. Add 1 teaspoon of whole black peppercorns, one or two garlic cloves, and any other spices desired.[19]

MRS. PUTNAM'S 1860 FRIED PIG'S FEET

Combine flour, water, a $1/2$ teaspoon of salt, and 1 egg to make a thick batter. Dip washed and dried pig's feet into the batter until well covered, and then fry in hot fat in a skillet until golden brown. Serve by pouring a little melted butter and 1 teaspoon of vinegar over them.[20]

MRS. HASKELL'S LARD

Trim all the fat from a pig skin and fry over low to moderate heat until it liquefies. Continue adding fat and a little salt, and at the same time, use a ladle to remove the liquid fat as it forms, straining it through a jelly bag to remove impurities. When the fat cools, it will congeal. Use it for future cooking.[21]

PORK AND BEANS

Soak 2 pounds of salt or pickled pork overnight in water. Also soak 2 quarts of dried beans overnight. Drain both, put the pork in a pot of cold water, and boil until the meat is tender, skimming off any fat that rises to the surface. Bring the beans to a boil in another pot of water, and cook until they start to split and are soft. Remove and drain the beans, put the pork on the bottom of a baking pan, and cover it with the beans. Add a little of the cooking water from the pork, cover the pan, and bake in a 375° oven until the top is browned.[22]

MISS LESLIE'S STEWED MUTTON CHOPS

Cut a loin or neck of mutton into chops, and trim away the fat and bones. Beat and flatten, season them with pepper and salt, put them into a pan, and barely cover with water. Add sliced carrots, turnips, onions, potatoes, and sweet herbs to taste, or a few tomatoes. Cover and stew over low heat, skimming occasionally, for 3 hours or until everything is tender.[23]

FRIED VENISON STEAK

Heat a $^1/_2$ cup of lard of bacon fat to sizzling in a skillet. Take venison steaks about 1 inch thick and dust with salt and pepper; then dredge in wheat flour or cracker meal and fry until a dark brown, turning just once, about 8 minutes to a side. Add 2 tablespoons of flour to the fat remaining in the pan and stir until brown. Then add 1 cup of boiling water and stir into a gravy. Strain if necessary to remove lumps, and pour over the steaks.[24]

ROASTED RABBIT ON A SPIT

Clean and skin a rabbit, remove the head, run a spit through it lengthwise, and tie the front and back feet to the spit with string. Place it over a bed of hot coals or beside a blazing fire. Roast, turning frequently, for 90 minutes to 2 hours.

FRIED RABBIT

Heat $^1/_3$ cup of lard in a heavy frying pan until very hot. Skin, clean, and joint a rabbit, and dredge the pieces in a mixture of 1 cup of flour with 1 teaspoon each of salt and black and red peppers. Put the pieces in the hot lard, and fry until a golden brown, turning once. Pour off excess, and add a chopped onion, 1 cup of beef stock, and 1 tablespoon of cider vinegar. Simmer for 1 hour or until the rabbit is tender. Remove the rabbit from the pan and keep warm. Pour a $^2/_3$ cup of cream into the skillet and stir constantly, scraping up any bits stuck to the pan, until it has thickened into a gravy. Pour over the rabbit when served.

SQUIRREL

Dredge a skinned squirrel in $^1/_4$ cup of flour, and then fry in 1 cup of hot fat until done. Eat as with a chicken. Another option is to fry until brown, and then to place in a pan and cover with water, simmering for about 1 hour. Add a sliced onion, two small quartered potatoes, and a sliced carrot, with herbs to taste, and simmer another 30 minutes.[25]

BROILED SQUIRREL

Clean and skin squirrels, and split them open along the back, washing carefully in cold water. Dust with salt and pepper; and then broil on a grill or gridiron over hot coals. Baste occasionally with melted butter, and turn twice on each side until golden brown. Serve dusted with bread crumbs, and pour over them a few ounces of melted butter.[26]

POSSUM WITH SWEET POTATOES

Skin a possum, and remove the head and feet. Wash carefully and salt heavily inside and out. Place the possum in a deep, covered pan with a few cups of water, and stew it for at least 1 hour. Then boil eight sweet potatoes in salted water, adding 2 tablespoons of butter and 1 tablespoon of sugar. Place the potatoes in the pot with the possum, lay a $^1/_2$ dozen strips of bacon over the possum, sprinkle the top with thyme and marjoram, and place uncovered in an oven to brown at 400°, basting frequently.[27]

PHOEBE PEMBER'S CHIMORAZO PLANKED RAT

"The rat must be skinned, cleaned, his head cut off and his body laid open upon a square board, the legs stretched to their full extent and secured upon it with small tacks, then baste with bacon fat and roast before a good fire quickly like canvas-back ducks."[28]

RAT

Cook as with squirrel and rabbit, either fried or stewed, or broil over an open fire on a ramrod or toasting fork.

LOUISIANA ALLIGATOR

Dice 4 pounds of alligator meat, and marinate in 1 cup of water seasoned with a $^1/_2$ teaspoon of cayenne pepper and the juice of one lemon. In a hot skillet, heat 1 cup of oil until very hot, and then gradually stir in 1 cup of flour. Keep stirring until the flour browns into a roux. Add and brown two diced onions, and then add one mashed tomato and a $^1/_2$ teaspoon of sugar. Allow to simmer for 5 minutes; then add one diced green pepper, two stalks of chopped celery, and a dozen small mushrooms sliced. Stir, and finish with 1 cup of water. Simmer for 1 hour. Then add the alligator and 3 chopped green onions, with salt and cayenne pepper to taste. Cook for a $^1/_2$ hour or until the meat is tender.[29]

FISH AND FOWL

FISH CHOWDER

In 2 tablespoons of hot oil in a skillet, sauté a finely diced onion and a piece of salt pork. In a separate pan, combine two large cleaned and cubed fish, such as cod or catfish, with a $^1/_2$ pound of cubed potatoes and a dash of salt and pepper to taste. Cover with water and simmer for 15 minutes. Meanwhile, make a white sauce by melting 4 tablespoons of butter, and stir in a $^1/_2$ cup of flour. Cook for 1 minute, stirring often. Then remove from heat, and stir in 1 cup of milk. Add the white sauce and the sautéed onions and salt pork to the potatoes and fish. Simmer for 10 minutes, seasoning to taste.[1]

MRS. HASKELL'S 1861 PICKED COD

Clean and bone a fresh cod, and then with forks pick the meat apart into very small pieces. Set them in water for 1 hour, drain, and replace with fresh water. Then bring to a simmer. Drain again, and just cover with fresh water. For each quart of the soaked fish, add 3 tablespoons of butter, 1 teaspoon of flour, and a $^1/_2$ teaspoon of fine ground pepper. Simmer over low heat. Meanwhile, beat two eggs. Then remove the fish from the fire and slowly stir in the beaten eggs.[2]

SOUTHERN BOILED FISH

Clean and wash any firm-fleshed fish, and dust with salt and pepper inside and out 2 hours before cooking. Bring 1 quart of water to lukewarm in a suitable pot, and then place the fish in the water. Bring to a boil for 20 to 30 minutes, depending on the size of the fish.[3]

GENERAL PICKETT'S FIVE FORKS SHAD BAKE

Carefully clean and scale as many fresh shad as are caught, removing the roe intact from the females. Then split them along the spine and affix them flat, skin side down, on oak boards or shingles. Stand the boards on end in the ground beside a blazing fire, and cook for 7 or 8 minutes. Then turn the fish on the boards and cook for another 7 or 8 minutes on the other side, until golden brown. Dredge the roe in cornmeal, and fry in bacon fat.

KENTUCKY OVEN BAKED SHAD

Clean and scale fresh shad, and then stuff the interior with a mixture made of a $^1/_2$ cup each of grated ham, bread crumbs, and mashed potato, seasoned with 1 tablespoon of butter, $^1/_4$ teaspoon each of pepper and mace, and a little chopped parsley. Rub the outside of the shad with a beaten egg yolk, and sprinkle bread crumbs over it. Then place in a pan containing 2 cups of water, $^3/_4$ cup of white or red wine, 3 teaspoons of vinegar, and 1 teaspoon of horse-radish. Dot the top of the fish with 4 ounces of butter broken into little bits and rolled in flour. Then cover the pan or dish and bake at 350° for 30 minutes, basting occasionally. Serve by removing from the pan and pouring the gravy over it.[4]

FRIED FISH

For any fresh-caught fish such as carp, perch, or catfish, cut off the head and fins and clean the fish; then roll it in flour or cornmeal, or finely crushed hard-tack, and fry in a skillet in hot lard or pork fat, perhaps 8 minutes on each side. Lighter fish like catfish will only need 3 or 4 minutes to a side. Use melted butter mixed with mushroom catsup (see chapter on sauces) as a sauce.

SALMON STEAK

Cut a cleaned salmon into steaks about 1 inch thick. Then dip each slice in a beaten egg yolk, and dredge in flour or bread crumbs. Place on a cool gridiron to prevent sticking. Broil them about 10 minutes on each side, turning the steaks just once. When served, pour melted butter flavored with lemon juice over them, or use mushroom catsup or soy (see chapter on sauces).[5]

MRS. CORNELIUS'S 1863 OYSTERS

Wash fresh, unopened oysters, and then lay them on hot coals or a griddle, with the larger side of the shell on the bottom to preserve the juice. Remove from heat when the top shell has opened. Using a knife, remove the upper shell and either eat the oysters from the shells while warm or scoop them out and eat with catsup or mustard catsup (see chapter on sauces).[6]

MRS. CORNELIUS'S 1863 PICKLED OYSTERS

Drain the juice from 100 fresh oysters and bring it to a boil. While still hot, pour it over the shucked oysters and allow to stand a few minutes. Then drain the liquid, and bring it to a boil once more, adding a 1/2 cup of vinegar, 1 teaspoon of whole black peppercorns, and 1 teaspoon of mace. Remove from the fire, pour over the oysters, and cover securely. Do not attempt to keep them more than a few days.[7]

KENTUCKY OYSTER FRITTERS

Shuck, wash, and trim any gristle from large oysters. Then dust them with nutmeg, salt, and pepper. Take large, fresh oysters, trim them, and season them with salt, pepper, and nutmeg. Make a thick batter of 1 pint of milk, 1 pint of flour or cornmeal, and three beaten eggs. Melt 1 cup of butter in a skillet and bring to a sizzle; then drop tablespoonfuls of batter into the butter, and immediately place an oyster on top of each fritter, covering it with another tablespoon of batter. Fry until golden brown on each side, turning as necessary.[8]

FRIED OYSTERS

Shuck oysters and wash them carefully. Then dredge them in stale bread crumbs mixed with salt and pepper. Drop them into a skillet with a 1/2 pound of butter melted and heated to a sizzle, and fry until golden brown on both sides. After removing from the pan and draining, scatter finely chopped parsley over them.[9]

MRS. HASKELL'S 1861 STEWED MUSSELS

Take any quantity of freshwater mussels and place in a pot with a little water, a chopped onion, and a little lemon juice. Bring to a simmer and stew for 15 minutes. As the mussels open, their own juice will add to the broth. Add a 1/2 cup of parsley and serve.[10]

LOUISIANA CRAWFISH

Heat 3 quarts of water to a boil. Add two lemons cut in half, two chopped onions, two or three stalks of celery chopped coarsely, and several cloves of crushed garlic. Allow the broth to boil for a 1/2 hour, and then quickly immerse 2 dozen live, whole crawfish. When the water returns to a boil, keep at a simmer for 15 to 20 minutes, or until the shells turn a brilliant red. Remove the crawfish from the broth, twist off the tails, and remove the meat to eat. If desired, ears of corn cut in half and halved potatoes may be cooked in the broth before adding the crawfish, to make an accompaniment.

TURTLE STEAK

Cut 1-inch-thick steaks from the thick part of the turtle's fin; dust with salt, pepper, and mace; and then dredge in flour and fry in a skillet containing a $^1/_2$ cup of melted butter and lard combined. Turn once to brown on both sides. When about done, add a $^1/_4$ cup of water and simmer for 15 minutes. Remove and serve with squeezed lemon juice over the steak.[11]

ANDERSONVILLE ROAST SWALLOW

If inclined to eat any very small bird, scald and pluck the bird first; then remove the head and feet and clean the interior cavity. Place a few slices of onion inside the cavity, and then wrap one or two strips of bacon around the carcass and roast on a toasting fork over an open fire until done.

ROAST TURKEY

First prepare a stuffing of fried pork sausage, adding the meat and its fat to one beaten egg and mixing it with one diced onion and enough bread crumbs to form stuffing balls. Pluck and clean the turkey, and then loosely pack the stuffing into the breast and body cavities. Stitch them closed, tie the wings to the body, and dust the bird with flour. Push a spit lengthwise through the bird, and then set it over hot coals or beside a blazing fire. Turn and baste with melted butter for 15 minutes for each pound the bird weighs. If using an oven, roast at 325° for 20 minutes per pound. When it is about half done, dust it with flour once more, and continue to roast until golden brown. Serve garnished with whatever is at hand, including sausages, dumplings, and boiled or roasted vegetables, and with gravy (see chapter on sauces).[12]

ROAST DUCK

Clean and pluck the duck; then make a stuffing of one finely chopped onion, a $^1/_2$ cup of sage leaves, 1 tablespoon of butter, and salt and pepper to taste. Stuff the breast and body cavities of the bird, and sew or tie them closed. Then run onto spits lengthwise, baste with a little salt water, and place over hot coals or beside a blazing fire. Turn and roast for 1 hour, basting occasionally with retained drippings from the bird. Meanwhile, boil the livers, gizzard, and heart; chop them; and put them into the drippings. Then thicken it with a little flour to make a gravy. Serve the duck with the gravy and perhaps with a wine jelly (see chapter on desserts) as an accompaniment.[13]

STEWED DUCK

Split a cleaned and plucked duck in two, dust with salt and pepper, and place the halves in a covered pot with a slice of pork or ham and just enough water to cover the bird. Stew for 15 minutes or until a fork shows the meat to be tender. Remove the duck and add two diced onions, 2 tablespoons of butter, a $1/2$ teaspoon of pepper, 2 tablespoons of flour slowly stirred in, and enough cream to make a thick, creamy gravy.[14]

FRIED PARTRIDGE

Take partridges that have already been roasted and cut into quarters. Dip them into beaten egg yolks seasoned with salt and pepper, and then place in a skillet containing a $1/2$ pound of butter melted and sizzling. Reduce heat and fry until the birds are golden brown.[15]

BOILED CHICKEN WITH OYSTERS

Clean and pluck a large chicken, stuff the cavity with shucked and washed oysters and close, place the fowl cavity side down in a close-fitting jar or pot, and place the jar in a pan of boiling water. Keep it at a boil for 90 minutes; then remove. Take the juice from the jar and stir in one beaten egg, 1 tablespoon of flour, 1 tablespoon of melted butter, and enough cream to make a thick sauce; serve over the fowl.[16]

POTTED PIGEON

Pluck and clean fat pigeons. Then make a stuffing of equal numbers of crushed hardtack and whole eggs sufficient to meet your needs. Add 3 tablespoons of butter for each egg used and a $1/2$ teaspoon of sage or marjoram for each bird to be stuffed. Place a few tablespoons of stuffing into each pigeon's body cavity, along with a piece of salt pork, and then dust the pigeons with flour. Place them in the bottom of a roasting pan, with just enough water to cover. Add 2 or 3 tablespoons of butter, and stew over moderate heat for about 90 minutes. Remove and serve.[17]

VEGETABLES

CAPTAIN SANDERSON'S COMMISSARY BEANS

Prepare beans as for Captain Sanderson's Commissary Pork and Bean Soup, but drain and then heat in a skillet over moderate heat. Finely chop an onion and sauté it; then scatter it over the beans with pepper, salt, and a little vinegar. Serve with soft bread and coffee.[1]

KENTUCKY SNAP BEANS

Cut a $1/4$ inch from each end of a pound of fresh green beans, and remove the strings from the pods. Break them in half and soak in a pot of cold water for 1 hour. Drain and put in a pan of fresh water, enough to cover the beans. Bring to a boil, and then simmer until the beans are tender. Drain the beans and put them back into enough cold water to cover. Add a chunk of salt pork or several slices of bacon and 1 teaspoon of salt. Bring again to a boil until they are very soft and the water reduced considerably. Remove from heat and dust bread crumbs or crushed hardtack over the top. Then place beside an open fire or in an oven and allow to brown. Drain all remaining liquid, and serve with the pork or bacon on top.[2]

CAPTAIN SANDERSON'S COMMISSARY BOILED HOMINY

Fill a kettle half full of dried hominy, and cover with water to within 1 inch of the top. Add 1 tablespoon of salt, and bring to a boil over a moderate fire for at least 1 hour, stirring constantly to avoid scorching. The hominy is done when a toothpick or knife easily penetrates the kernels.[3]

CAPTAIN SANDERSON'S COMMISSARY FRIED HOMINY

Take leftover boiled hominy and allow it to cool and dry into a congealed mass. Slice it a $1/2$ inch thick by 3 inches in length, drop into a skillet of very hot fat and fry until a golden brown on each side. Remove and drain on cloth or paper to allow fat to drain off; then sprinkle a little salt over it before eating.[4]

CAPTAIN SANDERSON'S COMMISSARY BOILED POTATOES

Wash potatoes, but do not peel. Place them in a clean kettle. Add salt to taste and cover with water; then place over the fire and bring to a boil. Add a little cold water, just enough to halt the full boil, and repeat this process two or three times. When a knife slides easily into the center of a potato, they are nearly done. Remove from the fire, and drain all of the water. Then put the kettle over the fire once more until it stops steaming. Remove and serve.[5]

CAPTAIN SANDERSON'S COMMISSARY FRIED POTATOES

Cut potatoes into thin slices and immerse in cold water for a $^1/2$ hour. Heat pork fat in a skillet until it hisses when a slice of potato is dropped in. Place the potatoes in the pan and fry, turning frequently, until they are a golden brown.[6]

QUARTERMASTER POOLE'S CRUISER BREAKFAST SCOUSE

In this variant of lobscouse (see chapter on stews and hashes), boil and quarter several potatoes, crumble a $^1/2$ dozen hardtack, mix all well, and fry in a pan with butter.[7]

MRS. HASKELL'S 1861 MASHED POTATOES

Peel and quarter four medium potatoes, and then drop into a pot of boiling water, adding 1 teaspoon of salt. Reduce heat to a simmer, and cook until the potatoes are tender. Drain the water, and allow the potatoes to steam and dry for 15 minutes. Then mash them in the kettle until they are smooth. Return the kettle to the heat, and cook over medium heat, stirring continually to prevent scorching, for 15 minutes. Remove and empty into a dish or pan, add 3 tablespoons of butter and a $^1/2$ cup of milk or cream, and mix thoroughly. Add salt and pepper to taste.[8]

CAPTAIN SANDERSON'S COMMISSARY BOILED RICE

Fill a kettle or pan one-third full of rice, and add water to come within 1 inch of the top of the pan. Boil gently, stirring constantly, until the rice is very soft; constant stirring is essential to prevent burning or scorching. When done, drain in a colander or through a piece of coarse fabric like muslin; then pour through the rice and colander a kettle full of cold water. When it has strained through, put the rice back in a clean pan, set close to the heat of the fire, and allow it to dry. It can then be served hot or cold, topped with molasses.[9]

MISS VIOLETTA'S
CONFEDERATE HOSPITAL CHRISTMAS SWEET POTATO PONE

Peel and quarter four or five large sweet potatoes, and put in boiling water, cooking them until very soft. Remove, drain, and allow the potatoes to steam and cool for 15 minutes. Then mash them into a smooth pulp and force through a sieve to remove any strings. Allow 1 tablespoon of butter to melt into the pulp while it cools. Beat three eggs until fluffy, and then stir in a $^1/_2$ pint of milk and 1 teaspoon of salt. To this add 1 quart of the cooled sweet potato pulp. Bake in a 400° oven for 90 minutes to 2 hours, until done.[10]

BROILED SWEET POTATOES

Boil a large sweet potato until half done. Then cut it into $^1/_2$-inch-thick slices, and broil them on a greased grill over hot coals. Turn them over once, and when both sides are of light brown, remove and pour a little melted butter over them to serve. As an alternative, the slices may be dusted with flour and fried in butter or lard.[11]

STEWED SWEET POTATOES

Cut three or four large sweet potatoes in half, place them in the bottom of a kettle, and cover with slices of cooked ham. Over the ham, place a layer of pieces of a cut-up chicken. Dust with salt and pepper, cover with water, and insert sprigs of marjoram, bay, sassafras, rosemary, or other herbs tied in a bundle. Bring to a boil, and then simmer for 1 hour or more, until the chicken is tender and ready to come away from the bone. Remove the herb bundle and drain the stew. Bring the liquid to a boil and reduce, thickening with flour to make a gravy. Then return the stew to the pot and simmer for a few minutes.[12]

SWEET POTATO BALLS

Boil, peel, and mash four or five sweet potatoes; then strain them through a colander. Add 2 tablespoons of butter to the pulp, with 1 teaspoon each of nutmeg and cinnamon. Mix well, and then form the mixture into small balls. Place on a greased baking sheet or pan, and cook at 400° for 20 minutes or until light brown.[13]

TURNIP GREENS

Cut the leafy tops from turnips, and wash and soak in water for 1 hour. Then rinse and place in a pot of boiling water. Add 1 teaspoon of salt and other root vegetables that are available, or a piece of salt pork well diced. Boil for 20 minutes; then drain and serve.[14]

STEWED GOURDS

Skin six or eight gourds, cover with water in a pot, and add 1 teaspoon of salt, 1 tablespoon of lemon juice, 1 tablespoon of butter, and a large slice of salt pork. Bring to a boil; then reduce to a simmer and stew until the gourds are tender.[15]

FRIED GOURDS

Thinly slice six or eight small gourds, dry thoroughly, and then fry for about a minute in a skillet in very hot lard until golden brown. Remove and drain on porous paper; then dust with pepper and salt, and serve.[16]

MRS. CORNELIUS'S 1865 PICKLED TOMATOES

Wash and stem a 1/2 dozen ripe firm tomatoes. Pierce them in several places with an ice pick or thick needle. Then set into an earthenware crock, dusting well between them with salt. Cover and let sit in a cool place for 2 days. Remove, wash, place in a jar, and cover with vinegar, adding 2 tablespoons of whole black pepper, 2 tablespoons of whole mustard seed, and 1 sliced onion. Cover and store in a cool place.[17]

MRS. CORNELIUS'S 1865 BROILED TOMATOES

Cut whole tomatoes in half, and lay face down on a gridiron over hot coals. Cook for 5 or 6 minutes; then turn them and repeat on the top. Remove and dust lightly with salt and pepper and a thin pat of butter on top of each.[18]

FRIED CORN

Shuck several ears of corn and remove the silk. With a knife, cut along the length of each ear to remove the kernels. Then use the edge to scrape off the remainder from the cobs. Put the corn in a frying pan with a little water, salt and pepper to taste, and 1 tablespoon of butter. Cover and fry over low heat, occasionally stirring the kernels, until thoroughly cooked and slightly browned.[19]

MRS. NICHOLSON'S 1865 CORN PUDDING

With a knife or grater, remove the kernels from 2 dozen fresh ears of corn. Mix with 1 teaspoon of salt, 1 teaspoon of sugar, 1 quart of milk, two beaten eggs, and 3 tablespoons of soft butter. Put in a baking dish or pan, and bake at 275° for 4 hours or until nicely browned and done to the consistency of mush.[20]

PEAS PUDDING

Soak 1 pint of dried split peas in warm water overnight. Drain and tie them in a cloth bag, and place in a pan of hot water. Then boil until they are quite soft. Remove, drain, and beat them together with 3 or 4 tablespoons of butter and 1 teaspoon of salt. Serve with boiled pork or beef.[21]

STEWED PEAS

Place 1 pint of dried peas, a thick slice of ham, and 1 teaspoon of sugar in 1 pint of water in a pot. Cover and bring to a boil; then reduce heat and simmer for 2 hours or until the peas are tender. Remove the ham, and then add 1 teaspoon of butter rolled in flour. Stir and continue to simmer for 5 minutes. Serve with the ham.[22]

SAUCES

CONFEDERATE CATSUP

Mix 4 quarts of crushed tomatoes, 1 pint of vinegar, 3 tablespoonfuls of salt, 2 tablespoonfuls of mustard, 2 tablespoonfuls of black pepper, 3 crushed red peppers, and a $^1/_2$ ounce each of allspice and mace. Bring to a boil; and then reduce heat, simmering until desired thickness is achieved.[1]

BOSTON CATSUP

Wash, stem, and crush one peck of tomatoes. Add 1 tablespoon of salt, and bring to a boil. Boil for 1 hour, stirring often; then drain the liquid in a colander, and force the tomatoes through a sieve to remove seeds. Add them to the liquid. Return to the fire, adding a $^1/_2$ pint of finely chopped onions and $^1/_8$ ounce of mace, with 1 tablespoon of whole black peppercorns. Boil until thickened and reduced to catsup consistency.[2]

MRS. NICHOLSON'S 1865 TOMATO MUSTARD

Wash, stem, and crush 1 gallon of tomatoes. Add 1 pint of white vinegar, and bring to a boil. Then simmer for 4 hours. Strain through a colander to remove seeds, and return to a boil until very thick. Add 4 tablespoons of salt, 1 tablespoon of coarse ground black pepper, 1 tablespoon of ground mustard, and a $^1/_2$ tablespoon of allspice. Boil for a $^1/_2$ hour or until of spreadable consistency. Stir to prevent scorching. Add vinegar in a ratio of one part vinegar for four parts sauce, mix, and bottle. If thick enough, it will not pour. Place in widemouthed bottles to admit a spoon or knife.[3]

BOSTON MUSTARD

In a mortar, mix and grind 1 ounce of ground mustard seed, a $^1/_2$ teaspoon of salt, and a $^1/_2$ teaspoon of sugar. Gradually stir into this 3 tablespoons of milk or cream. Continue to stir until very smooth.[4]

CAMP MORTON CONFEDERATE "LUXURY" BONE BUTTER

Split beef bones and break into small pieces. Then place in a pot with just enough water to cover. Boil until all of the fat is cooked out of the bones and the water has evaporated. While hot, strain through a sieve to remove any bone fragments. Allow to cool and congeal.[5]

MUSHROOM "DOGSUP"

Line the bottom of a stoneware crock with mushroom caps, and sprinkle salt over them. Place another layer of mushrooms, salt, and repeat until there are at least a $^1/_2$ dozen layers. Let stand 2 or 3 hours; then mash the mushrooms into a pulp in the crock. Cover, and let stand for 2 days, stirring and mashing again once or twice each day. Pour into another stoneware crock, and add a $^1/_2$ ounce of allspice and $1^1/_2$ ounces of whole black peppercorns. Cover the jar tightly, and set in a pot of boiling water for at least 2 hours. Without squeezing or pressing the mushroom pulp, pour and strain through a sieve into a fresh pot, and simmer until the liquid is reduced by half and becomes very thick. Skim any scum from the surface, and pour into clean jars. Cover, and let stand overnight. Pour through a jelly bag or cloth sieve until the liquid is completely clear; then add 1 tablespoon of brandy for every pint of catsup. Again, let stand overnight and strain in the morning. Bottle and store in a cool, dry place.[6]

CAROLINA SOY

Into 1 quart of mushroom catsup and 1 quart of walnut pickle, pour 1 gallon of Madeira wine and 1 tablespoon of mustard seed. Add 1 cup of anchovies, and bring to a boil for a $^1/_2$ hour. Then bottle and seal tightly. Allow to sit in a cool place for 10 days before using.[7]

MRS. CORNELIUS'S 1863 KNICKERBOCKER PICKLE

Pour $4^1/_2$ pounds of salt, $1^1/_2$ pounds of granulated brown sugar, $1^1/_2$ ounces of saltpeter, a $^1/_2$ ounce of baking soda, and 2 quarts of molasses into 3 gallons of water. Bring to a boil, and skim any scum from the surface until it is clear. Upon cooling, this can be used as a sauce over meats or as a pickling preservative for beef and pork.[8]

CONFEDERATE VINEGAR

Mix 1 pint of molasses with 1 gallon of warm water, cover, and let stand for 2 months, to make a vinegar substitute.[9]

CAROLINA BEEF GRAVY

Melt a $^1/_4$ pound of butter in a skillet, and cook until browned. Then gradually stir in 2 tablespoons of flour. Add 1 pound of very finely chopped beef and 2 or 3 medium onions finely diced. Sauté until well browned, and then add 1 teaspoon of whole black peppercorns, a carrot coarsely cut, rosemary or marjoram to taste, and 3 pints of water. Boil until reduced by two-thirds, strain, and serve with beef or fowl.[10]

KENTUCKY WHITE GRAVY

Take 1 quart of beef or chicken stock produced from boiling meat and bring to a simmer. Add 2 tablespoons of butter, and after it has melted gradually, stir in 3 tablespoons of flour until smooth. Continue to simmer and add cream slowly to bring the gravy to the desired thickness. Then flavor with a little mushroom catsup and/or Worcestershire sauce or vinegar.[11]

KENTUCKY PANCAKE SYRUP

Into 1 pint of boiling water, stir 1 tablespoon of butter, 1 tablespoon of flour, 4 tablespoons of sugar or molasses, and 2 teaspoons of grated nutmeg. Simmer until smooth and thick, and then pour over pancakes, dumplings, or cakes.[12]

DESSERTS

DUNN BROWNE'S 14TH CONNECTICUT PUMPKIN PIE

Browne called for using one pumpkin, 8 dozen eggs, and 1 gallon of milk, which would make a very peculiar pie, indeed. He had the basic ingredients correct, however, and if he had cut down on the eggs, he would have had almost all of the makings of a proper pie. To approximate his recipe, bake or boil a seeded pumpkin and cut into large pieces, until it is soft. Peel and mash, and then strain the pulp until you have 2 quarts of pulp. Boil 4 quarts of milk, and then stir in the pumpkin pulp, 8 cups of sugar, and sixteen well-beaten eggs, with 1 tablespoon of salt. If spices such as ginger, cinnamon, or nutmeg are available, 2 teaspoons of one or a mixture may be added, along with 4 tablespoons of butter. Use the pie crust recipe below, and bake in a 375° oven for about 30 minutes, or until a toothpick inserted in the center comes out clean. Makes four to six pies, depending on size of pan.[1]

MRS. CORNELIUS'S 1863 OPEN APPLE PIE

Peel and quarter eighteen tart apples. Make a thick syrup by boiling 1 quart of water and then adding 4 cups of sugar. Reduce until thick and of the same weight as the apples; add sugar and water if more weight is needed. Grate the zest from one lemon, cut up the lemon itself, remove the seeds, and add to the boiling syrup. When the syrup is clear, add half the apples and boil until soft but not mushy. Take them out and repeat with the rest of the apples. Remove them and boil the syrup until thick. Meanwhile, place the apples in three or four pie pans lined with pie crust (see below), laying them in layers. Sprinkle the lemon zest on top, and then pour over them enough syrup to rise to the rim of the crust. Bake at 500° for a $^1/_2$ hour or until browned on top. A little granulated sugar can be sprinkled on top.[2]

MRS. CORNELIUS'S MOLASSES APPLE PIE

Make a pie crust (see below), and place in a deep dish. Fill it with peeled, sliced apples, dust 1 teaspoon of nutmeg over them, and then put several thin shavings of butter on top. Pour over this 1 cup of molasses, set on the upper crust, and crimp the edges to seal. Bake for 1 hour in a 400° oven.[3]

CONFEDERATE APPLE PIE WITHOUT THE APPLES

Bring $1^3/4$ cups of water, 2 cups of sugar, and 2 tablespoons of cream of tartar to a boil; then simmer for 15 minutes. Add 2 tablespoons of lemon juice and grated zest of one lemon. Allow the mixture to cool, and line a 9-inch pie pan with pastry. Place in the crust $1^3/4$ cups of crumbled soda crackers or even crumbled hardtack. Pour the cooled liquid over the crackers, dust the top with a $1/2$ teaspoon of cinnamon and 2 tablespoons of butter finely diced, and place a top crust over the pie, crimping the edges and making several holes in it with a fork or knife. Bake in a 425° oven for 30 to 35 minutes.[4]

KENTUCKY FRIED PIES

Stew dried apples, peaches, or other fruit until tender, and then mash and sweeten to taste with sugar or molasses. Make pie crust (see below), roll out $1/4$ inch thick, and cut into circular disks about 6 inches in diameter. Spoon several tablespoons of the mashed fruit onto half of each disk; then fold over the other half and crimp the edges to seal. Melt enough butter or lard in a skillet sufficient to cover a pie when inserted, and fry the pies one at a time until browned. Remove and drain each pie; then dust with granulated sugar.[5]

CONFEDERATE MOLASSES PIE

Make a pie crust (see below) and line a pie pan. Bring to a low boil 2 cups of sorghum molasses; then gradually stir in $1/4$ cup of flour and 2 cups of chopped walnuts until well mixed. Simmer, stirring constantly, until well thickened. Pour into the pie crust and bake at 425° for a $1/2$ hour.[6]

1865 PIE CRUST

Into 1 pound of flour rub 6 ounces of lard, 6 ounces of butter, 1 teaspoon of salt, and a $1/2$ teaspoon of baking powder. Mix well together, and then add tablespoons of water until dough is stiff but not sticky. Roll out on a floured surface and let stand for 10 minutes. Then ball it up again and roll it out a second time. Use for meat or fruit pies alike.[7]

FLANNEL CAKE

Mix 1 quart of flour and a $1/4$ cup of yeast with water sufficient to make into a batter, with 1 teaspoonful of salt. Set covered in a warm place and allow to rise overnight. Just before baking, stir in 1 teaspoon of baking soda. Then pour out on a greased griddle and bake at 400° until browned.[8]

LINCOLN CAKE

Beat two eggs. Add 2 cups of sugar, a $^1/_2$ cup of softened butter, and 1 cup of milk. Gradually add 3 cups of flour, 1 teaspoon of cream of tartar, a $^1/_2$ teaspoon of soda, and 1 teaspoon of lemon extract or the zest of 1 lemon. Stir until the batter is creamy, and then pour into a greased cake pan. Bake in a 375° oven for 45 minutes or until done.[9]

JOSEPHINE PEFFER'S 1860 WISCONSIN GINGERBREAD

In a bowl combine 1 cup of molasses, a $^1/_2$ cup of softened butter, a $^1/_2$ cup of buttermilk, two eggs, 1 tablespoon of brown sugar, 1 teaspoon of ginger, and 1 teaspoon of baking powder. While stirring, gradually add flour until it forms a stiff batter. Pour it into a greased 9- or 10-inch baking pan, and bake for a $^1/_2$ hour at 350° or until a toothpick inserted in the center comes out clean.[10]

MRS. H. W. HAYES'S 1860 WISCONSIN SPONGE CAKE

Beat ten eggs, and then gradually stir into them 3 cups of flour and 3 cups of sugar. Stir until smooth. Bake in a 375° oven for 45 minutes or until done.[11]

KENTUCKY SWEET COOKIES

Rub 1 pound of cubed butter into 3 pounds of flour. Then dust in 1 pound of powdered sugar and 1 teaspoon of powdered nutmeg. Stir in $^1/_4$ cup of wine mixed with $^1/_4$ cup of brandy if available. Dissolve 1 teaspoon of baking powder into a few spoonfuls of boiling water. Then add it to the flour mixture and mix it with as much buttermilk as will make the whole into a firm dough. Knead well. Roll out a $^1/_2$ inch thick, and cut into small cookie-size disks. Place on a sheet and bake at 400° for 15 minutes or until well browned.[12]

KATE CUMMING'S LUXURIOUS PUDDING

Dessert: "a luxurious baked pudding, made of the same materials as the batter-cakes, with molasses for sweetening, with the addition of spices."[13]

MRS. PUTNAM'S BATTER PUDDING

Into 1 quart of milk, stir four well-beaten eggs, 6 spoonfuls of flour, and a little salt. Bake in a 400° oven for 20 minutes or until done.[14]

MRS. CORNELIUS'S OUNCE PUDDING

Beat six eggs well, and fold into six finely chopped apples and 6 ounces of stale bread crumbs. Stir in 6 ounces of currants, 6 ounces of sugar, and a little salt and nutmeg. Tie in a waterproof bag, and place in a pot of boiling water to boil for 2 hours. Serve with a sweet sauce (see below).[15]

MRS. HALE'S ARROWROOT PUDDING

In 1 cup of milk mix 3 tablespoons of arrowroot. Then stir it into 3 cups of boiling milk. Allow to cool; then stir in four beaten eggs, 2 ounces of granulated sugar, and 2 ounces of butter. Stir until the butter is melted. Then add 1 teaspoon of nutmeg. Pour into a greased baking dish or pan, and bake 20 minutes at 400°, or until a knife inserted in the center comes out clean.[16]

MRS. RANDOLPH'S PUMPKIN PUDDING

Cut up, seed, and stew a medium-size pumpkin until soft. Then force the pieces through a sieve. To the pulp, add six beaten eggs, $1/4$ pound of butter, a $1/2$ pint of milk, a $1/2$ cup of brandy, and ginger, nutmeg, and sugar to taste. Pour into a pie dish lined with pie crust, and bake at 400° for 1 hour or until a knife inserted in the center comes out clean.[17]

GROUND RICE PUDDING

Stir 4 ounces of ground rice into 1 pint of milk, and beat until it makes a smooth batter. Boil 3 pints of milk, and while it is boiling, gradually stir into it the rice batter until it is very smooth. Add 6 ounces of butter and stir until melted. Then remove from the fire and stir in a $1/2$ pound of powdered white sugar. Allow the mixture to cool, stirring frequently. When cold, stir in the juice and grated rind of one lemon and eight beaten eggs. Pour into a buttered dish. Bake at 325° for about 45 minutes or until a knife inserted in the center comes out clean. Remove and allow to cool completely; then dust heavily with granulated sugar.[18]

DEEP WATER PLUM DUFF

Put a $^1/_2$ ounce of fresh yeast and $1^1/_2$ tablespoons of brown sugar in a bowl. Add a few teaspoons of warm water and stir; then set aside until frothy. In a large bowl, put 2 cups of flour. Make a hole in the center, and pour in the yeast mixture. Stir, adding enough flour to make a stiff dough. Cover, and set in a warm place to rise for 2 hours. Then punch down the dough and add 1 cup of chopped plums, $1^1/_2$ tablespoons of brown sugar, 1 teaspoon of nutmeg, and enough milk to soften the dough. Tie the dough loosely in muslin cloth, and place it in a pot of boiling water. Cover and boil for 90 minutes.[19]

MRS. RUTLEDGE'S SWEET POTATO PONE

Stir together in a bowl 1 quart of grated sweet potato, $^3/_4$ pound of sugar, a $^1/_2$ pint of milk, 3 tablespoonfuls of powdered ginger, and the grated peel of a sweet orange. Rub in 10 ounces of butter, and mix the ingredients well. Bake in a shallow plate or dish at 350° for 1 hour or until a knife inserted in the middle comes out clean.[20]

BREAD PUDDING

Crumble several slices of stale bread into a bowl, and cover with enough milk to soak thoroughly overnight. Beat three eggs thoroughly and fold into the bread mixture. Add a dash of salt and sugar or molasses to taste. Then tie the mixture tightly in a waterproof bag, and place in a pot of boiling water for 1 hour.[21]

MRS. RUTLEDGE'S RICE PUDDING

Stir $^1/_4$ cup of sugar into 1 quart of milk, add a $^1/_2$ cup of uncooked white rice, and pour into a baking dish or pan. Place 1 tablespoon of butter on top in the center. Put the dish in a 400° oven, and bake for 1 hour or until set.[22]

MRS. HASKELL'S BOILED CUSTARD

Bring 1 quart of milk to a boil, preferably in a double boiler or over a pot of hot water. Beat four eggs with 6 tablespoons of sugar until light and frothy; then stir them into the milk and remove from heat. When the mixture has cooled, add a pinch of salt. Then place over the fire again, and stir until it thickens like cream. Pour into cups while hot, and eat, or allow to cool and set.[23]

MRS. CORNELIUS'S BOILED CUSTARD

Bring 3 cups of milk to a boil in a kettle. Mix 3 tablespoonfuls of flour in 1 cup of milk until smooth, adding a pinch of salt. When the rest of the milk boils, stir it in. Simmer for a $^1/_2$ hour, stirring often. Beat one or two eggs with 2 or 3 tablespoonfuls of sugar, and stir into the milk. Add vanilla, cinnamon, nutmeg, or any other spice to taste. Cool until set.[24]

GEN. SILAS CASEY'S DRIED APPLES

Stew sliced apples in water until soft. Then drain and add $^1/_4$ teaspoon of ginger and/or clove. The same can be done with peaches, making "desirable articles."[25]

MRS. CORNELIUS'S CODDLED APPLES

Place a $^1/_2$ peck of peeled and quartered apples in a kettle containing a $^1/_2$ pint of water. Add $^3/_4$ cup of brown sugar, cover, and bring to a low boil. Simmer until the apples are tender.[26]

MRS. HASKELL'S GRIDDLE CAKES WITHOUT EGGS

Dissolve 1 teaspoon of baking soda in 1 pint of milk, adding 1 heaping teaspoon of salt. Sift 2 teaspoons of cream of tartar with 1 pint of flour, and then mix in 1 pint of milk, stirring well until the batter is smooth. Mix with the milk and soda, pour onto a griddle, and bake immediately, turning once, until browned on both sides.[27]

CRULLERS

Mix 2 pounds of flour, $^3/_4$ pound of sugar, a $^1/_2$ pound of softened butter, nine eggs, 1 teaspoon of mace, and 1 tablespoon of rose water. Beat until the batter is smooth, and then drop by tablespoonfuls into a skillet of hot butter or lard. Fry until golden brown. Remove and drain.[28]

SOUR CREAM SAUCE

Mix 1 cup of sugar and $1^1/_2$ cups of thick sour cream. Beat for 5 minutes, and then dust grated nutmeg over it. Serve on cornmeal puddings or boiled suet puddings.[29]

A PLAINER SAUCE

Mix 3 tablespoons of brown sugar with $1^1/2$ tablespoons of melted butter and a $^1/2$ tablespoon of flour. Stir until smooth. Then pour in a $^1/2$ cup of boiling water. Bring to a boil; then remove quickly, adding a $^1/2$ teaspoon of rose water, lemon juice, or other flavoring.[30]

ELEGANT PUDDING SAUCE

Add 4 tablespoons of granulated sugar and 1 tablespoon of flour to 2 tablespoons of melted butter, and stir until creamy. Beat one egg white until stiff, and fold it into the sauce. Then pour in a $^1/2$ cup of boiling water, stirring rapidly. Stir in a little extract of lemon or vanilla or $^1/4$ teaspoon of grated spice to taste, and pour over a baked pudding.[31]

PHOEBE PEMBER'S CONFEDERATE JELLY

Add one box of plain gelatin to 1 pint of cold water, and let sit for 1 hour. Then add 3 tablespoons of citric acid, $1^3/4$ pounds of granulated sugar, 1 pint of whiskey, a $^1/2$ cup of brandy, and $3^1/2$ cups of boiling water. Stir and strain. Then refrigerate or set in a cool place for several hours or overnight; and allow to set.[32]

TRYPHENA FOX'S LOUISIANA PUMPKIN PRESERVES

Clean and cut up a medium-size pumpkin and boil in water for 3 hours or until soft. Make a thin syrup of 2 cups of sugar and 4 cups of water, and bring to a boil. Place the cooked pumpkin in it, and continue to boil, occasionally skimming the top until scum no longer rises and the pumpkin is very tender. Remove and skin the pumpkin, cutting it into 1-inch cubes. Meanwhile, boil the syrup until it is reduced and thick. Place the pumpkin cubes in a crock or canning jar, add a little vanilla or lemon extract to the syrup, and pour the hot syrup over the pumpkin, sealing the container. Serve hot or cold.[33]

TEA ICE CREAM

Put 2 tablespoonfuls of tea leaves in a pot, pour on enough boiling water to cover, and let them steep for a $^1/2$ hour. Stir into 1 quart of sweet cream the beaten yolks of eight eggs. Simmer slowly over moderate heat until the mixture becomes thick. Strain the tea and stir it into the cream; then cool and freeze.[34]

ICE CREAM

Beat together two eggs and 6 ounces of granulated white sugar. Bring 1 quart of milk to a boil; then immediately reduce the heat and stir in 3 teaspoons of arrowroot that has been dissolved in a few teaspoons of the milk. Remove from heat, adding immediately the eggs and sugar; at the same time, stir briskly to prevent the eggs from cooking. Then set aside to cool completely. Boil one vanilla bean in 1 cup of water for 1 hour or more, or until the water is reduced by at least half. Then remove the bean and add sugar, stirring as it boils, until a thick, clear syrup forms. Remove from heat and allow to cool completely, adding to the ice cream mixture just before placing it in the freezer.[35]

PINEAPPLE ICE CREAM

Core and skin one pineapple; then mince it very small and place in a dish, pouring 1 pound of white granulated sugar over it. Cover and let stand for 3 hours; then strain through a sieve, being sure to mash out all the juice from the fruit. Gradually stir the juice into 1 quart of sweet cream, beating vigorously, and then place in the freezer.[36]

MRS. HASKELL'S CANDY SYRUP

Dissolve 2 pounds of granulated sugar in 1 pint of cold water, add an egg white and beat the mixture well. Put over heat, and bring to a boil. Remove immediately, and skim material from the surface. Then bring to a boil again, repeating the skimming and boiling process until no more material forms on the top and the syrup is reduced by about one-third. Pour onto a cold surface in teaspoonfuls, and allow to cool and harden.[37]

MRS. HASKELL'S 1863 MOLASSES CANDY

Bring 1 quart of molasses slowly to a boil, and continue boiling until 1 teaspoon of it dropped in cold water becomes brittle and cracks when bent. Grease a flat baking sheet, and pour the candy onto it. Allow to cool. When it is lukewarm and easily handled, pick it up and pull it by hand, folding it over on itself and pulling again. Repeat until the candy turns white. Pull and roll into ropes, and cut into bite-size pieces.[38]

MRS. HASKELL'S 1863 MAPLE SUGAR TAFFY

In 2 cups of water in a saucepan, add and dissolve 5 pounds of maple sugar and a $1/2$ ounce of cream of tartar. Bring to a boil, remove from heat, and skim the scum from the surface. Then bring again to a boil, and repeat this process until no more scum is produced. Bring again to a boil, stirring steadily, and continue until a teaspoon of the syrup dropped into cold water turns hard and brittle. Pour onto greased flat pans, and cool by setting on ice or on cold water. As soon as it can be comfortably handled by hand, lift and pull the taffy, folding it over on itself and repeatedly pulling and stretching until it turns white. Then twist or roll it into small ropes, and break or cut it into pieces.[39]

BEVERAGES

CAPTAIN SANDERSON'S COMMISSARY COFFEE

Roast green coffee beans over a moderate heat, taking care not to burn them, until they are brown. Let them cool, and then grind them into grounds (or simply use purchased coffee grounds). Fill a coffee boiler or pot with clean, fresh water, and bring to a boil over high heat. Add coffee grounds in the normal proportion of grounds to water, and boil briskly for 2 minutes. Immediately add 1 cup of cold water, remove from heat, and let stand for 5 minutes. Pour it through a flannel or muslin cloth—or a fine mesh strainer—to separate from the grounds, and serve.[1]

MERCURY RYE COFFEE

Take rye, boil it, but not so much as to burst the grain; then dry it, either in the sun, on the stove, or in a kiln, after which it is ready for parching. Then grind like the real coffee bean.[2]

YORKVILLE CHINQUAPIN COFFEE

Boil chinquapin nuts, dry thoroughly, and roast until very hard. Grind and brew as with regular coffee.[3]

CONFEDERATE BAPTIST POTATO AND PERSIMMON COFFEE

Boil persimmons and then sieve the fruit to save the seeds. Wash, dry, and roast the seeds; then grind. Meanwhile, dry potatoes thoroughly, roast until hard, and grind. Mix two parts potato grounds to one part persimmon grounds, and brew coffee.[4]

GEORGIA CANE SEED COFFEE

If sugarcane seed can be obtained, dry it, roast and parch, and grind as coffee beans. It requires longer brewing than regular coffee to make a proper drink.[5]

GEORGIA *REPUBLICAN* PEA COFFEE

Take dried peas and roast until they turn a cinnamon brown. Crush and grind as with coffee beans and brew.[6]

PICAYUNE "INSTANT" COFFEE

Bake or roast brown sugar until it is completely black, and then add hot water until it forms a thick syrup. Place 5 tablespoons of syrup in the coffee pot, and then put 1 tablespoon of real coffee grounds in the percolator or "dripper" basket. Pour boiling water through the coffee grounds and into the syrup. The syrup will keep for some time and can be turned into coffee by mixing 1 tablespoon of syrup into boiling water.[7]

GEORGIA *FIELD AND FIRESIDE* GRAPE COFFEE

Boil grape seeds, and then dry and roast. Crush and use as with coffee grounds.[8]

SUMTER *WATCHMAN* COFFEE

Coffee can be stretched by mixing 1 spoonful of regular coffee grounds with an equal amount of toasted cornmeal. Percolate or boil, and strain as with coffee.[9]

LAURENSVILLE BEET COFFEE

Dice freshly washed and peeled beets, and toast them until thoroughly dry but not burned. Grind in a mill, and then put $1^{1}/_{2}$ cups in 1 gallon of water with one egg, stir to mix thoroughly, and bring to a boil. Serve with cream and sugar.[10]

CONFEDERATE COFFEE

Gather 1 quart of ripe acorns, wash and dry them, then bake them until the shells open. Roast the kernels in a little bacon fat, and then grind and use to brew a drink.[11]

CONFEDERATE CREAM SUBSTITUTE

Beat one egg white, and then mix into it 1 tablespoon of soft butter. Place in a cup and slowly pour coffee into the cup, taking care not to do it so fast as to curdle the egg.[12]

YANKEE "INSTANT" COFFEE SYRUP

Take a $^1/_2$ pound of ground coffee, and boil in 3 quarts of water until the quantity is reduced to 1 quart. Strain until all grounds are removed, and then put in a clean pan and boil again, gradually adding granulated sugar until it forms a thick syrup the consistency of molasses. Allow to cool, and then seal tightly in bottles. To make "instant" coffee, place 2 teaspoons of the syrup in a coffee cup and fill with boiling water.[13]

MRS. HASKELL'S 1861 MOCK COFFEE CREAM

Bring 1 quart of milk to a simmer, and then add 1 teaspoon of flour dissolved into a little milk. Allow $1^1/_2$ teaspoons of butter to melt in the milk, and then bring to a boil while stirring constantly for 5 minutes. Remove from heat, and continue beating. Then add two well-beaten eggs, mix and strain through a fine sieve, and beat once more until frothy and light. Add to coffee as one would cream.[14]

KATE CUMMING'S CORINTH HOSPITAL MILK SUBSTITUTE

Mix powdered arrowroot and water to the consistency of milk, and heat to a simmer. Add one beaten egg to each quart, and stir in while hot; then add 1 teaspoon of wine or citrus preserves. Let cool and drink.[15]

GERMAN CHOCOLATE

In a double boiler, melt 4 tablespoons of grated chocolate, and then gradually add 2 quarts of milk. Beat four egg whites and two yolks until light and frothy, and pour in a $^1/_2$ cup of cold milk. Beat this well, and then add 1 cup of the heated chocolate while beating. Remove the rest of the chocolate from heat, and gradually pour the egg mixture into it, stirring constantly. Dust with nutmeg or cinnamon and a bit of vanilla, and add sugar to taste.[16]

CARBONATED SYRUP WATER

In a standard drinking glass, pour $^1/_4$ cup of unsweeted syrup of lemon, raspberry, strawberry, pineapple, or other citric fruit. Fill the glass half full with ice water, and add a $^1/_2$ teaspoon of soda bicarbonate and stir. Drink while foaming.[17]

1862 LEMONADE

Slice three lemons and place in a pitcher or bowl. Pour a $^1/_2$ pound of granulated white or brown sugar over the fruit, and mash it together. Then pour in 1 gallon of water. Stir well.[18]

CONFEDERATE HOSPITAL LEMONADE

Squeeze the juice from one large lemon, and add to 2 pints of water. Stir in $1^1/_2$ ounces of sugar.[19]

CONFEDERATE HOSPITAL BARLEY WATER

In 5 pints of water, mix 2 ounces of sugar and 2 ounces of very finely ground barley.[20]

CONFEDERATE HOSPITAL RICE WATER

In 5 pints of water, combine 2 ounces of sugar and 2 ounces of finely ground rice flour.[21]

CONFEDERATE GINGER BEER

In a 4-quart pot, combine 1 pint of molasses and 2 spoonfuls of ground ginger. Add 2 quarts of boiling water and stir. Then add 2 quarts of cold water. Add 1 pint of liquid yeast when the beer has cooled to lukewarm. Cover and store in a warm place overnight, and then bottle.[22]

MRS. CORNELIUS'S 1863 GINGER BEER

Boil 4 quarts of water, and pour over $1^1/_2$ ounces of grated ginger root, 1 ounce of cream of tartar, 1 pound of brown sugar, and 2 thinly sliced lemons. Mix in 1 cup of liquefied yeast, and let stand for 24 hours. Then strain and bottle. It will be at its best after a few weeks.[23]

CONFEDERATE SPRUCE BEER

Heat 3 gallons of water to about 100°, and add 3 cups of molasses, 1 tablespoon of ground ginger, and 1 tablespoon of spruce essence made by boiling a $^1/_2$ pound of spruce needles in 1 quart of water. Add a $^1/_2$ cup of liquid yeast, let stand overnight, and bottle. In another day, it will be ready to drink.[24]

CONFEDERATE WINE

Into 4 gallons of water, mix 20 pounds of sugar and 1 gallon of sour orange juice. Beat two egg whites and stir into the liquid. Bring to a boil for 10 minutes, and skim any scum from the surface. Then strain through a flannel or other porous cloth. Stir in 1 quart of sour orange juice. Pour into a large jug or crock, and cover. Store in a cool place and allow to ferment for 5 or 6 months, then strain, bottle, and seal.[25]

FISH HOUSE PUNCH

In a punch bowl, combine 1/4 pint of brandy, a 1/2 pint of cognac, 1/4 pint dark rum, 1/3 pint of lemon juice, 3/4 pound of granulated sugar, and 2 1/2 pints of cold water. Stir thoroughly until the sugar dissolves, and serve.[26]

APPLE PUNCH

Cover the bottom of a large bowl with a layer of sliced apples. Top that with powdered sugar and then a layer of lemons covered with sugar. Alternate until the bowl is half full. Then pour a bottle of red wine over the fruit, cover, and let sit for 6 hours. Strain and drink.[27]

SPREAD EAGLE PUNCH

Combine one bottle of Islay Scotch whiskey and one bottle of rye whiskey. Mix in the grated peel of two lemons and 1 pound of granulated sugar. Stir in 1 pint of boiling water and drink.[28]

CHAMPAGNE PUNCH

In a large punch bowl, combine 1 quart of champagne, 1/4 pound of sugar, one orange slice, the juice of one lemon, three slices of pineapple, and a 1/2 cup of raspberry or strawberry syrup. Mix thoroughly to dissolve the sugar and serve.[29]

HOT BRANDY AND RUM PUNCH

Take 1 pound of sugar cubes and rub them over the skin of four lemons until the cubes have absorbed the zest; then put the cubes in a punch bowl. Pour in 3 quarts of boiling water, and stir until the sugar dissolves. Then stir in 1 quart of dark rum, 1 quart of cognac, and 1 teaspoon of nutmeg, and serve.[30]

SANTA CRUZ RUM FIX

Fill a glass two-thirds full of crushed ice, and then pour in a $^1/_2$ cup of dark rum, $^1/_4$ cup of water, 1 teaspoon of sugar, and one-fourth of a lemon. Stir and garnish the rim with other fruit slices.[31]

GIN AND PINE

Split a piece of the heart of a green pine log into fine splints, about the size of a cedar lead pencil. Take 2 ounces of the same, and put into a 1-quart decanter. Fill the decanter with gin. Let the pine soak for 2 hours, and the gin will be ready to serve.[32]

BRANDY TODDY

In a small glass, combine a $^1/_2$ cup of brandy, a $^1/_2$ cup of cold water, and 1 teaspoon of sugar. Add a lump of ice, or for a hot toddy, use boiling water instead of cold water, and do not add the ice.[33]

SAILOR'S GROG

Mix two parts of whiskey or dark rum to 1 part of water.

PINE-TOP WHISKEY

Confederates fermented pine boughs to distill homemade whiskey. This can be approximated by boiling a $^1/_2$ pound of pine needles in 1 quart of water for a $^1/_2$ hour and then adding the strained liquid to pure grain alcohol at a ratio of one part pine juice to six parts alcohol. It does not taste very good.

GEN. JUBAL EARLY'S STONE WALL

Fill a large schooner glass with cracked ice. Pour over the ice 1 tablespoon of sugar and, over that, a double shot of bourbon whiskey. Fill the glass to within $1^1/_2$ inches of the top with hard cider, and then pour on top a $^1/_2$ inch of Virginia Concord grape wine. According to Bvt. Brig. Gen. Edward B. Grubb, who shared one with Early in 1870, "when I awoke the next morning, I had a headache so severe that I spent 75 cents for relief at a drug store and then had reminiscences of it during the day."[34]

GEN. SIMON BUCKNER'S MINT JULEP

Pound or crush ice into tiny pebble-size bits. Place a heaping teaspoon of granulated sugar in the bottom of a silver tumbler, and pour in enough spring water to cover. Add 1 slightly crushed mint leaf. Fill the tumbler one-fourth full of Kentucky bourbon, and then fill to the rim with the ice, while sprinkling in a little sugar at the same time. Place one or two three-inch sprigs of mint in the tumbler, and then with a spoon, gently stir the contents until a frost forms on the outside of the tumbler.[35]

GEORGE VENNIGARHOLTZ'S NATCHEZ MINT JULEP

Fill a glass tumbler to the brim with cracked ice. Dust 1 tablespoon of sugar over the ice, lay three mint leaves on top, and pour over the sugar and mint equal parts of cognac, Jamaica rum, and port.[36]

BRANDY MINT JULEP

Dissolve 1 tablespoon of white pulverized sugar in $2^1/_2$ tablespoons of water. Take two sprigs of fresh mint, press them well into the sugar water, until the flavor of mint is extracted, and pour into a tumbler. Add $^3/_4$ cup of cognac, and then fill the glass with fine-shaved ice. Garnish the top of the glass with mint leaves, strawberries or raspberries, and a slice of orange, and put a dash of Jamaica rum on top. Sprinkle with white sugar.[37]

1862 APPLE TODDY

Fill a glass two-thirds full with boiling water. Add 1 tablespoon of confectioners' sugar, half of a baked apple cut into small pieces, and a $^1/_4$ cup of hard apple cider. Sprinkle nutmeg on top.[38]

1862 BRANDY SOUR

Fill a glass two-thirds full of shaved ice. Pour over it $^1/_4$ cup of brandy, $^1/_8$ cup of water, the juice from one-fourth of a lemon, and 1 tablespoon of sugar. Stir.[39]

SANGAREE

Fill a small glass two-thirds full of shaved ice. Dissolve 1 teaspoon of sugar in $^1/_4$ cup of water. Then pour into the glass along, with a $^1/_2$ cup of wine, brandy, gin, port, or sherry. Shake well. Strain the liquid into a small glass, and sprinkle a little nutmeg on top. May also be garnished with a slice of lemon or pineapple.[40]

BRANDY SHRUB

In a 5-quart bowl, add 2 quarts of brandy to juice from five lemons and the grated zest from two lemons. Cover, and let sit for 3 days. Then add 1 quart of sherry and 2 pounds of granulated sugar. Strain and serve.[41]

RUM FLIP

Warm 1 quart of ale over a fire. Beat four eggs, and add 4 ounces of sugar moistened in as little water as will make a paste, 1 teaspoon of ground nutmeg or ginger, and 1 gill of rum or brandy. Mix well. Then add to the hot ale, and rapidly pour it back and forth between 2 pitchers until smooth and creamy.[42]

WHISKEY COBBLER

Into a glass filled with ice, pour 1 cup of whiskey, 1 tablespoon of sugar, and two or three slices of orange. Shake well and drink.[43]

TALLY SIMPSON'S 3RD SOUTH CAROLINA EGGNOG

Separate 1 dozen eggs, and beat whites and yolks separately. Then for each egg, mix 3/4 cup of rum or whiskey and the same amount of boiling water with 1 tablespoon of molasses. Mix thoroughly; then stir in the beaten eggs, stirring constantly to prevent curdling. Then stir in 3/4 cup of milk, and serve.[44]

GEN. WILLIAM HENRY HARRISON'S "OLD TIPPECANOE" EGGNOG

Combine one beaten egg, 1 1/2 teaspoons of granulated sugar, and two or three small ice cubes in a large glass. Fill it with hard cider, and shake well.[45]

NOTES

INTRODUCTION

1. Stephen Sears, ed., *Mr. Dunn Browne's Experiences in the Army: The Civil War Letters of Samuel W. Fiske* (New York: 1998), 178.
2. Amos Breneman to My dear friend, April 26, 1865, Amos Breneman Papers, Civil War Miscellaneous Collection, United States Army Military History Institute, Carlisle Barracks, PA (hereafter USAMHI).
3. Alfred J. Bollet, *Civil War Medicine: Challenges and Triumphs* (Tucson, AZ: 2002), 358.
4. "Cooking the Hell Broth," *The Old Guard* II (June 1864), 140.
5. Richmond *Examiner*, October 1, 1863.

CHAPTER ONE: SKIM, SIMMER, AND SCOUR

1. James P. Jones and William Warren Rogers, eds., "Montgomery as the Confederate Capital: View of a Nation," *Alabama Historical Quarterly* 23 (Spring 1964), 78–79.
2. Ibid., 79–80.
3. United States War Department, *General Regulations for the Army* (Washington, D.C.: United States War Department, 1825), as quoted in Barbara K. Luecke, *Feeding the Frontier Army 1775–1865* (Eagan, MN: 1990), 109.
4. Ibid., 108.
5. Jones and Rogers, "Montgomery," 113–14.
6. Spencer Talley Memoir, 1918, in possession of Frances Martin, Lebanon, Tennessee.

7. William Dennison to Thomas A. Scott, October 10, 1861; W. H. Clement to Scott, October 11, 1861; D. E. Wade to Dennison, October 5, 1861; T. H. Smith et al. to Dennison, October 5, 1861, Records of the Office of the Quartermaster General, Entry 225, Quartermaster's Consolidated Correspondence File, Correspondence of J. M. Sanderson and W. S. Chapman concerning Army Cooking, Record Group 92, National Archives, Washington, D.C. (hereafter cited as NA).

8. James M. Sanderson to Military Affairs Committee, July 22, 1861, Entry 224, Record Group 92, NA.

9. Edwin D. Morgan endorsement on Sanderson to Military Affairs Committee, July 22, 1861; Elisha Harris endorsement, July 22, 1861; J. F. Callum to Simon Cameron, July 24, 1861, Entry 225, Record Group 92, NA.

10. James M. Sanderson, *Camp Fires and Camp Cooking; or Culinary Hints for the Soldier: Including Receipt for Making Bread in the "Portable Field Oven" Furnished by the Subsistence Department* (Washington, D.C.: 1862), 1.

11. Ibid., 1–3.

12. Ibid., 5, 6, 7, 10, 11, 13.

13. Circular, November 19, 1862, Entry 714, General Orders, Provisional Brigades and Mobile Units in the Department of Washington and 22d Army Corps, Record Group 393, Records of U.S. Army Continental Commands, Part 2, NA.

14. United States War Department, *Manual for Army Cooks* (Washington, D.C.: United States War Department, 1879), 3–9, 160, 166–67, and passim.

CHAPTER 2: EVERY FELLOW FOR HIMSELF

1. Wilbur Fisk, *Anti-Rebel: The Civil War Letters of Wilbur Fisk* (Croton-on-Hudson, NY: 1983), 3.

2. Ibid., 10.

3. James I. Robertson, Jr., *Soldiers Blue and Gray* (Columbia, SC: 1988), 65.

4. William Richardson to parents, February 22, 1862, Gordon C. Jones, ed., *"For My Country": The Richardson Letters* (Wendell, NC: 1984), 35.

5. Lawrence VanAlstyne, *Diary of an Enlisted Man* (New Haven, CT: 1910), 31.

6. William E. Coleman to parents, January 19, 1862, Coleman Family Papers in possession of R. E. Coleman, Decatur, GA.

7. John D. Billings, *Hard Tack and Coffee* (Boston: 1887), 133.

8. William Richardson to parents, March 18, 1863, Jones, *Richardson Letters*, 90–91.

9. VanAlstyne, *Diary*, 29–31.

10. Fisk, *Anti-Rebel*, 10.

11. David Donald, ed., *Gone for a Soldier: The Civil War Memoirs of Private Alfred Bellard* (Boston: 1975), 119.

12. Robertson, *Soldiers*, 65.
13. Charles E. Davis, *Three Years in the Army: The Story of the Thirteenth Massachusetts Volunteers from July 16, 1861, to August 1, 1864* (Boston: 1894), 98–99.
14. William Richardson to parents, January 28, 1862, Jones, *Richardson Letters*, 30.
15. Ibid., 68.
16. "The Haversack," *Land We Love* II (March 1867), 369.
17. Fisk, *Anti-Rebel*, 32.
18. Ibid., 93.
19. Donald, *Gone for a Soldier*, 120.
20. Susan W. Benson, ed., *Berry Benson's Civil War Book* (Athens, GA: 1992), 53–54.
21. Billings, *Hard Tack*, 136.
22. Ibid., 136–37.
23. Patricia B. Mitchell, *Union Army Camp Cooking* (Chatham, VA: 1990), 25.
24. New York, *Harper's Weekly Illustrated Newspaper*, April 18, 1863.
25. Spencer Talley Memoir, 16.
26. "Query Box," *Southern Bivouac* I (October 1882), 80–81.
27. Harold A. Small, ed., *The Road to Richmond: The Civil War Memoirs of Major Abner R. Small of the 16th Maine Volunteers* (Berkeley, CA: 1939), 197–98.
28. Davis, *Three Years*, 99–100.
29. Billings, *Hard Tack*, 138–39.
30. United States War Department, *War of the Rebellion: Official Records of the Union and Confederate Armies* (Washington, D.C.: United States War Department, 1880–1901), Series I, Vol. 14, 351 (hereafter cited as *Official Records*, I, 14, etc.).
31. Bollet, *Civil War Medicine*, 337.
32. W. O. Dodd, "Recollections of Vicksburg during the Siege," *Southern Bivouac* I (September 1882), 5–6.
33. Billings, *Hard Tack*, 133.
34. Ibid., 131.
35. Ibid., 135–36.
36. Ibid., 134–35.
37. "Query Box," 80–81.
38. Linn Tanner, "The Meat Diet at Port Hudson," *Confederate Veteran* XXVI (November 1918), 484.
39. Dodd, "Recollections of Vicksburg during the Siege," 6.
40. Clarence Poe, ed., *True Tales of the South at War* (Chapel Hill, NC: 1961), 88.
41. Patricia B. Mitchell, *Civil War Celebrations* (Chatham, VA: 1998), 8–9.
42. Benson, *Berry Benson*, 36.
43. Robertson, *Soldiers*, 72.
44. Ibid., 66–67.

45. VanAlstyne, *Diary*, 327, 331.

46. John W. Haley, *The Rebel Yell & the Yankee Hurrah: The Civil War Journal of a Maine Volunteer* (Camden, ME: 1985), 276.

47. Donald, *Gone for a Soldier*, 122.

48. Haley, *Rebel Yell*, 276.

49. Donald, *Gone for a Soldier*, 122.

50. Fisk, *Anti-Rebel*, 32.

51. "Query Box," 80–81.

52. Benson, *Berry Benson*, 50.

53. William C. Davis, ed., *Diary of a Confederate Soldier, John S. Jackman of the Orphan Brigade* (Columbia, SC: 1990), 83.

54. Billings, *Hard Tack*, 110.

55. Robertson, *Soldiers*, 65.

56. Robert K. Krick to the author, September 17, 2002.

57. Fisk, *Anti-Rebel*, 32.

58. Robertson, *Soldiers*, 66.

59. Donald, *Gone for a Soldier*, 119.

60. Billings, *Hard Tack*, 112.

61. Sears, *Experiences*, 23–26.

62. Nelson D. Lankford, ed., *An Irishman in Dixie: Thomas Conolly's Diary of the Fall of the Confederacy* (Columbia, SC: 1988), 55–56.

63. Benson, *Berry Benson*, 50.

64. A. P. Ford, "Service on the Carolina Coast," *Southern Bivouac*, New Series, I (November 1885), 325.

65. Dayton E. Flint to his sister, February 1, 1863, Dayton E. Flint Letters, Civil War Miscellaneous Collection, USAMHI.

CHAPTER THREE: HARD CRACKERS, COME AGAIN NO MORE

1. Quoted in Bruce Catton, *American Heritage Picture History of the Civil War* (New York, 1960), 492.

2. Sanderson, *Camp Fires and Camp Cooking*, 12.

3. James F. Preston to Jackson, June 4, 1861, with endorsement by Jackson, Joseph Rubenfine List 69, "C.S.A." (Pleasantville, NJ, n.d.), item 41.

4. Benson, *Berry Benson*, 14–15.

5. Ibid., 80.

6. "Query Box," 80–81.

7. Patricia B. Mitchell, *Cooking for the Cause* (Chatham, VA: 1988), 10.

8. Robertson, *Soldiers*, 68.

9. *Confederate Receipt Book: A Compilation of over One Hundred Receipts, Adapted to the Times* (Richmond, VA: 1863), 16.

10. Benson, *Berry Benson*, 30.

11. Dodd, "Recollections of Vicksburg during the Siege," 5–6.

12. Harold E. Simon, "As I Cannot Get Letter I Must Drink Whiskey, Brandy," *Confederate Philatelist* XXIV (March-April 1979), 61.

13. "Query Box," 80–81.

14. Robertson, *Soldiers*, 70; Benson, *Berry Benson*, 13.

15. Mitchell, *Cooking*, 16.

16. Ibid., 12–14.

17. *Bread and Bread Making* (Washington, D.C.: 1864), 1, Entry 225, Records of the Quartermaster General, Box 84, Record Group 92, NA.

18. Ibid., 2, 4, 5, 40, 43, 46.

19. Ibid., 5–10, 44.

20. Ibid., 10–14.

21. Ibid., 16–18, 23.

22. Ibid., 24–34.

23. Ibid., 35–39.

24. Ibid., 49.

25. Alvin Voris to his wife, November 29, 1862, Alan Johnson Collection, Akron, OH.

26. Dayton E. Flint to his sister, February 1, 1863, Civil War Miscellaneous Collection, USAMHI.

27. Robertson, *Soldiers*, 68–69.

28. Catton, *Civil War*, 385.

29. "Hardtack Anyone?" Roanoke Civil War Round Table, *Civil War Dispatch* (September 2000), 7

30. J. J. Scroggs, "How Hardtack Was Made," *Civil War Times Illustrated* XI (October 1972), 34.

31. Henry Clay Trumbull, *War Memories of an Army Chaplain* (New York: 1898), 52–53.

32. Robertson, *Soldiers*, 69.

33. Ibid., 69.

34. Voris to wife, March 2, 1862, Johnson Collection.

35. Fisk, *Anti-Rebel*, 10.

36. Haley, *Rebel Yell*, 276.

37. Fisk, *Anti-Rebel*, 88.

38. Billings, *Hard Tack*, 117.

39. Robertson, *Soldiers*, 69.

40. Ibid., 68.

41. Billings, *Hard Tack*, 118–19.

CHAPTER FOUR: VISIONS OF FAT AND SAVORY BEEFSTEAKS

1. Sears, *Experiences*, 178.
2. *Official Records*, III, 1, 399.
3. Fisk, *Anti-Rebel*, 89.
4. United States War Department, *Revised Regulations of the Army, 1861* (Washington, D.C.: United States War Department, 1861), 243.
5. *Official Records*, I, 5, 835–36.
6. Bell I. Wiley, *The Life of Billy Yank* (Indianapolis: 1952), 224.
7. William A. Richardson to his parents, October 19, 1861, Jones, *Richardson Letters*, 13.
8. William Richardson to parents, December 1, 1861, Jones, *Richardson Letters*, 21.
9. William Richardson to parents, July 7, 1862, Jones, *Richardson Letters*, 51.
10. G. S. Bradley, *The Star Corps; or, Notes of an Army Chaplain* (Milwaukee: 1865), 274–76.
11. Catton, *Civil War*, 373.
12. Voris to wife, December 14, 1862, Johnson Collection.
13. Voris to wife, June 7, 1862, Johnson Collection.
14. Voris to wife, February 14, 1863, Johnson Collection.
15. Voris to wife, March 13, 1862, Johnson Collection.
16. William Richardson to parents, November 13, 1862, Jones, *Richardson Letters*, 73–74.
17. Poe, *True Tales*, 72.
18. "The Haversack," *Land We Love* IV (December 1867), 164.
19. Poe, *True Tales*, 72.
20. Voris to wife, June 7, 1862, Johnson Collection.
21. William E. Coleman to his parents, January 19, 1862, Coleman Family Papers.
22. William Richardson to parents, August 23, 1863, Jones, *Richardson Letters*, 126.
23. Fisk, *Anti-Rebel*, 131–32.
24. Shelby Foote, *The Civil War: A Narrative* (New York: 1958), II, 383.
25. Fisk, *Anti-Rebel*, 27.
26. Catton, *Civil War*, 373.
27. Voris to wife, June 30, 1862, Johnson Collection.
28. Mitchell, *Union Army Camp Cooking*, 10–11.
29. Sears, *Experiences*, 5.
30. Haley, *Rebel Yell*, 188.
31. Voris to wife, February 10, 1863, Johnson Collection.
32. Voris to wife, June 16, 1863, Johnson Collection.
33. Voris to wife, February 14, 1863, Johnson Collection.
34. Sears, *Experiences*, 12.
35. "Coffee-Boiler Rangers," *Southern Bivouac* I (July 1883), 442–43.

36. "Heel and Toe," *Southern Bivouac* I (February 1883), 258.

37. "The Haversack," *Land We Love* II (March 1867), 377.

38. *Official Records*, I, 25, part 2, 730.

39. Robert K. Krick to author, September 17, 2002.

40. *Official Records*, I, 25, part 2, 687; Clifford Dowdey, ed., *The Wartime Papers of Robert E. Lee* (Boston: 1961), 418.

41. "A Southern Woman's Letter," *Southern Bivouac* I (November 1882), 115.

43. Mitchell, *Union Army Camp Cooking*, 32.

43. Catton, *Civil War*, 373.

44. *Official Records*, I, 38, part 2, 695.

45. "The Haversack," *Land We Love* VI (April 1869), 488.

46. John O. Casler, *Four Years in the Stonewall Brigade* (Marietta, GA: 1951), 78.

47. "The Haversack," *Land We Love* IV (December 1867), 163.

48. "Beef Seekers," *Southern Bivouac* I (October 1882), 70–72.

49. "The Haversack," *Land We Love* V (August 1868), 359.

50. "High Price for Needles and Thread," *Southern Bivouac* III (January 1885), 237.

51. "The Haversack," *Land We Love* II (March 1867), 373.

52. Benson, *Berry Benson*, 36.

53. James O. Morehead, ed., *History of Bland County* (Radford, VA: 1961), 256.

54. Fisk, *Anti-Rebel*, 164.

55. Ibid., 122.

56. Sears, *Experiences*, 247–48.

57. Billings, *Hard Tack*, 112.

58. Sears, *Experiences*, 3.

59. William Richardson to parents, October 28, 1861, Jones, *Richardson Letters*, 15.

60. Fisk, *Anti-Rebel*, 164.

61. Ibid., 165.

62. Sears, *Experiences*, 183, 199.

63. Virginia Matzke Adams, ed., *On the Altar of Freedom: A Black Soldier's Civil War Letters from the Front* (Amherst, MA: 1991), 17.

64. Benson, *Berry Benson*, 50.

65. Ibid., 18–19.

66. Maud Carter Clement, *War Recollections of Confederate Veterans of Pittsylvania County* (Chatham, VA: 1892), 25–26.

67. "The Haversack," *Land We Love* III (September 1867), 425.

68. Catton, *Civil War*, 216.

69. Davis, *Diary of a Confederate Soldier*, 162.

70. Fisk, *Anti-Rebel*, 152.

71. Davis, *Diary of a Confederate Soldier*, 46.

72. Fisk, *Anti-Rebel*, 113.

73. Poe, *True Tales*, 130.

74. Benson, *Berry Benson*, 18–19.

75. Clement, *Recollections*, 61–63.

76. "The Last Ration," *Southern Bivouac* I (January 1883), 217–18.

CHAPTER FIVE: THE GREAT TROUBLE ABOUT HOSPITALS

1. Joseph J. Woodward, *The Hospital Steward's Manual* (Philadelphia, 1862), 183, 191, 197.

2. Barbara Haber, *From Hardtack to Home Fries: An Uncommon History of American Cooks and Meals* (New York: 2002), 52–53.

3. Florence Nightingale, *Notes on Nursing and Notes on Hospitals* (London: 1859), 11.

4. A. Wittenmyer, *A Collection of Recipes for the Use of Special Diet Kitchens in Military Hospitals* (Mattituck, NY: 1864), 3 and passim.

5. Mary A. Livermore, *My Story of the War* (Hartford, CT: 1888), 490.

6. Ibid., 536.

7. Ibid., 207–8.

8. Ibid., 320, 324.

9. Haber, *Hardtack to Home Fries*, 50.

10. Ibid., 51–52.

11. Ibid., 57.

12. Livermore, *My Story*, 528.

13. George Richardson to parents, March 30, 1863, Jones, *Richardson Letters*, 93.

14. Fisk, *Anti-Rebel*, 45.

15. Bollet, *Civil War Medicine*, 372.

16. Joseph J. Woodward, *Outlines of the Chief Camp Diseases of the United States Armies* (Philadelphia: 1863), 186, 204.

17. Edmund Boemer file LL457, Record Group 153, Records of General Courts Martial, NA, Washington, D.C. (Hereafter, these records will be cited as Boemer file LL457, NA, etc.)

18. Robertson, *Soldiers*, 165.

19. Irwin Miller files nn3639 and nn361, NA.

20. Thomas Gillian file ii365, NA.

21. Livermore, *My Story*, 481.

22. Edward Mullen file 112080, NA.

23. Thomas P. Lowry and Jack D. Welsh, *Tarnished Scalpels: The Court-Martials of Fifty Union Surgeons* (Mechanicsburg, PA: 2000), 90–91, 100.

24. George Richardson to parents, December 8, 1863, Jones, *Richardson Letters*, 138.

25. Fisk, *Anti-Rebel*, 51.

26. Livermore, *My Story*, 683–84.

27. Walt Whitman, "Memoranda during the War," *Two Rivulets: Author's Edition*, on Major Authors on CD-ROM: Walt Whitman.

28. Diet Tables for Military Hospitals—Articles composing the Different Diets for a Day, Order Book, January–July 1864, Samuel Hollingsworth Stout Papers, Center for American History, University of Texas, Austin.

29. *Regulations for the Medical Department of the Confederate States Army* (Richmond, VA: 1863), 73–76.

30. Glenna R. Schroeder-Lein, *Confederate Hospitals on the Move: Samuel H. Stout and the Army of Tennessee* (Columbia, SC: 1994), 72–73.

31. Ibid., 112.

32. Richard B. Harwell, ed., *The Journal of Kate Cumming, A Confederate Nurse 1862–1865* (Athens, GA: 1975), 84.

33. Schroeder-Lein, *Confederate Hospitals*, 113.

34. Sam Watkins, *Co. Aytch, Maury Grays, First Tennessee Regiment* (New York: 1862; reprint), 187–88.

35. Talley Memoir, 32.

35. Davis, *Diary of a Confederate Soldier*, 143.

37. Harwell, *Cumming*, 84.

38. Schroeder-Lein, *Confederate Hospitals*, 88.

39. Haber, *Hardtack to Home Fries*, 40–41.

40. Bell I. Wiley, ed., *A Southern Woman's Story: Life in Confederate Richmond* (Jackson, TN: 1959), 29, 31.

41. Ibid., 86.

42. Ibid., 156.

43. Ibid., 125.

44. Ibid., 107.

45. Harwell, *Cumming*, 18.

46. Schroeder-Lein, *Confederate Hospitals*, 114.

47. Ibid., 111.

48. Harwell, *Cumming*, 74–76.

49. Wiley, *Southern Woman's Story*, 78.

50. Schroeder-Lein, *Confederate Hospitals*, 113–14.

51. Ibid., 103.

52. Ibid., 139.

53. Wiley, *Southern Woman's Story*, 83–84, 86.

54. Ibid., 69.

55. Davis, *Diary of a Confederate Soldier*, 150.

56. Jean V. Berlin, ed., *A Confederate Nurse: The Diary of Ada W. Bacot* (Columbia, SC: 1994), 171.

57. Edward B. Williams, ed., *Rebel Brothers: The Civil War Letters of the Truehearts* (College Station, TX: 1995), 69.

58. Kate Cumming, *Gleanings from Southland* (Birmingham, AL: 1895), 159.

59. Wiley, *Southern Woman's Story*, 176.

60. Violetta, "The Last Confederate Christmas," *Southern Bivouac* II (February 1884), 273–75.

61. Benson, *Berry Benson*, 43–44.

CHAPTER SIX: GETTING IN A PICKLE

1. Case file ii447; John Lucy files nn3567 and nn354, NA. Writing this chapter would have been impossible without the generosity of Thomas and Beverly Lowry, who have poured through more than 80,000 Union court-martial files in this record group and shared those involving food.

2. Victor Monier file mm1615; Edward Hubby file kk84; Walter Delastatius file mm3208, NA.

3. Joseph Delevan file kk312; Sherman Streeter file 111763; Charles F. Hill file nn159, folder 1; William H. Pool file 111554, folder 1, NA.

4. James Stinson file 113054; Johnson Owen file 111588, NA.

5. Andrew A. Braden file 112363; John Bay file 112363; Blinn Sweeting file 1126826, folder 2; Joseph Marshall file 112686, folder 1; Daniel Patterson file nn3311, NA.

6. Nathan Kotchland file kk664; James Downs file ii921; Lewellyn Dearing file ii537; Dennis Kelly file ii902, NA.

7. William Grant file kk610; Louis Williams file mm2103; Abram Franklin files mm1659 and oo368; Thomas Stockwell file kk80; Commodore P. Jackson file oo727, NA.

8. Untitled anecdote, *Southern Bivouac* I (December 1882), 147.

9. Charges and Specifications, October 31, 1861, Confederate States of America Records, Center for American History, University of Texas, Austin; Nelson Isham file 11160, NA.

10. H. T. Shaw file kk487; James P. Shallcross file nn3517, NA.

11. Haley, *Rebel Yell*, 96.

12. Thomas Coyne file oo739; James Woodsome files 00930 and mm2109; John Meigs file nn3003; Samuel E. Clark file mm2503, NA.

13. William Cane file oo566; George Flake file nn1697, NA.

14. Robert Taliaferro file nn81, folder 1a; Thomas Tewhoy file nn2072; William Bush file nn1770; Abraham Allen file oo135, NA.

15. Adam Serr file 111799; Thomas McEvoy file nn1955; Charles Wilson file 11589, folder 1, NA.

16. John Sullivan ii799; Smiley Craig file nn130, NA.

17. Joseph Mason file kk263; Alexander Plunkett file 112758; Reuben Shroat file 112719, NA.

18. James B. Roney file 1162; Henry J. Sherman file mm1602; John Williams file nn3852, NA.

19. Samuel C. Barr file 111161; Ruben Wilson file nn2497; Thomas Bentley file nn2529; Alfred Chapman file nn3641, NA.

20. William Wurster file kk437; Leopold Weishar file mm2628, folder 1; Edward Donohoe file ii378; Hermann Temps files 112691 and 112695, NA; Beverly Lowry to the author, n.d., c. 1997.

21. R. E. Looker files mm2387 and mm2; John Snow file mm297, NA.

22. Simon, "I Cannot Get Letter," 61.

23. W. H. Catlin, "An Incident at Long Bridge," *Confederate Philatelist* XXIII (March-April 1978), 40.

24. "Price's Commissary Department," *Southern Bivouac* III (February 1885), 262.

25. "What the Confederates Drank for Whiskey," *Southern Bivouac* I (July 1883), 441–42.

26. D. E. Henderson, "Confederate Moonshiners," *Southern Bivouac* III (April 1885), 347–48.

27. Edward Doherty file kk715; Benjamin R. Helmes file mm3373, NA.

28. George F. Blinn file kk594; John Spanhake files mm1537 and oo368, NA.

29. William P. Thompson file oo677; Thomas Hastie file 112602, folder 2; T. B. Williamson files mm1540 and nn36; George Kelley files mm1540 and nn35; Martin V. Vann file 111346, NA.

30. Thomas Flynn file 111465; William Loeb file mm1759, NA.

31. Charles Wakeman file k496; Frank Biliol file oo507, NA.

32. Whittier (first name not given) file kk417, NA.

33. Emanuel Faust file nn2567; Edward Davis file mm3559; Frederick Reimers file 2139; Amos Fielding file mm3131; James Lynch file oo926; George E. Weaver file ii622, NA.

34. Charles R. Call file nn3688; A. Zorne file 111626; John B. Williams file 111626; George Mackley files nn3181 and nn357; Thomas Jones file kk297; Peter Holder file i503; Benedict Emler file kk207, folder 1; John Chadwick file ii486, NA.

35. Talbot Williams file nn3064; George A. May file ii567, NA.

36. Archer C. Johnson file mm1802; Jasper Laster files mm1331 and nn14; William Dormody file 112; J. C. Blair file 112426, folder 1, NA.

37. Christopher Hyde file nn2877; J. S. Ruffin file mm2392; Henry E. Johnson file oo1150, NA.

CHAPTER SEVEN: HOW STRANGE A THING IT IS TO BE HUNGRY

1. "Louisville during the War," *Southern Bivouac* I (December 1882), 158.

2. Lonnie R. Speer, *Portals to Hell: Military Prisons of the Civil War* (Mechanicsburg, PA, 1997), 21–22.

3. Patricia B. Mitchell, *Yanks, Rebels, Rats, & Rations: Scratching for Food in Civil War Prison Camps* (Chatham, VA: 1993), 9.

4. George Levy, *To Die in Chicago: Confederate Prisoners at Camp Douglas, 1862–1865* (Evanston, IL: 1994), 52.

5. Edward T. Downer, "Johnson's Island," in William B. Hesseltine, ed., *Civil War Prisons* (Kent, OH: 1962), 102.

6. William Marvel, *Andersonville, The Last Depot* (Chapel Hill, NC: 1994), 80.

7. Michael Dougherty, *Diary of a Civil War Hero* (New York: 1960), 99.

8. Marvel, *Andersonville*, 80.

9. Levy, *Camp Douglas*, 154.

10. Hattie Lou Winslow and Joseph R. H. Moore, *Camp Morton 1861–1865, Indianapolis Prison Camp* (Indianapolis: 1940), 337–38, 349.

11. *Official Records*, II, 7, 512–13, 554; Winslow and Moore, *Camp Morton*, 354–55.

12. Marvel, *Andersonville*, 57–58.

13. Speer, *Portals*, 268–69.

14. Levy, *Camp Douglas*, 125, 127, 130.

15. Ibid., 164.

16. Benson, *Berry Benson*, 122–23.

17. Speer, *Portals*, 193.

18. *Official Records*, II, 7, 560, 691; 8, 997.

19. Speer, *Portals*, 175.

20. Levy, *Camp Douglas*, 51.

21. Sears, *Experiences*, 84–86.

22. Benson, *Berry Benson*, 122–23.

23. Speer, *Portals*, 278.

24. John McElroy, *Andersonville, A Story of Rebel Military Prisons* (Greenwich: CT, 1962), 43.

25. Speer, *Portals*, 203.

26. *Official Records*, II, 7, 518–19.

27. Winslow and Moore, *Camp Morton*, 337–38, 349.

28. Ibid., 266–67 and n.

29. Levy, *Camp Douglas*, 195.

30. Poe, *True Tales*, 144.

31. Miles O. Sherrill, *A Soldier's Story, Prison Life and Other Incidents in the War of 1861–'65* (Raleigh, NC: 1911), 10.

32. Levy, *Camp Douglas*, 235.

33. Marvel, *Andersonville*, 80–81.

34. Dougherty, *Diary*, 89.

35. Speer, *Portals*, 204.

36. A. P. Day, "Narrative of Prison Life," *Confederate Philatelist* XXIII (March-April 1978), 42.

38. McElroy, *Andersonville*, 192–93.

38. Marvel, *Andersonville*, 60.

39. Speer, *Portals*, 275.

40. Marvel, *Andersonville*, 80.

41. McElroy, *Andersonville*, 43.

42. Dougherty, *Diary*, 96.

43. John L. Ransom, *John Ransom's Andersonville Diary* (Middlebury, VT: 1986), 83.

44. Speer, *Portals*, 128.

45. McElroy, *Andersonville*, 192–93.

46. Levy, *Camp Douglas*, 131.

47. Speer, *Portals*, 125.

48. Ibid., 216.

49. Ibid., 262.

50. Bollet, *Civil War Medicine*, 371.

51. Ibid., 344.

52. Speer, *Portals*, 203.

53. Marvel, *Andersonville*, 79.

54. Ibid., 52.

55. Speer, *Portals*, 275.

56. Hugh Mercer file mm3424, NA.

57. Marvel, *Andersonville*, 52.

58. Ibid., 79.

59. Poe, *True Tales*, 143.

60. Robertson, *Soldiers*, 199.

61. Anthony M. Keiley, *In Vinculis; or, the Prisoner of War* (Petersburg, VA: 1866), 145–46.

62. Mitchell, *Cooking for the Cause*, 33.

63. Ibid., 33–34.

64. Levy, *Camp Douglas*, 195.

65. *Official Records*, II, 8, 52–53.

66. Poe, *True Tales*, 144.

67. Speer, *Portals*, 252.

68. Winslow and Moore, *Camp Morton*, 337–38, 349.

69. Ibid., 382–83.

70. Levy, *Camp Douglas*, 179.

71. Ibid., 189.

72. Robertson, *Soldiers*, 197–98.

73. Winslow and Moore, *Camp Morton*, 350–52.

74. *Official Records*, II, 7, 512–13, 554; Winslow and Moore, *Camp Morton*, 354–55.

75. *Official Records*, II, 7, 73.

76. Ibid., 183, 367.

77. Ibid., II, 8, 62.

78. Winslow and Moore, *Camp Morton*, 358–59.

79. Ibid., 368.

80. Mitchell, *Scratching for Food*, 8–9.

81. William M. Armstrong, "Cahaba to Charleston: The Prison Odyssey of Lt. Edmund E. Ryan," in Hesseltine, *Prisons*, 119–20.

82. John N. Opie, *A Rebel Cavalryman with Lee Stuart and Jackson* (Chicago: 1899), 319.

83. Levy, *Camp Douglas*, 239.

84. *Official Records*, II, 7, 1185.

85. Levy, *Camp Douglas*, 158.

86. Mitchell, *Scratching for Food*, 18.

87. Ibid., 9.

88. Frank L. Byrne, "A General behind Bars: Neal Dow in Libby Prison," in Hesseltine, *Prisons*, 72.

89. Levy, *Camp Douglas*, 139.

90. Ibid., 104.

91. Winslow and Moore, *Camp Morton*, 359–60.

92. Benson, *Berry Benson*, 133.

93. Ibid., 133.

94. Speer, *Portals*, 185.

95. Robertson, *Soldiers*, 199.

96. Speer, *Portals*, 184.

97. Joseph T. Durkin, ed., *John Dooley, Confederate Soldier: His War Journal* (Georgetown, D.C.: 1945), 163.

98. Speer, *Portals*, 183.

99. E. C. Colgan, "What Became of the Dog," *Southern Bivouac* II (October 1883), 79–81.

100. Levy, *Camp Douglas*, 152–53.

101. Mitchell, *Scratching for Food*, 4–5.

102. Opie, *Cavalryman*, 322.

103. Mitchell, *Scratching for Food*, 14.

104. Ransom, *Diary*, 83.

105. Speer, *Portals*, 278.

106. Winslow and Moore, *Camp Morton*, 360.

107. John R. King, *My Experiences in the Confederate Army and in Northern Prisons* (Clarksburg, WV: 1917), 42.

108. Levy, *Camp Douglas*, 190.

109. Speer, *Portals*, 205.

110. Dougherty, *Diary*, 119.

111. Colgan, "What Became of the Dog," 79–81.

112. Mitchell, *Cooking for the Cause*, 34–35.

113. James I. Robertson, Jr., "The Scourge of Elmira," in Hesseltine, *Prisons*, 88.

114. Speer, *Portals*, 195–96.

115. Marvel, *Andersonville*, 80.

116. Levy, *Camp Douglas*, 257.

117. McElroy, *Andersonville*, 311.

118. Marvel, *Andersonville*, 228.

119. Mitchell, *Scratching for Food*, 12–13.

120. Opie, *Cavalryman*, 319.

121. Speer, *Portals*, 266–67.

122. Ibid., 284.

123. Winslow and Moore, *Camp Morton*, 360.

124. H. Clay Holmes, *The Elmira Prison Camp* (New York: 1912), 326.

125. King, *My Experiences*, 45.

126. Levy, *Camp Douglas*, 182.

127. Speer, *Portals*, 183.

128. Dougherty, *Diary*, 38.

129. Mitchell, *Scratching for Food*, 32.

130. Robertson, "The Scourge of Elmira," 88.

CHAPTER EIGHT: THE "IRREPRESSIBLE" TURKEY

1. Leander Stillwell, *The Story of a Common Soldier of Army Life in the Civil War 1861–1865* (Erie, KS: 1920), 69–71.

2. William Richardson to parents, November 17, 1861, Jones, *Richardson Letters*, 18.

3. Stillwell, *The Story of a Common Soldier*, 69–71.

4. Willoughy M. Babcock, *Selections from the Letters and Diaries of Brevet Brigadier Willoughby Babcock of the Seventy-Fifth New York Volunteers: A Study of Camp Life in the Union Armies during the Civil War* (Albany, NY: 1922), 94–95.

5. Billings, *Hard Tack*, 217–18.

6. Billings, *Hard Tack*, 218–19.

7. Coleman to parents, January 19, 1862, Coleman Family Papers.

8. William and George Richardson to parents, February 1, 1862, Jones, *Richardson Letters*, 32.

9. George Richardson to parents, April 2, 1863, Jones, *Richardson Letters*, 95.

10. Billings, *Hard Tack*, 222.

11. Sears, *Experiences*, 227–29.

12. Billings, *Hard Tack*, 219.

13. "Beef Seekers," *Southern Bivouac* I (October 1882), 70.

14. Fisk, *Anti-Rebel*, 58.

15. Billings, *Hard Tack*, 218–19.

16. Voris to wife, December 24, 1862, Johnson Collection.

17. George Richardson to parents, December 25, 1861, Jones, *Richardson Letters*, 25.

18. William Richardson to parents, December 27, 1861, Jones, *Richardson Letters*, 26.

19. George Richardson to parents, December 1861, Jones, *Richardson Letters*, 23.

20. William Richardson to parents, December 25, 1862, Jones, *Richardson Letters*, 77.

21. Voris to wife, December 12, 1863, Johnson Collection.

22. Voris to wife, December 23, 1863, Johnson Collection.

23. Adams, *Altar of Freedom*, 95–96.

24. Oscar O. Winthur, ed., *With Sherman to the Sea: The Civil War Letters, Diaries, and Reminiscences of Theodore F. Upson* (Bloomington, IN: 1958), 145.

25. Livermore, *My Story*, 684.

26. Mitchell, *Celebrations*, 16.

27. Fredericksburg, *Virginia Star*, December 23, 1882.

28. Austin C. Dobbins, ed., *Grandfather's Journal* (Dayton, OH: 1988), 116.

29. Terry L. Jones, ed., *The Civil War Memoirs of Captain William J. Seymour: Reminiscences of a Louisiana Tiger* (Baton Rouge, LA: 1991), 104.

30. Dobbins, *Grandfather's Journal*, 174.

31. Richard Beard, "My Christmas Dinner in 1863," *Confederate Veteran* XXXVI (December 1928), 447.

32. Davis, *Diary of a Confederate Soldier*, 102.

33. Spencer G. Welch, *A Confederate Surgeon's Letters to His Wife* (New York: 1911), 39.

34. Guy R. Everson, ed., *"Far, Far from Home": The Wartime Letters of Dick and Tally Simpson* (New York: 1994), 102.

35. Poe, *True Tales*, 176.

36. Mitchell, *Celebrations*, 26.

37. Dobbins, *Grandfather's Journal*, 225, 227.

39. Time-Life Books, *Voices of the Civil War—Atlanta* (Alexandria, VA: Time-Life Books, 1996), 23.

40. Mitchell, *Celebrations*, 7–8.

41. Allan Nevins, ed., *A Diary of Battle: The Personal Journals of Colonel Charles S. Wainwright 1861–1865* (New York: 1962), 433.

42. Robert Hunt Rhodes, ed., *All for the Union: The Civil War Diary and Letters of Elisha Hunt Rhodes* (New York: 1985), 167.

43. Fisk, *Anti-Rebel*, 32–33.
44. Ibid., 133–34.
45. Voris to wife, November 26, 1863, Johnson Collection.
46. Sears, *Experiences*, 202–204.
47. Ibid., 46–48.
48. Nevins, *Wainwright*, 129–30.
49. Fisk, *Anti-Rebel*, 283.
50. Voris to wife, November 17, 20, 1864, Johnson Collection.
51. Voris to wife, November 23, 1864, Johnson Collection.
52. Florance Grugan to Clara Grugan, November 26, 1864, Florance W. Grugan Papers, Civil War Miscellaneous Collection, USAMHI.
53. Voris to wife, November 30, 1864, Johnson Collection; Mitchell, *Celebrations*, 12.
54. Nevins, *Wainwright*, 482–83.
55. Rhodes, *All for the Union*, 197.
56. Mitchell, *Celebrations*, 12.
57. Ibid., 13–14.
58. Katherine M. Jones, *Heroines of Dixie: Winter of Desperation* (New York: 1955), 33.
59. Mitchell, *Celebrations*, 15.
60. Bertram Korn, *American Jewry and the Civil War* (Philadelphia: 1951), 90–92.
61. Robert Rosen, *The Jewish Confederates* (Columbia, SC: 2000), 198, 200–201.
62. Mitchell, *Celebrations*, 30.

CONCLUSION

1. E. B. Long, *The Civil War Day by Day* (New York: 1971), 710–12.

RECIPES: BREADS, BISCUITS, AND YEASTS

1. *Bread and Bread Making*, 12–15, 32.
2. Sanderson, *Camp Fires and Camp Cooking*, 12–14.
3. Civil War Interactive Civil War Cookbook, http://www.civilwarinteractive.com/cookbooks.html (hereafter cited as CWICWC).
4. Ibid.
5. Lily May Spaulding and John Spaulding, *Civil War Recipes: Receipts from the Pages of Godey's Lady's Book* (Lexington, KY: 1999), 84.
6. CWICWC.
7. Ibid.
8. Ibid.
9. Ibid.
10. Dayton E. Flint to his sister, February 1, 1863, Dayton E. Flint Letters.

11. Mitchell, *Celebrations*, 12.

12. Spaulding and Spaulding, *Civil War Recipes*, 72–73.

13. Levy, *Camp Douglas*, 257.

14. CWICWC.

15. Edgefield, South Carolina, *Edgefield Advertiser*, March 1, 1863.

16. CWICWC.

17. Spaulding and Spaulding, *Civil War Recipes*, 77–78.

18. Ibid., 77.

19. *Confederate Receipt Book*, 12.

20. Ibid.

21. Haber, *Hardtack to Home Fries*, 57.

22. CWICWC.

23. Ibid.

24. *Confederate Receipt Book*, 10.

25. Ibid., 10; William C. Davis, *The Civil War Cookbook* (Philadelphia: 1993), 92.

26. Mitchell, *Scratching for Food*, 9.

27. CWICWC.

28. Ibid.

RECIPES: SOUPS

1. Circular, November 19, 1862, Record Group 393, NA.

2. Sanderson, *Camp Fires and Camp Cooking*, 5–6.

3. CWICWC.

4. Ibid.

5. Rosen, *Jewish Confederates*, 198, 200–201.

6. Spaulding and Spaulding, *Civil War Recipes*, 66–67.

7. Ibid., 64.

8. Wiley, *Southern Woman's Story*, 30–31.

9. Haber, *Hardtack to Home Fries*, 58.

10. Marvel, *Andersonville*, 80.

11. CWICWC.

12. Sanderson, *Camp Fires and Camp Cooking*, 7.

13. Ibid., 6.

14. CWICWC.

15. Ibid.

16. *Official Records*, I, 14, 351.

17. Sanderson, *Camp Fires and Camp Cooking*, 6–7.

18. CWICWC.

19. Ibid.

20. Ibid.

21. Ibid.

22. Ibid.

23. Wiley, *Southern Woman's Story*, 69.

24. *Regulations for the Medical Department of the Confederate States Army*, 76.

25. Atlanta, *Southern Field and Fireside*, January 31, 1863.

26. CWICWC.

27. Ibid.

RECIPES: STEWS AND HASHES

1. Circular, November 19, 1862, Record Group 393, NA.

2. Sanderson, *Camp Fires and Camp Cooking*, 8–9.

3. Ibid., 9.

4. *Southern Recorder*, September 2, 1862.

5. Donald, *Bellard*, 122.

6. Mitchell, *Union Army Camp Cooking*, 20–21.

7. Fisk, *Anti-Rebel*, 93.

8. Luecke, *Frontier Army*, 27–28.

9. CWICWC.

10. Luecke, *Frontier Army*, 27.

11. CWICWC.

12. Basil W. Duke, *Reminiscences of General Basil W. Duke, C.S.A.* (New York: 1911), 26.

13. Sanderson, *Camp Fires and Camp Cooking*, 9–10.

14. Ibid., 9.

15. Naval History Department, *Civil War Naval Chronology 1861–1865* (Washington, D.C.: Naval History Department, 1971), VI, 60n.

RECIPES: MEATS

1. Circular, November 19, 1862, Record Group 393, NA.

2. CWICWC.

3. Ibid.

4. Ibid.

5. Ibid.

6. Ibid.

7. Ibid.

8. Ibid.

9. Circular, November 19, 1862, Record Group 393, NA.

10. CWICWC.

11. Ibid.

12. Ibid.

13. Ibid.

14. Sanderson, *Camp Fires and Camp Cooking*, 10.

15. Ibid., 10.

16. Ibid., 10.

17. Naval History Division, *Civil War Naval Chronology*, VI, 64n.

18. Spaulding and Spaulding, *Civil War Recipes*, 172.

19. CWICWC.

20. Ibid.

21. Ibid.

22. Ibid.

23. Ibid.

24. Ibid.

25. Luecke, *Frontier Army*, 52.

26. CWICWC.

27. Ibid.

28. Wiley, *Southern Woman's Story*, 86.

29. CWICWC.

RECIPES: FISH AND FOWL

1. Davis, *Civil War Cookbook*, 88.

2. CWICWC.

3. Ibid.

4. Ibid.

5. Spaulding and Spaulding, *Civil War Recipes*, 126–27.

6. CWICWC.

7. Ibid.

8. Ibid.

9. Ibid.

10. Ibid.

11. Ibid.

12. Spaulding and Spaulding, *Civil War Recipes*, 141–42.

13. CWICWC.

14. Ibid.

15. Spaulding and Spaulding, *Civil War Recipes*, 145.

16. CWICWC.

17. Ibid.

RECIPES: VEGETABLES

1. Sanderson, *Camp Fires and Camp Cooking*, 8.
2. CWICWC.
3. Sanderson, *Camp Fires and Camp Cooking*, 8.
4. Ibid., 8.
5. Ibid., 10.
6. Ibid., 11.
7. Dennis J. Ringle, *Life in Mr. Lincoln's Navy* (Annapolis, MD: 1998), 74.
8. CWICWC.
9. Sanderson, *Camp Fires and Camp Cooking*, 11.
10. Violetta, "The Last Confederate Christmas," 273–75.
11. CWICWC.
12. Ibid.
13. Ibid.
14. Ibid.
15. Ibid.
16. Ibid.
17. Ibid.
18. Ibid.
19. Ibid.
20. Ibid.
21. Ibid.
22. Ibid.

RECIPES: SAUCES

1. *Confederate Receipt Book*, 15.
2. CWICWC.
3. Ibid.
4. Ibid.
5. Winslow and Moore, *Camp Morton*, 359–60.
6. CWICWC.
7. Ibid.
8. Ibid.
9. *Confederate Receipt Book*, 15.
10. CWICWC.
11. Ibid.
12. Ibid.

RECIPES: DESSERTS

1. Sears, *Experiences*, 202.
2. CWICWC.
3. Ibid.
4. Haber, *Hardtack to Home Fries*, 39.
5. CWICWC.
6. Mary Elizabeth Massey, *Ersatz in the Confederacy* (Columbia, SC: 1952), 67.
7. Spaulding and Spaulding, *Civil War Recipes*, 183.
8. CWICWC.
9. Spaulding and Spaulding, *Civil War Recipes*, 203.
10. CWICWC.
11. Ibid.
12. Ibid.
13. Harwell, *Cumming*, 84.
14. CWICWC.
15. Ibid.
16. Ibid.
17. Ibid.
18. Ibid.
19. Davis, *Civil War Cookbook*, 88.
20. CWICWC.
21. Ibid.
22. Ibid.
23. Ibid.
24. Ibid.
25. Circular, November 19, 1862, Record Group 393, NA.
26. CWICWC.
27. Ibid.
28. Ibid.
29. Ibid.
30. Ibid.
31. Ibid.
32. Wiley, *Southern Woman's Story*, 125.
33. Wilma King-Hunter, ed., *A Northern Woman in the Plantation South* (Columbia, SC: 1993), 116.
34. CWICWC.
35. Spaulding and Spaulding, *Civil War Recipes*, 232–33.
36. CWICWC.
37. Ibid.
38. Ibid.
39. Ibid.

RECIPES: BEVERAGES

1. Sanderson, *Camp Fires and Camp Cooking*, 11–12.
2. Charleston, South Carolina, *Mercury*, February 8, 1862.
3. Yorkville, Georgia, *Enquirer*, September 30, 1863.
4. Columbia, South Carolina, *Confederate Baptist*, November 18, 1863.
5. Yorkville, Georgia, *Enquirer*, January 21, 1863.
6. Albany, Georgia, *Patriot*, June 30, 1864.
7. Milledgeville, Georgia, *Southern Federal Union*, May 13, 1862.
8. Augusta, Georgia, *Field and Fireside*, August 8, 1863.
9. Sumter, South Carolina, *Tri-Weekly Watchman*, July 8, 1861.
10. Laurensville, South Carolina, *Herald*, September 20, 1861.
11. *Confederate Receipt Book*, 21.
12. Ibid., 21.
13. Spaulding and Spaulding, *Civil War Recipes*, 50.
14. CWICWC.
15. Harwell, *Cumming*, 18.
16. CWICWC.
17. Spaulding and Spaulding, *Civil War Recipes*, 49–50.
18. Sharon Peregrine Johnson and Byron A. Johnson, *The Authentic Guide to Drinks of the Civil War Era* (Gettysburg, PA: 1992), 86.
19. Diet Tables for Military Hospitals, Order Book, Stout Papers, Texas.
20. Ibid.
21. Ibid.
22. *Confederate Receipt Book*, 14.
23. CWICWC.
24. *Confederate Receipt Book*, 14.
25. Confederate Wine Recipe, n.d., Tulane University Library, New Orleans.
26. Johnson and Johnson, *Drinks*, 120.
27. Ibid., 95.
28. Ibid., 128.
29. Ibid., 102.
30. Ibid., 109.
31. Ibid., 70.
32. Ibid., 54.
33. Ibid., 144.
34. Edward Burd Grubb to W. Erwin Schermerhorn, April 15, 1910, *The Burlington Story* X, no. 1 (1980), 1–3.
36. William C. Davis, *A Way through the Wilderness: The Natchez Trace and the Civilization of the Old Southern Frontier* (New York: 1995), 245–46.

37. Johnson and Johnson, *Drinks*, 80.

38. Ibid., 143.

39. Ibid., 141.

40. Ibid., 137–38.

41. Ibid., 98.

42. Ibid., 75.

43. Ibid., 37.

44. Everson, *"Far, Far from Home,"* 102.

45. Johnson and Johnson, *Drinks*, 109.

BIBLIOGRAPHY

MANUSCRIPTS

Breneman, Amos. Papers. Civil War Miscellaneous Collection, United States Army Military History Institute, Carlisle, PA.

Coleman Family Papers. In possession of R. E. Coleman, Decatur, GA.

Confederate States of America Records. Center for American History, University of Texas, Austin.

Confederate Wine Recipe, n.d. Tulane University Library, New Orleans.

Flint, Dayton E. Letters. Civil War Miscellaneous Collection. United States Army Military History Institute, Carlisle, PA.

Grugan, Florance W. Papers. Civil War Miscellaneous Collection. United States Army Military History Institute, Carlisle, PA.

Record Group 92. Records of the Office of the Quartermaster General: Entry 225, Quartermaster's Consolidated Correspondence File, Correspondence of J. M. Sanderson and W. S. Chapman concerning Army Cooking. National Archives, Washington, D.C.

Record Group 153. Records of General Courts Martial. National Archives, Washington, D.C.

Record Group 393. Records of U.S. Army Continental Commands, Part 2: Entry 714, General Orders, Provisional Brigades and Mobile Units in the Department of Washington and 22d Army Corps. National Archives, Washington, D.C.

Stout, Samuel Hollingsworth. Papers, Center for American History, University of Texas, Austin.
Talley, Spencer. Memoir, 1918. In possession of Frances Martin, Lebanon, TN.
Voris, Alvin C. Papers. Alan Johnson Collection, Akron, OH.

NEWSPAPERS
Albany, Georigia, *Patriot*
Atlanta, Georgia, *Southern Field and Fireside*
Augusta, Georgia, *Field and Fireside*
Charleston, South Carolina, *Mercury*
Columbia, South Carolina, *Confederate Baptist*
Edgefield, South Carolina, *Edgefield Advertiser*
Fredericksburg, *Virginia Star*
Laurensville, South Carolina, *Herald*
Milledgeville, Georgia, *Southern Federal Union*
New York, *Harper's Weekly Illustrated Newspaper*
Richmond, *Examiner*
Southern Recorder
Sumter, South Carolina, *Tri-Weekly Watchman*
Yorkville, Georgia, *Enquirer*

ELECTRONIC SOURCES
Civil War Interactive Civil War Cookbook
  http://www.civilwarinteractive.com/cookbook.html.
Walt Whitman, "Memoranda during the War," *Two Rivulets: Author's Edition,* on Major Authors on CD-ROM: Walt Whitman.

GOVERNMENT PUBLICATIONS
Confederate States War Department. *Regulations for the Medical Department of the Confederate States Army.* Richmond, VA: Surgeon General's Office, 1863.
Naval History Department. *Civil War Naval Chronology 1861–1865.* Washington, D.C.: Government Printing Office, 1971.
Sanderson, James M. *Camp Fires and Camp Cooking; or Culinary Hints for the Soldier: Including Receipt for Making Bread in the "Portable Field Oven" Furnished by the Subsistence Department.* Washington, D.C.: Government Printing Office, 1862.

United States Quartermaster General. *Bread and Bread Making.* Washington, D.C.: Government Printing Office, 1864.

United States War Department. *General Regulations for the Army.* Washington, D.C.: Government Printing Office, 1825.

United States War Department. *Manual for Army Cooks.* Washington, D.C.: Government Printing Office, 1879.

United States War Department. *Revised Regulations of the Army, 1861.* Washington, D.C.: Government Printing Office, 1861.

United States War Department. *War of the Rebellion: Official Records of the Union and Confederate Armies.* Washington, D.C.: Government Printing Office, 1880–1901.

Woodward, Joseph J. *The Hospital Steward's Manual.* Philadelphia: J. B. Lippincott, 1862.

———. *Outlines of the Chief Camp Diseases of the United States Armies.* Philadelphia: J. B. Lippincott, 1863.

COOKBOOKS, CONTEMPORARY AND MODERN

Confederate Receipt Book: A Compilation of Over One Hundred Receipts, Adapted to the Times. Richmond, VA: West and Johnson, 1863.

Davis, William C. *The Civil War Cookbook.* Godalming, UK: Colour Library, 1993.

Haber, Barbara. *From Hardtack to Home Fries: An Uncommon History of American Cooks and Meals.* New York: Free Press, 2002.

Johnson, Sharon Peregrine, and Byron A. Johnson. *The Authentic Guide to Drinks of the Civil War Era.* Gettysburg, PA: Thomas Publications, 1992.

Luecke, Barbara K. *Feeding the Frontier Army 1775–1865.* Eagan, MN: Grenadier Publications, 1990.

Mitchell, Patricia B. *Civil War Celebrations.* Chatham, VA: Privately published, 1998.

———. *Cooking for the Cause.* Chatham, VA: Privately published, 1988.

———. *Union Army Camp Cooking.* Chatham, VA: Privately published, 1990.

———. *Yanks, Rebels, Rats, & Rations: Scratching for Food in Civil War Prison Camps.* Chatham, VA: Privately published, 1993.

Spaulding, Lily May, and John Spaulding. *Civil War Recipes: Receipts from the Pages of Godey's Lady's Book.* Lexington, KY: University Press of Kentucky, 1999.

Wittenmyer, Anne. *A Collection of Recipes for the Use of Special Diet Kitchens in Military Hospitals.* Mattituck, NY: United States Christian Commission, 1864.

BOOKS, PRIMARY AND SECONDARY

Adams, Virginia Matzke, ed. *On the Altar of Freedom: A Black Soldier's Civil War Letters from the Front.* Amherst, MA: University of Massachusetts Press, 1991.

Babcock, Willoughy M. *Selections from the Letters and Diaries of Brevet Brigadier Willoughby Babcock of the Seventy-Fifth New York Volunteers: A Study of Camp Life in the Union Armies during the Civil War.* Albany, NY: State University of New York Press, 1922.

Benson, Susan W., ed. *Berry Benson's Civil War Book.* Athens, GA: University of Georgia Press, 1992.

Berlin, Jean V., ed. *A Confederate Nurse: The Diary of Ada W. Bacot.* Columbia, SC: University of South Carolina Press, 1994.

Billings, John D. *Hard Tack and Coffee.* Boston: George M. Smith and Co., 1887.

Bollet, Alfred J. *Civil War Medicine: Challenges and Triumphs.* Tucson, AZ: Galen Press, 2002.

Bradley, G. S. *The Star Corps; or, Notes of an Army Chaplain.* Milwaukee: Jermain and Brightman, 1865.

Casler, John O. *Four Years in the Stonewall Brigade.* Marietta, GA: Continental Book Co., 1951.

Catton, Bruce. *American Heritage Picture History of the Civil War.* New York: Doubleday, 1960.

Clement, Maud Carter. *War Recollections of Confederate Veterans of Pittsylvania County.* Chatham, VA: Pittsylvania Historical Society, 1892.

Cumming, Kate. *Gleanings from Southland.* Birmingham, AL: Roberts and Son, 1895.

Davis, Charles E. *Three Years in the Army: The Story of the Thirteenth Massachusetts Volunteers from July 16, 1861, to August 1, 1864.* Boston: Estes and Lauriat, 1894.

Davis, William C., ed. *Diary of a Confederate Soldier, John S. Jackman of the Orphan Brigade.* Columbia, SC: University of South Carolina Press, 1990.

———. *A Way Through the Wilderness: The Natchez Trace and the Civilization of the Old Southern Frontier.* New York: HarperCollins, 1995.

Dobbins, Austin C., ed. *Grandfather's Journal.* Dayton, OH: Morningside Press, 1988.

Donald, David, ed. *Gone for a Soldier: The Civil War Memoirs of Private Alfred Bellard.* Boston: Little, Brown, 1975.

Dougherty, Michael. *Diary of a Civil War Hero*. New York: Pyramid Books, 1960.

Dowdey, Clifford, ed. *The Wartime Papers of Robert E. Lee*. Boston: Little, Brown, 1961.

Duke, Basil W. *Reminiscences of General Basil W. Duke, C.S.A.* New York: Doubleday, 1911.

Durkin, Joseph T., ed. *John Dooley, Confederate Soldier: His War Journal*. Georgetown, D.C.: Georgetown University Press, 1945.

Everson, Guy R., ed. *"Far, Far from Home": The Wartime Letters of Dick and Tally Simpson*. New York: Oxford, 1994.

Fisk, Wilbur. *Anti-Rebel: The Civil War Letters of Wilbur Fisk*. Croton-on-Hudson, NY: Privately published, 1983.

Foote, Shelby. *The Civil War: A Narrative*. New York: Random House, 1958.

Haley, John W. *The Rebel Yell & the Yankee Hurrah: The Civil War Journal of a Maine Volunteer*. Camden, ME: Down East Books, 1985.

Harwell, Richard B., ed. *The Journal of Kate Cumming, A Confederate Nurse 1862–1865*. Athens, GA: University of Georgia Press, 1975.

Holmes, H. Clay. *The Elmira Prison Camp*. New York: G. P. Putnam's Sons, 1912.

Jones, Gordon C., ed. *"For My Country": The Richardson Letters*. Wendell, NC: Privately published, 1984.

Jones, Katherine M. *Heroines of Dixie: Winter of Desperation*. New York: Ballantine, 1955.

Jones, Terry L., ed. *The Civil War Memoirs of Captain William J. Seymour: Reminiscences of a Louisiana Tiger*. Baton Rouge, LA: Louisiana State University Press, 1991.

Keiley, Anthony M. *In Vinculis; or, the Prisoner of War*. Petersburg, VA: Petersburg, *Daily Index*, 1866.

King, John R. *My Experiences in the Confederate Army and in Northern Prisons*. Clarksburg, WV: Privately published, 1917.

King-Hunter, Wilma, ed. *A Northern Woman in the Plantation South*. Columbia, SC: University of South Carolina Press, 1993.

Korn, Bertram. *American Jewry and the Civil War*. Philadelphia: Jewish Publication Society, 1951.

Lankford, Nelson D., ed. *An Irishman in Dixie: Thomas Conolly's Diary of the Fall of the Confederacy*. Columbia, SC: University of South Carolina Press, 1988.

Levy, George. *To Die in Chicago: Confederate Prisoners at Camp Douglas, 1862–1865.* Evanston, IL: Evanston Publishing, 1994.

Livermore, Mary A. *My Story of the War.* Hartford, CT: A. D. Worthington, 1888.

Lowry, Thomas P., and Jack D. Welsh. *Tarnished Scalpels: The Court-Martials of Fifty Union Surgeons.* Mechanicsburg, PA: Stackpole Books, 2000.

Marvel, William. *Andersonville, The Last Depot.* Chapel Hill, NC: University of North Carolina Press, 1994.

Massey, Mary Elizabeth. *Ersatz in the Confederacy.* Columbia, SC: University of South Carolina Press, 1952.

McElroy, John. *Andersonville, A Story of Rebel Military Prisons.* Greenwich, CT: Fawcett, 1962.

Morehead, James O., ed. *History of Bland County.* Radford, VA: Commonwealth Press, 1961.

Nevins, Allan, ed. *A Diary of Battle: The Personal Journals of Colonel Charles S. Wainwright 1861–1865.* New York: Harcourt, Brace, 1962.

Nightingale, Florence. *Notes on Nursing and Notes on Hospitals.* London: Harrison, 1859.

Opie, John N. *A Rebel Cavalryman with Lee Stuart and Jackson.* Chicago: Lokey, 1899.

Poe, Clarence, ed. *True Tales of the South at War.* Chapel Hill, NC: University of North Carolina Press, 1961.

Ransom, John L. *John Ransom's Andersonville Diary.* Middlebury, VT: Eriksson, 1986.

Rhodes, Robert Hunt, ed. *All for the Union: The Civil War Diary and Letters of Elisha Hunt Rhodes.* New York: Orion Books, 1985.

Ringle, Dennis J. *Life in Mr. Lincoln's Navy.* Annapolis, MD: Naval Institute Press, 1998.

Robertson, James I., Jr. *Soldiers Blue and Gray.* Columbia, SC: University of South Carolina Press, 1988.

Rosen, Robert. *The Jewish Confederates.* Columbia, SC: University of South Carolina Press, 2000.

Rubenfine, Joseph. *List No. 69, "C.S.A."* Pleasantville, NJ: Privately published, n.d.

Schroeder-Lein, Glenna R. *Confederate Hospitals on the Move: Samuel H. Stout and the Army of Tennessee.* Columbia, SC: University of South Carolina Press, 1994.

Sears, Stephen, ed. *Mr. Dunn Browne's Experiences in the Army: The Civil War Letters of Samuel W. Fiske*. New York: Fordham University Press, 1998.

Sherrill, Miles O. *A Soldier's Story, Prison Life and Other Incidents in the War of 1861–'65*. Raleigh, NC: Edwards and Broughton, 1911.

Small, Harold A., ed. *The Road to Richmond: The Civil War Memoirs of Major Abner R. Small of the 16th Maine Volunteers*. Berkeley, CA: University of California Press, 1939.

Speer, Lonnie R. *Portals to Hell: Military Prisons of the Civil War*. Mechanicsburg, PA: Stackpole Books, 1997.

Stillwell, Leander. *The Story of a Common Soldier of Army Life in the Civil War 1861–1865*. Erie, KS: Franklin Hudson, 1920.

Time-Life Books. *Voices of the Civil War—Atlanta*. Alexandria, VA: Time-Life Books, 1996.

Trumbull, Henry Clay. *War Memories of an Army Chaplain*. New York: Scribner's, 1898.

VanAlstyne, Lawrence. *Diary of an Enlisted Man*. New Haven, CT: Tuttle, Morehouse, and Taylor, 1910.

Watkins, Sam. *Co. Aytch, Maury Grays, First Tennessee Regiment*. New York: Collier, 1962.

Welch, Spencer G. *A Confederate Surgeon's Letters to His Wife*. New York: Neale Publishing, 1911.

Wiley, Bell I. *The Life of Billy Yank*. Indianapolis: Bobbs-Merrill, 1952.

———, ed. *A Southern Woman's Story: Life in Confederate Richmond*. Jackson, TN: McCowatt-Mercer, 1959.

Williams, Edward B., ed. *Rebel Brothers: The Civil War Letters of the Truehearts*. College Station, TX: Texas A&M University Press, 1995.

Winslow, Hattie Lou, and Joseph R. H. Moore. *Camp Morton 1861–1865, Indianapolis Prison Camp*. Indianapolis: Indiana Historical Society, 1940.

Winthur, Oscar O., ed. *With Sherman to the Sea: The Civil War Letters, Diaries, and Reminiscences of Theodore F. Upson*. Bloomington, IN: Indiana University Press, 1958.

ARTICLES

Armstrong, William M. Armstrong. "Cahaba to Charleston: The Prison Odyssey of Lt. Edmund E. Ryan." In William B. Hesseltine, ed., *Civil War Prisons*. Kent, OH: 1962, 114–23.

Beard, Richard. "My Christmas Dinner in 1863." *Confederate Veteran* XXXVI, (December 1928), 447.

"Beef Seekers." *Southern Bivouac* I (October 1882), 70–72.

Byrne, Frank L. "A General behind Bars: Neal Dow in Libby Prison." In Hesseltine, *Prisons*, 60–79.

Catlin, W. H. "An Incident at Long Bridge." *Confederate Philatelist* XXIII (March-April 1978), 40.

"Coffee-Boiler Rangers." *Southern Bivouac* I (July 1883), 442–43.

Colgan, E. C. "What Became of the Dog." *Southern Bivouac* II (October 1883), 79–81.

"Cooking the Hell Broth." *The Old Guard* II (June 1864), 140.

Day, A. P. "Narrative of Prison Life." *Confederate Philatelist* XXIII (March-April 1978), 42.

Dodd, W. O. "Recollections of Vicksburg during the Siege." *Southern Bivouac* I (September 1882), 2–11.

Downer, Edward T. "Johnson's Island." In Hesseltine, *Prisons*, 98–113.

Ford, A. P. "The Last Battles of Hardee's Corps." *Southern Bivouac* New Series, I (August 1888), 140–43.

———. "Service on the Carolina Coast." *Southern Bivouac* New Series, I (November 1885), 325–27.

Grubb, Edward, to W. Erwin Schermerhorn, April 15, 1910. *The Burlington Story* X, no. 1 (1980), 1–3.

"Hardtack Anyone?" Roanoke Civil War Round Table, *Civil War Dispatch* (September 2000), 7.

"The Haversack." *Land We Love* II (March 1867), 366–77.

"The Haversack." *Land We Love* III (September 1867), 423–33.

"The Haversack." *Land We Love* IV (December 1867), 159–66.

"The Haversack." *Land We Love* IV (April 1868), 525–34.

"The Haversack." *Land We Love* V (August 1868), 352–62

"The Haversack." *Land We Love* V (October 1868), 530–38.

"The Haversack." *Land We Love* VI (March 1869), 413–21.

"The Haversack." *Land We Love* VI (April 1869), 486–90.

"Heel and Toe." *Southern Bivouac* I (February 1883), 255–59.

Henderson, D. E. "Confederate Moonshiners." *Southern Bivouac* III (April 1885), 347–48.

"High Price for Needles and Thread." *Southern Bivouac* III (January 1885), 237.

Jones, James P. and William Warren Rogers, eds. "Montgomery as the Confederate Capital: View of a Nation." *Alabama Historical Quarterly* XXIII (Spring 1964), 1–125.

"The Last Ration." *Southern Bivouac* I (January 1883), 217–18

"Louisville during the War." *Southern Bivouac* I (December 1882), 157–60.

"Price's Commissary Department." *Southern Bivouac* III (February 1885), 262.

"Query Box." *Southern Bivouac* I (October 1882) 80–81

Robertson, James I., Jr. "The Scourge of Elmira." In Hesseltine, *Prisons*, 80–97.

Scroggs, J. J. "How Hardtack was Made." *Civil War Times Illustrated* XI (October 1972), 34.

Simon, Harold E. "As I Cannot Get Letter I Must Drink Whiskey, Brandy." *Confederate Philatelist* XXIV (March-April 1979), 61.

"Soldiers of '61 and '65." *Southern Bivouac* I (March 1883), 308–10.

"A Southern Woman's Letter." *Southern Bivouac* I (November 1882), 114–16.

Stokes, J. W. "The Retreat from Laurel Hill, West Virginia." *Southern Bivouac* III (October 1884), 61–66.

Tanner, Linn. "The Meat Diet at Port Hudson." *Confederate Veteran* XXVI (November 1918), 484.

Untitled anecdote. *Southern Bivouac* I (December 1882), 147.

Violetta. "The Last Confederate Christmas." *Southern Bivouac* II (February 1884), 273–75.

Walter. "High Price for Needles and Thread." *Southern Bivouac* III (January 1885), 236–37.

"What the Confederates Drank for Whiskey." *Southern Bivouac* I (July 1883), 441–42.

INDEX

References in italics are to photographs, which can be found between
pages 66 and 67, and between pages pages 98 and 99.

217